Development and Management of Virtual Schools: Issues and Trends

Table of Contents

Preface

For more than a century, children have learned at a distance from their teachers. Correspondence lessons were the primary education mechanism for children of remote farmers, migrant workers, and others. Beginning in the 1990s, the Internet replaced mail, radio, and fax transmissions for many students. So far tens of thousands of students at the primary and secondary levels in the U.S. have taken online courses. The total represents a very small proportion of the more than 50 million students, but the number of students in virtual schools on a full-time or part-time basis is growing rapidly. The primary and elementary school levels are experiencing the greatest rate of growth. The number of virtual schools in North America is currently around 100, and the number continues to grow. The movement of students and teachers into virtual schools has important implications for education at all levels. It is time to explore the impact of virtual schools on elementary and secondary education.

Virtual schools are a result of widespread changes in knowledge about learning, in available technology, and in society. As we learn more about learning styles, brain-based learning, and differentiated instruction, we realize the value of technology, including distance education, in meeting the unique needs of all learners. The U.S. Census Bureau in 2001 reported that two-thirds of children lived in homes with computers, and 90 percent of school age children have access to computers. Half of homes were able to access the Internet, and children lead adults in their use of computer-mediated communication technologies. As adult use of distance learning grows in postsecondary education and professional development, parents will be more welcoming of distance learning for their children. Because today's students grow up as natives in the digital world, they think and work fluently with multimedia and technology, and they expect teachers to incorporate technology into teaching and learning. Students who are unsatisfied with the disconnect between traditional schooling and their natural digital habitat may be drawn to and succeed in virtual schools. A challenge will be keeping up with demand for virtual schools and upholding quality in virtual schools.

Not all parents, administrators, or community members agree that virtual schooling is an effective answer to the changing educational needs of digital-age children. Many students and parents choose virtual schooling because of the independent nature of the study, the flexibility of the scheduling, or the opportunities offered that may be absent in local schools. However, some say that distance education is unproven at primary and secondary levels, and that many of the issues have not been satisfactorily addressed. Critics and skeptics of virtual schooling say that students experience social isolation, that cheating is easy, that the human dimension of education is missing, and that "seat time" or "contact time" in virtual schools between teacher and student is not equivalent to that in schools and classrooms. Will virtual school students be prepared for life in a diverse culture? Will they succeed in the workplace and in family life?

While scholarly examination of distance learning at the primary and secondary levels is extensive, encompassing decades of study and a wide range of delivery methods, study of virtual schools at the K-12 level is in its infancy. Enough is known to bring together a review of best practice from concept and development, through implementation and evaluation. Virtual schooling will continue to attract students because of the benefits it offers over traditional schooling, and clients of virtual schools need information to guide their decisions. For the foreseeable future, virtual schools will continue to meet diverse students' needs, and to evolve in response to further change.

The purpose for this book is to share knowledge of issues and trends in virtual schooling, from the perspectives of virtual school administrators, course developers, educators, students, and other stakeholders. At a time when virtual schools represent the preferred education choice for steadily growing numbers of students, it is essential that we understand their strengths and limitations, the unique contributions and requirements of virtual schools. The information presented in the following chapters will aid virtual school planners, managers and educators to maximize their efforts for the education of students.

Organization of the Book

The book is organized into four sections. The first section raises issues related to the administration of virtual schools. This section presents an overview of virtual schools including a look at their emergence. Benefits are discussed, along with problems, solutions and future trends. The unique nature of virtual schools gives rise to unique challenges for administrators and planners of virtual schools. Virtual school managers must balance the needs of children, teachers, parents, and others in the education community, none of whom are likely to meet in person. In addition, the virtual school must make its curriculum accessible to learners who "attend" from many locations, at any time of day, for many reasons. The chapters in this section offer lessons learned from experienced virtual school developers and administrators.

The second section delves into standards used by virtual schools to ensure quality and accessibility of the educational experience. Virtual schools are operated by several types of organizations, ranging from states, public school systems and universities to private schools and home schools. As a way of communicating to stakeholders its interest in high quality education, a virtual school may choose to pursue accreditation by a local, regional or national accrediting agency. Accreditation standards vary according to the mission of the accrediting agency. Virtual schools, operating largely online, may also choose to meet accessibility standards to ensure that their curriculum is accessible by all students. This section describes the accreditation and accessibility standards in the context of virtual schools.

Section III concentrates on the people at the front lines of virtual schooling: the teachers and course developers. It has been said that the practices in instructional design and teaching that work in face-to-face education are also effective in distance learning, but there are many distinctive features of virtual schooling. While the values and philosophies that make great teachers are shared by all teachers, they are expressed in special ways in the online environment. Gifted online teachers require special forms of support and specific forms of course design. The chapters in Section III provide case studies of successful virtual school educators and the professional development programs that enable them to continually improve.

The final section focuses on the processes of education in the virtual school. The nature of digital content presents possibilities for teaching and learning that have the potential to transform and enhance learning. The roles of teachers and students shift in the virtual school setting, and the challenge of course designers is exploiting the strengths of the virtual classroom. The tools available to virtual course designers and teachers are continually developing and changing. One of the responsibilities in online education is selecting and using the tools that are best suited to the needs of students and the demands of curriculum. Section IV describes new tools and their applications in specific virtual school situations.

Chapter I investigates some of the critical issues associated with virtual schools. It reviews historical forms of school education, and the different types of virtual schools that are currently emerging. The educational value of virtual schooling is considered in terms of cognitive and affective outcomes, and some of the factors that promote the rise of virtual schools are outlined. The implications of related philosophical viewpoints and communication theory are explored, together with the benefits and disadvantages of virtual schools for society. A number of problems associated with virtual schools are identified, and some possible solutions are outlined. Future trends in the growth of virtual schooling and the characteristics of the next generation of virtual schools are discussed in terms of their implications for school education.

Chapter II takes us on a tour of the design, development, and implementation of a virtual school. There were no other public schools in the state which had initiated such a program, and no other public school in the country had developed a distance learning system for middle school students. Lang identifies budgetary and evaluation issues as well as perceptions of staff. She also identifies future trends in technology which may result in new pedagogy.

Chapter III describes the Canadian experience with virtual schooling, discusses administrative issues, and outlines trends. Haughey and Muirhead begin with a brief overview of the development of virtual schooling in Canada from its initial development in Alberta in 1996 with more than 20 schooling programs, to its rapid expansion across Canada. The chapter identifies administrative issues that have arisen and that are in some ways unique to online schooling, ranging from admission requirements to course development, and from parent support to funding. Also included are ongoing issues related to educational leadership such as issues of supervision of teachers, quality of instruction, and provision of professional development. The chapter concludes with an outline of likely trends and their implications.

Chapter IV centers on quality guidelines and standards. C. Cavanaugh outlines a distance learning development and implementation cycle consisting of three stages: (1) procurement and preparation of the resources necessary to meet the distance education goals, (2) delivery of instruction using the best practices from education, business and research, and (3) analysis of the results of distance education to gauge achievement of the goals. The chapter explores the interconnect between the success factors of the Resources - Practices - Results (RPR) cycle and standards published by agencies accrediting virtual schools. A survey of 67 virtual schools in the U.S. in the spring of 2003 resulted in identification of accrediting standards applied to virtual schools at national, regional and state levels. The standards of accrediting bodies are examined and compared to the RPR success factors.

Chapter V addresses the important role of virtual schools in educating students with special needs. When creating online instruction it is important to follow the accessibility standards and guidelines such as the Section 508 and W3C accessibility standards to enable persons with disabilities access to educational material. Within the U.S., more than 26,000 K-12 students classified as hospital/homebound received education through some form of distance education. Case studies of a hospital/homebound program, online programs used by a school for students with disabilities, and a state public online school and its interactions with students with disabilities are presented. The results of a survey of online schools and the schools' services for students with disabilities are also reported.

Chapter VI takes us inside the teaching process at Florida Virtual School as the following essential characteristics of online teaching are highlighted: communication, teamwork, flexibility, student-centered learning and love of students. Using technology as a tool to design and deliver curriculum and instruction, the virtual learning environment mirrors the technological world that students live in today and will work in tomorrow. Virtual education changes the way teachers teach and interact with other teachers, with students, and with parents. Virtual educators are reshaping the routine learning modes of the traditional school day into a dynamic interactive, real-world learning environment that presents choices to parents and students and requires students to take ownership of the learning process.

Chapter VII continues the focus on teachers by describing the effective professional development that is needed to help educators learn to organize content for online delivery, convert instructional materials to online formats, use advanced multimedia tools, and integrate technology resources in online learning environments. Hinson and Bordelon address standards for technology-supported instruction and staff development, models of effective face-to-face professional development along with adaptations for online educators and professional development programs currently available to online educators. Recommendations for effective professional development are also provided.

Chapter VIII discusses ways that the nature of digital content and tools coupled with the communications capabilities available through online instruction can, if leveraged properly, provide opportunities for quality instructional delivery. Schnitz and Azbell propose that even in an environment of remote, asynchronous, web-based instructional approaches and the best of effective classroom practices may not be sufficient to address the full range of capabilities the technology provides. Through work done by IBM and the Florida Virtual School (FLVS), principles and models for leveraging the advantages offered by the technology environment and overcoming the difficulties inherent have been worked out that offer significant promise to all providers of virtual schooling.

Chapter IX presents the viewpoint of managing virtual classes in rural school districts. As rural communities and schools decline in size, educational policy makers often question their viability. In the Canadian province of Newfoundland and Labrador and in New Zealand, new educational structures based on digital networking, using the Internet, have been developed for the delivery of education to rural schools. Within these electronic educational structures senior students in rural high schools have been provided with extended curriculum choice through a combination of on-site and on-line instruction. This has led to three challenges: the administration of electronically inter-connected rural schools; the integration of physical and virtual classes and the need to find pedagogy that is appropriate for e-teaching and e-learning. The new educational structures in rural Newfoundland and New Zealand have extended traditional classrooms in terms of time, space, organisation and capacity.

Chapter X provides a set of case studies and vignettes of actual delivery and receiving classes to highlight pedagogical limitations and potentials of the Virtual Schooling Service in Queensland, Australia. Critical success factors for pedagogical effectiveness are documented along with a reflection on these elements using Activity Theory. The chapter concludes with an update of the current initiatives being undertaken to enhance the pedagogical effectiveness of the Virtual Schooling Service. Pendergast and Kapitske focus on one element of the evaluation of the service-pedagogical effectiveness.

Chapter XI illustrates an evaluation tool used by teachers and researchers to study the impact of computer-mediated collaborative and communication technologies used in K-12 education. Standard usability engineering methods and tools focus on individual users at a single workstation. Networked collaborative systems, however, present the challenge of multiple users interacting at a variety of times and places. Carroll, Neale and Isenhour developed a web forum tool to capture and display user critical incident reports and threaded discussions of these reports by users, evaluators, and system developers. The Collaborative Critical Incident Tool (CCIT) is effective at evoking detailed usability evaluation information, as well as reflective analysis of usability issues from diverse points of view among stakeholders in the system.

Chapter XII outlines a university-science center partnership called Science Net that has been functioning as a virtual school for the extension education of the global public in general and the Singapore public in particular. Tan Wee Hin and Subramaniam describe the design, implementation mechanics and learning potential of this online school for non-formal science education, and suggest that it is an innovative experiment to expand the communicative space of learning in society.

The Appendix offers a Directory of Online K-12 Schools that, while not exhaustive, is comprehensive and includes schools in several countries. The schools' names, locations and web addresses are included.

Scholarly study and reporting on K-12 virtual schools has now begun, and further development of the literature of virtual school research is important for several reasons. Virtual schools serve a population of students at the primary and secondary levels who have characteristics and needs different from those of adult learners served by other forms of distance education. Virtual schools are a relatively new form of education, but one that is growing rapidly in importance. Teaching at a distance requires special skills, and teaching children at a distance requires specific adaptation of those skills. The trends in technology, education, and society that have led to the creation of virtual schools show signs of continuing rapid change. If the education community hopes to influence the future direction of virtual schooling, continued research and reports such as the chapters in this book are needed in order to inform the practice of virtual schooling.

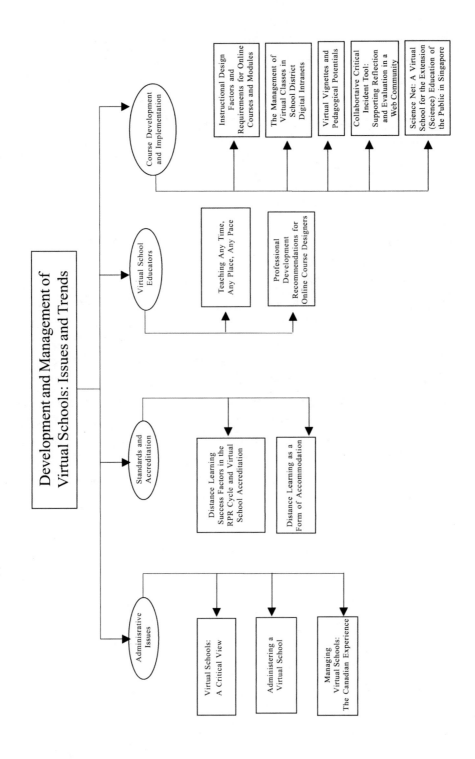

Acknowledgments

The editor wishes to acknowledge the many professionals who contributed to this book at all stages of its development. I am grateful for the creativity and enthusiastic cooperation of each author of chapters included here. It has been a delight and a much appreciated learning opportunity. Most of the authors served as referees for chapters submitted for inclusion. Thanks to all who provided thorough and thoughtful reviews. Reviewers whose critical and constructive comments were highly valued include Deborah Abbott, Rachel Bordelon, Roger Carlsen, Terry Cavanaugh, Leland Clabots, Gerry Cowles, Jace Hargis, Margaret Haughey, Jan Hinson, Gaye Lang, Dennis Neale, Glenn Russell, Jim Schnitz, Richard Stein, Ken Stevens, Merry Stewart, R. Subramaniam, Tony Turrin, Maggie Veres, and Madonna Wise.

Special thanks are due to the editorial staff of Idea Group Publishing, including Mehdi Khosrow-Pour's support of the concept.

I am most indebted to my husband and collaborator, Terry Cavanaugh, for his unflagging contributions and love.

Catherine Cavanaugh
Jacksonville, Florida, USA
March 2003

Section I

Administrative Issues

Chapter I

Virtual Schools: A Critical View

Glenn Russell
Monash University, Australia

Abstract

This chapter investigates some of the critical issues associated with virtual schools. It reviews historical forms of school education and the different types of virtual schools that are currently emerging. The educational value of virtual schooling is considered in terms of cognitive and affective outcomes, and some of the factors that promote the rise of virtual schools are outlined. The implications of related philosophical viewpoints and communication theory are explored, together with the benefits and disadvantages of virtual schools for society. A number of problems associated with virtual schools are identified and some possible solutions are outlined. Future trends in the growth of virtual schooling and the characteristics of the next generation of virtual schools are discussed in terms of their implications for school education.

The Emergence of the Virtual School

Forms of school education have been with us for around 2,000 years, and perhaps longer. Schools are known to have existed in Plato's time (Marrou, 1956), and histories of many societies refer to the ways in which the young have been educated. Modes of schooling over time have shown diversity that has sometimes been related to the social class and religion of the students and the facilities available to teach them. Until quite recent times, however, they have been characterised by the physical presence of teachers and students together. Usually a building is used for instruction, and teaching materials such as books or blackboards are often in evidence.

During the 19th century, education by correspondence was established in some areas of England, Germany, the U.S. and Sweden (Simonson, Smaldino, Albright, & Zvacek, 2000). The 20th century saw the emergence of additional alternatives to what may be called "bricks-and-mortar" schools. These were forms of distance education where children could learn without attending classes on a regular basis. The technologies used included mail, for correspondence schools, and the 20th century technologies of radio and television. The schools that used these technologies were particularly valuable for students who lived in remote areas, for those whose parents were frequently on the move, for students who were too ill to attend school, or for those who had been excluded. In Australia, a Correspondence School was established in Melbourne as early as 1914 (Correspondence School, 1978), and the Alice Springs School of the Air commenced radio broadcasts in the Northern Territory in 1951 (School of the Air, 2002).

However, although a number of examples of distance education schools can be identified during the 20th century, they rarely became the principal mode of education. There is little indication that parents wanted to abandon conventional schools in favor of distance education, although criticism of schooling has been constant.

Virtual schools can be seen as a variant of distance education. They emerged in the closing years of the 20th century, and can be understood as a form of schooling that uses online computers to provide some or all of a student's education. Typically, spatial and temporal distancing is employed, and this results in students being able to use their computers at a convenient time in their homes or elsewhere, rather than being subject to meeting at an agreed time in a school building.

Asynchronous technology is often used for virtual schools. This has the advantage that students are able to interact with web sites and send and receive emails when it is convenient for them. It is also possible to use synchronous technologies, such as electronic chat and desktop video conferencing, but these are sometimes seen as less attractive because the timetabling involved reduces flexibility.

The concept of a virtual school is agreed on only in broad terms, as there are a number of variants. Some virtual schools insist on an agreed minimum of face-to-face contact, while others are so organized that a student might never set foot in a classroom. Indeed, it is possible for a virtual school to have no physical presence at all for students to visit, and an office building in one state or country can be used to deliver virtual school services to interstate or international students.

One way of categorizing virtual schools is by imagining where they might be placed on a scale of face-to-face contact between students and teachers. At the conservative end of this scale there would be conventional schools where students use online computers in classrooms or labs for some of their lessons. A trained teacher in the same subject area might be available to help students, or other teachers, volunteers or parents could supervise them. Isenhour, Caroll, Neale, Rosson, and Dunlap (2000) describe one variation of this type of virtual school where a collaborative online environment exists between schools.

Towards the middle of such a scale would be found mixed-mode examples, where some subjects are offered in virtual mode, but students are asked to visit the school on a regular basis to monitor their progress or to participate in other face-to-face subjects such as sport, drama or art. At the other end of the scale are virtual schools where the student and teacher never meet, and there is no requirement for the student to enter a school building for the duration of the course. Schools of this type can also be seen as the "Out-of-School Model" (Schnitz & Young, 2002), and they are exemplified by Florida High School. In this school, "there is no Florida High School building and students and teachers can be anywhere in the world" (Florida High School Evaluation, 2002, p. 12).

Virtual school characteristics can be better appreciated by identifying the provider. Figure 1, adapted from Clark (2001), gives examples of different types of virtual schools in the U.S.

Clearly, the education that a student might receive from each of these types of virtual schools would vary considerably in its nature, and further differences could be identified within each category.

In addition, virtual schools can be seen in terms of their ability to supplement traditional schools when there is a perceived need for remediation, certification or extension. These schools, which Russell and Holkner (2000) refer to as the *coaching* aspect of virtual schools, enable students to complete missed school subjects that might be needed for university entrance, and provide an opportunity for students whose needs are not adequately catered for in conventional schools. In many cases, students can log onto a computer in their home to complete the required work after their day has been spent in a conventional school or in employment.

Figure 1: Types and Examples of Virtual Schools (Adapted from Data in Clark, 2001)

Virtual school type	School/organization	Web address
Virtual schools consortia	VHS (Virtual High School)	http://www.govhs.org/website.nsf
Virtual schools operated by districts and schools	HISD (Houston Independent School District Virtual School)	http://hs.houstonisd.org/virtualschool/
Virtual charter schools	Pennsylvania Virtual Charter School	http://www.pavcs.org/
University-based virtual schools	University of Nebraska-Lincoln College Independent Study	http://extended.unl.edu/cis/
Private virtual schools	Christa McCauliffe Academy	http://www.cmacademy.org/main.html
Related for-profit providers of curricula and content	Apex Learning	http://www.apexlearning.com/offerings/vs/default.asp
State-sanctioned virtual schools	Florida Virtual School	http://www.flvs.net/splashpage/doors.html

The Educational Value of Virtual Schools

Because virtual schools are relatively new, and are usually encountered only in cyberspace, there is not yet an extensive tradition of evaluating them. Recent reports (Clark, 2001; California Virtual School Report, 2001; Florida High School Evaluation, 2002; Kozma et al., 2000) have provided insights into their characteristics, and have identified both successes and problems that will have to be faced. However, evaluations of virtual schools are still uncommon. A study by Cavanaugh (2001) illustrates this problem:

Although distance learning is well documented with adults, fewer studies of effectiveness exist that center on the primary and secondary school levels. At a point when all states [in the U.S.A.] offered distance education in schools, very few had conducted formal evaluations (p. 75).

Cavanaugh's meta-analysis concluded that distance education in K-12 could be expected to result in achievement at least comparable to traditional instruction in most academic circumstances. There should be no difference with distance education when compared to face-to-face education. When implemented with the same care as face-to-face instruction, distance education has the potential to expand educational opportunities with intermediate, middle and upper grades.

Reliable longitudinal studies concerning students' socialisation after involvement in online virtual schools, or comparative studies on the affective domain, are currently unavailable. Indeed, it is difficult to think of a situation where such studies would be of real benefit. For example, a study that followed high school students for 10 years after they had left their virtual school, in order to determine whether they became well-adjusted citizens, would be of limited value. Communications and information technologies are changing very rapidly. The virtual school and its societal context would have undergone transformative change in this period. An additional interpretation that can be drawn from this realisation is that critics who foresee educational disaster ahead and the strongest proponents of virtual schools are only making informed guesses about what might lie ahead.

Factors Promoting the Rise of Virtual Schools

It is likely that the number of virtual schools will continue to increase. The principal factors that account for the growth of virtual schools include globalisation, technological change, availability of IT technology, economic rationalism, the model provided by higher education, perceptions about traditional schools, and the vested interest of those involved in them.

The first of these factors, globalisation, refers to a process in which traditional geographic boundaries are bypassed by international businesses that use information technology for globally oriented companies. A critical aspect of globalisation is the use of online computer and information technology to access markets, personnel and money. For education, this means that students who would once have used a textbook designed for their educational system can now access web sites from around the world. This enables corporations to provide alternatives that challenge traditional learning materials. It is now possible for curriculum to be delivered remotely from across state and national borders. Educational administrators can purchase online units of work for their school, and parents in developed countries can sometimes choose between a traditional school and its virtual counterpart. As Evans (1997) suggests, communications media allow educators to take their teaching around the globe, and it allows teachers to use global resources to enhance their own teaching. However, globalisation can be seen as both advantage and danger. The same online technology that permits teachers to locate rich learning materials for their students reveals forms of schooling that challenge existing educational beliefs.

As information technology continues to develop, there is a correspondingly increased capacity to deliver relevant curricula online. As broadband connections become more common, students will be less likely to encounter prolonged delays while web pages load or other information is downloaded. Advances in computers and software design have led to developments such as full-motion video clips, animations, desktop video conferencing, and online music. Collectively, what is referred to as the Internet is already very different from the simple slow-loading web pages of the early 1990s.

Around five years ago, it was common for commentators to marvel at the spread of the Internet and cite statistics that indicated what changes might eventuate. What is now apparent is that in developed countries the Internet is becoming commonplace. It is essential for many businesses, and households are adopting the Internet with such enthusiasm that it will eventually become an essential consumer item, along with televisions, refrigerators and mobile phones. As more people connect to the Internet its value increases, as there are more people to communicate with and more web pages with useful information. Segaller (1998) cites Netscape founder Marc Andreeson's interpretation of Metcalfe's Law:

The power of the network is N squared, where N is the number of nodes. So if you double the number of nodes, you actually double square or you quadruple the overall value of the network. The reason is that the network gets more valuable to me if you come on it. Even though I'm already there, the network's getting continually more valuable to me as more people come on, as more contact comes on, as important businesses are connected (p. 283).

Economic rationalism also drives the spread of virtual schools. Economic rationalism, as Smith and Sachs (1995) point out, puts a premium on productivity, efficient use of resources and value for money. The application of economic rationalism to education implies, as Rutherford (1993) suggests, that the collective or government provision of goods and services is a disincentive to private provision, and that deregulation and commercialisation should be encouraged. Consistent with this understanding is the idea that schools, as we know them, are inefficient and should be radically changed. Schools, for Tiffin and Rajasingham (1995), have been seen as part of a former industrial era, and Perelman (1992) believes that they ought to be replaced with technology:

...the nations that stop trying to "reform" their education and training institutions and choose instead to totally replace them with a brand new high-tech learning system will be the world's economic powerhouses through the 21st century (p. 20).

In this view, virtual schools provide an opportunity to apply the ideology of economic rationalism to school education. They provide a context where private providers can readily compete with governments, religious groups and local communities in offering educational programs. An added advantage is that the availability of online technology for this purpose parallels its use by business.

Collectively, the discussion that relates to the opposition of traditional school education can be referred to as "anti-school discourses" (Bigum & Kenway, 1998). The subsets of this discourse include the argument that multimedia and the Internet are more exciting than school experiences, the conviction that home schooling is preferable to traditional schools, and the belief that conventional school can be physically unsafe or psychologically harmful. The concerns that parents might have for the safety of their children are underscored by research cited by Elliot, Hamburg and Williams (1998) in the U.S., which indicated that 47 percent of all teens believed that their schools were becoming more violent, and one in ten reported a fear of being shot or hurt by classmates who carry weapons to school. A related concern is discussed by Epp (1996), who argues that schools are complicit in the abuse of children through the systematic violence resulting from exclusionary practices, discrimination, tolerance of abuse, and other practices that might prevent students from learning.

The ways in which higher education has adopted online teaching provides an example of how online education can be accepted as an alternative. The online courses provided by universities in recent years have proliferated (Russell & Russell, 2001). The spread of these courses has been so extensive that there have been predictions of a dramatic decline in the number of tertiary institutions in the U.S. (Dunn, 2000), and suggestions that the traditional university will be superseded (Noam, 1995). As increasing numbers of parents complete an online tertiary course, there is a corresponding growth in the conceptual understanding that virtual schooling may also be a viable alternative. The shaping of attitudes by the use of technology resonates with McLuhan's (1994) argument that the content of technologies is less important than the changes brought about by the technology itself. If parents are advised that virtual schooling is an option for their children, they would be in a better position to consider it if they had previously experienced online education themselves.

Those who are convinced that existing schools are unsatisfactory can see virtual schools as one alternative. Criticism of schools for not adequately meeting student needs, for providing inadequate skills required for employment, or not preparing students for examinations and entrance tests, are a continuing theme that can be identified in a number of educational systems. Discussions related to school reform can include funding, resourcing, teacher supply, curriculum change, and pedagogy, but they can also include more radical alternatives such as virtual schooling.

A disadvantage, which might follow the adoption of virtual schooling, however, is an exacerbation of existing problems of equity and access. Reports in the U.S. consistently show that people who are identified as belonging to lower-income or minority groups are less likely to have online computer access at home (Bikson & Paris, 1999; Falling through the Net, 2000). In the Pew Report (2002), 90 percent of white college students answered "yes" in response to the question "Have you ever gone online?," while only 74 percent of Blacks also answered "yes" to the same question.

Nevertheless, virtual schooling does offer flexibility in terms of access and curriculum choice for those who are able to use it. Proponents of virtual schooling sometimes refer to the motto of "any place, anytime, anywhere," and while this is sometimes an exaggeration, virtual schools are often able to offer a wider range of subjects than their traditional counterparts. They also have the advantage of often being asynchronous. If a student chooses to complete schoolwork at 2:00 a.m., the wait for the next scheduled class that would be required with a traditional school will not apply.

In one respect, virtual schooling builds on antecedent distance education technologies such as print-based materials, radio and telephone. It is not surprising that some virtual schools retain a combination of synchronous audio technologies, printed materials and the Internet. In Victoria, Australia, the curriculum materials available from the Distance Education Centre enable students to "choose to receive materials via CD-ROM, print-based booklets, or by accessing courses online" (DECV, 2002). In Queensland, Australia, the Virtual Schooling Service (2002) explains that its lessons "are delivered via 'real time' audio teleconferencing and shared computer graphics ('audiographics'), as well as activities placed in an online 'studyroom'."

Virtual schools can also be promoted because they are profitable, or because they advance the careers of those who promote them. Those involved in the IT industry can identify a market for hardware and software, and for educational modules designed to be used in online environments. A search of the World Wide Web, using the term *Virtual School* will soon reveal a number of targeted commercial products and services. The profit-making opportunities for those involved in virtual schools are potentially considerable. Virtual schools can also enable those involved in school education, administration, and academia and planning to contribute to a growing area.

Implications of Philosophical Viewpoints and Communication Theory for Virtual Schools

When humans use technology in their daily lives, there are usually some disadvantages to be considered. The decision to use a car to drive to work balances the convenience and comfort of privately owned transportation against the risk of being killed or injured in an accident. The electrical power available at the turn of a switch will often come at some cost to the environment, through the burning of fossil fuels or the hazards of nuclear energy. The choice to adopt virtual schools also has advantages and disadvantages.

While virtual schools can also be seen as convenient, there are some grounds for believing that face-to-face instruction can be superior to distance education. When we learn of the world through a computer, it is a mediated experience. It is a representation rather than a direct experience. Understanding and empathy are likely to be increased when the distance between a person and a perceived object is reduced, or when there are minimal changes to the nature of experience through a mediating technology.

Distance can be seen as both spatial and temporal. A student in a virtual school is likely to be physically distant from the teacher, and separated in time by the use of asynchronous technologies such as web pages and email. The affective domain is likely to be influenced by the distancing effect caused by mediating technologies, because the immediacy that accompanies face-to-face human interaction is absent. It follows, then, that students in a virtual school may have reduced opportunities for empathizing with others compared to their counterparts in a traditional school.

Arguments concerning the immediacy of experience are not new, and examples can be identified in antiquity that pre-date the online era by thousands of years. Aristotle (Cooper, 1932) argued in *The Rhetoric* that temporal distancing contributed to a lack of pity, because men could not feel pity for events that were many years off in the past or the future. Similarly, David Hume examined physical distancing in the 18th century. In *A Treatise on Human Nature* (1898), Hume argued that:

*...where an object is...far remov'd...its idea becomes...fainter and more
obscure...The* fewer *steps we take to arrive at an object, and the* smoother
the road is, this diminution of vivacity is less vividly felt (2.3.7).

Several writers have examined issues relating to the distancing effect caused by
mediating technologies. These include Wellen's (1986) theory that reduction
of telecommunication bandwidth leads to a progressive decrease in sensory
modalities, and Dede's (1991) discussion of bandwidth and rich learning
experience. Some of these arguments were first proposed in the pre-Internet
era, and they provide indications that face-to-face teaching has some advantages compared to its mediated counterparts.

Collectively, the implication of theories such as distancing effects, bandwidth
and media richness for virtual schools is that the teacher or administrator of a
virtual school has a reduced ability to monitor any student behaviours that might
result from online learning. In part, this may be because the information that is
transmitted to students in a virtual school environment is likely to be less rich
than in a traditional classroom.

Information in online schools is related to bandwidth, in that fewer channels are
used to transmit the information than when teacher and student are in the same
room together. Physical real-life proximity enables the observation of body
language, and social and relational cues. Parks (1996) argues that the cues
emanating from physical settings are missing in online contexts, and this concept
can be related to earlier theories of media richness (Daft & Lengel, 1984).
These writers discuss the concept of the potential information-carrying capacity of data, and suggest that wide bandwidth is related to the immediacy and
richness of student learning.

Although communication research indicates that there are some grounds for
reservations concerning virtual schools, it is important to remember that both
traditional and online schools are multi-dimensional learning environments that
cannot be readily explained in terms of theory. If difficulties in communication
were inherent in the technology used by virtual schools, it would be reasonable
to expect high levels of student dissatisfaction. However, evaluations of virtual
schools generally indicate high levels of student satisfaction. Virtual High
School students, for example, were interested in their courses and enjoyed
them (Kozma et al., 2000).

Problems of Virtual Schools and their Solutions

Virtual schools face a number of challenges related to the way that teaching and learning are implemented in online environments. While similar problems can also be identified in conventional schools, the different nature of virtual schools serves to highlight these concerns. Some of these problems are outlined in Figure 2.

The first of these problems, authenticity, relates to the verification of the student as the person who has completed the corresponding assignments and tests from a virtual school. Virtual schools may assign students a secure password to use over the Internet, but this procedure would not preclude students from giving their passwords to a parent or tutor who completed the work on their behalf. A possible solution that may have to be considered is for independent testing

Figure 2: Problems of Virtual Schools

Virtual school problem	Example of virtual school problem
Authenticity	Honesty in test taking and completion of assignments
Interactivity	Students directed to passive materials such as lecture notes on web pages
Socialization	Insufficient attention given to the teaching of community norms and values
Experiential learning	Using virtual schooling for activities that usually require face-to-face interaction or synchronous monitoring of physical processes
Responsibility, accountability and discipline	Uncertainty about allocation of responsibilities. Threats or unsuitable materials sent by email. Hacking into administrative computer servers. Unauthorized changes to school websites or posting of websites with offensive materials
Teacher training	Teachers not trained to work in online environments
Teacher certification	Use of unqualified teachers or tutors. Use of teachers not certified or registered for the corresponding school system
Class size	Large virtual classes lead to slower responses to student requests
Accreditation	Varying standards across geographic regions can mean that a course in one area is not recognized in another
Student suitability	Students' learning style and ability may be mismatched to the available course
Equity	Use of virtual schools can exacerbate existing educational disadvantage

of students to confirm that they have the understanding, knowledge and skills suggested by their submitted work.

Interactivity describes the relationship between the learner and the educational environment. For virtual school students there is an interactive relationship involving the multimedia, the online materials used and the teacher. Students would typically access materials on the World Wide Web, respond to them, and send completed work electronically to their teacher. The preferred way for students to become involved in online learning is for an active engagement involving a response. If a student is directed to a static web page containing a teacher's lecture notes, learning may be less effective, unless other teaching methods are used to supplement it.

The solution to this problem will be found in both the increased capability of students' online computers to operate in a rich multimedia environment, and the recognition by course designers that virtual schools should take advantage of advances in learning theory and technological capability. In the U.S., the National Education Association's *Guide to Online High School Courses* observes that:

Online courses should be informed by and reflect the most current research on learning theory. They should be designed to take advantage of the special circumstances, requirements and opportunities of the online learning environment and support the development of 21st century learning skills (NEA, 2002, p. 15).

Socialisation continues to be a problem with virtual schools because there is an expectation in conventional schooling that students will learn how to work cooperatively with others, and will internalize the norms and values necessary for living in a civilized community. Moll (1998) is concerned with possible disruption to a 200-year-old tradition of public education as the primary vehicle for the transference of national narratives, and humanistic and democratic values, while Russell (2002) argues that virtual schools may be less able to socialize students in expected values than their conventional counterparts.

An insight into the socialisation problem was provided recently when the author of this chapter had the opportunity to visit a primary school classroom in Victoria, Australia. The back wall of the classroom contained a large banner with the words "treat others as you would want to be treated." Posters on another wall urged students to take action against bullying, while a different classroom area advised students to take responsibility for their actions and accept consequences. During the class, boys and girls worked together cooperatively at large tables with the support of their teacher. Although the details might change, similar examples to this could probably be provided from classrooms in many parts of the world.

Clearly, socialization will still occur if students use online learning supplemented by some contact with teachers and opportunities for organized sport. However, students' ability to relate to others in society is likely to change. It would be challenging for the designers of a virtual school to offer the same opportunities to their students that would have been available in the preceding example.

Nevertheless, a partial solution to this problem is apparent if it is recalled that there is not one agreed variant of virtual schools. A type of virtual school that routinely insists on organized face-to-face learning and social situations, with peers, teachers and other adults will reduce the problems that otherwise are likely to arise. Indeed, there are virtual schools where some provision has been made for student socialization. One example is the Odyssey Charter School (2002) which notes: "students meet weekly with their teacher to review teacher in a one-to-one meeting that takes place in the student's home or at a designated location." Odyssey offers a range of extra-curricular activities to supplement its academic program, including field trips, skate nights, holiday events and choir. Children are also required to attend assigned group science class twice per month.

A related concern to that of socialization is the belief that web culture is inherently isolating, and that by encouraging students to pursue their education with a virtual school, an existing trend towards loss of community may be exacerbated. Putnam (1995) has argued that technology is associated with diminished civic engagement and social connectedness, but there is conflicting research evidence regarding social involvement and computers.

Kraut et al. (1998) originally suggested that Internet use could be associated with declines in participants' communication with family members in the household, declines in the size of their social circle, and increases in depression and loneliness. However, more recent research (Kraut, Kiesler, Boneva, Cummings, Helgeson, & Crawford, 2002) found that negative effects had largely dissipated. The researchers reported an increase in favorable effects, although there were less satisfactory outcomes for introverts and for those with less support. Support for the positive effects of online computers on society is also found in Katz and Aspden (1997), who maintain that there is no support for pessimistic theories of the effects of cyberspace on community involvement.

Similarly, Jansz (2001) believes that there will be increased possibilities of new friendships and a "veritable smorgasbord of new possibilities in education" (p. 53).

There are some teaching activities in conventional schools that may be referred to as experiential. These usually involve some form of hands-on activity or physical interaction with others. Typically, a teacher will provide a demonstration, explanation or modeling of what is to be learned, and activities that follow provide an opportunity for the correction of errors. While virtual schools commonly offer subjects such as mathematics and social studies, the study of physical education, drama, art, and the laboratory component of science is more problematic. Sometimes the problem does not arise, because students will enroll only for subjects that they have missed or are needed for credit towards a qualification.

A common solution to these problems is for the virtual school to provide online or print-based teaching materials, as with other subjects in the range to be offered. Students complete the activities and send evidence of the completed work to the school. The Open School (2002) in British Columbia, Canada, offers art in both elementary and secondary school. The year nine secondary course offers the foundation of drawing and design basics, and introduces students to painting, printmaking, crafts, art appreciation, and photography. The Open School also offers a secondary physical education program, where students plan their own program. At the Fraser Valley Distance Education Centre (2002), students are invited to participate in a science fair by sending in digital pictures and a digital video clip of their project to the supervising teacher. Online movies of student projects can be viewed at the school's web site. What is apparent from viewing examples of the activities on offer from virtual schools is that the teaching of experiential-based subjects is not impossible. The problem in many cases lies more in the use of appropriate teaching techniques.

Changing notions of responsibility, accountability and student discipline are also likely to arise in virtual school environments. In a traditional school, teachers accept responsibility for the students in their charge, including the prevention of physical injury, and accountability for using appropriate teaching techniques. When there is a spatial and temporal distance between teacher and student, teachers are unable to exercise some of their accustomed responsibilities. While there is still a requirement to act ethically, and to ensure that appropriate teaching materials and methods are used, much of the responsibility shifts to parents, students, and to the suppliers of the online materials.

However, responsibility is still unclear in some areas. When students are below the school-leaving age, and they work from home in a virtual school environment, they will usually be in the care of a parent or guardian. If a student uses his or her home computer to hack into the school's administrative computer, or send offensive emails to a teacher or fellow student, both parents and teachers would expect to be involved in solving the problem.

Teacher training is also emerging as an area of concern. Virtual teachers will find that some new skills are required, while others are less important. Class management skills in a face-to-face environment will differ from their online equivalent, as will many of the teaching practices. There will be an ongoing need to use not only technological skills, but to apply these skills to the appropriate educational context. However, it is unlikely that many teachers' colleges and other providers of trained teachers have modified their courses to reflect these changes. The California Virtual School Report (2002) provides an indication of the direction that teacher training for virtual schools is taking. It reports the use of online modules for teachers at Durham Virtual High School, Canada, a 15-week teacher-training program in Fairfax County School District, and professional development options at Virtual High School. There is also a mentoring program operating at Florida Virtual School, and a training program operating at the Cyber Schoolhouse associated with the Clark County School District in Nevada (USA).

Parents would normally expect that the virtual teacher working with their child would be a competent online teacher and certified or registered with the corresponding school system. Where a student is working from home, and the principal contact with the teacher is by email, the anonymity of the communication mode could conceivably cover the use of unqualified teachers. The necessity for demonstrating that a high quality educational experience is being supplied is, however, likely to reduce this possibility. Florida Virtual High School only uses certified classroom teachers (Schnitz & Young, 2002, p. 4). As the online environment becomes more competitive, it is likely that virtual schools will provide evidence of their teachers' certification.

With conventional schools, the issue of class sizes is a perennial problem. The diversity of virtual schools means that it is not easy to determine corresponding workloads. The evaluation of Virtual High School (Kozma et al., 2000) revealed that some of the teachers involved in the case study had to complete their VHS work at home in addition to their normal teaching load during the day. Where teachers are asked to take responsibility for large groups of students, the time available for individual attention is likely to be reduced, and the quality of the educational service provided may be less satisfactory. Some virtual schools have recognised this problem. Teachers in Odyssey Charter School (2002) have a caseload of 24 students, with visits to students of one hour per week, while Louisiana Virtual School (2002) is limited to 20 students per course.

Accreditation of courses across geographic regions will also become an increasing problem. Varying standards can mean that a course in one area is not recognized in another. In one sense, this problem is not new, as there have been movements of students from one area to another for as long as there has been an organized schooling system. What is different is that students will increasingly be able to choose programs across state and even national borders, and complete their schoolwork by sitting at home with their computer. In tertiary education, administrative systems have evolved to allow students credit for work undertaken at other institutions. It is likely that similar pressures will affect the online component of the school education sector, although response to these pressures may be slow.

An important item relating to the quality of a student's educational experience in a virtual school is the recognition that not all students are suited to online learning. Some virtual schools already try to determine whether the prospective student is suited to online learning. The Louisiana Virtual School (2002) and the Electronic Classroom of Tomorrow (ECOT, 2002) offer online questionnaires for students. Typically, these questionnaires ask students about their independent learning skills, motivation, time management abilities, and comfort with technology. In broad terms, the questions asked of students reflect Del Litke's (1998) conclusions from a case study that examined teacher beliefs about virtual schooling. Teachers in this study thought that student success was related to self-motivation, persistence, intelligence and supportive parents. The implications of studies such as Del Litke's, and of the existence of checklists used by some virtual schools, is that students must be carefully assessed before they commit to online education. Any educational choice should always be made in the best interests of the student involved. Hidden agendas, such as cost-cutting to traditional schools, promotion of the careers of those involved, or an unthinking commitment to an ideology of technology, should have no place in the decision.

If virtual schools are perceived to be advantageous for those enrolled in them, there are also concerns when the access to them is seen as inequitable. Early research on the use of information technologies by school-age children in the U.S. (Martinez, 1994) indicated that white students had more access to a computer at home than did black or Hispanic students. More recent research on adults' access to the Internet suggests that socio-economic status might also be an important variable. Bikson and Paris (1999) found that there were "highly significant differences in household computer access based on income" (p. 9), in the U.S. It is reasonable to assume that households with children will have less access to computers to use in a virtual school if they are part of a disadvantaged group. Unless there is careful planning, the use of technology-mediated education is likely, in the short term, to entrench further those inequalities that exist in society.

Nevertheless, the long-term prognosis for equitable access to virtual schools in industrialized countries is more hopeful. As online computers become cheap and ubiquitous, they will become as common in homes as telephones. While there may continue to be differences between the computers used by dominant and disadvantaged groups, debate is likely to focus on the comparative quality of the online educational experience for students rather than access.

Collectively, a range of problems related to teaching and learning confront students, teachers, parents, administrators, and educational providers. Some of the solutions to these problems are already being implemented. In other cases, resistance can be expected, either because there are financial or political reasons for not implementing change, or because the problem is not yet adequately recognized.

Future Trends in Virtual Schools

Two broad trends can be identified in the growth of virtual schools. These are the continued expansion in the number of virtual schools, and the trend from virtual high schools to virtual K-12 schools. Research by Clark (2001, p. 3) indicates that more virtual schools began their operations in the U.S. during the period 2000 or 2001 (43 percent) than in the previous four years combined. Fifty-one percent of virtual schools surveyed offered junior high and middle school courses as well as high school courses, and about one in four schools currently offered courses across the whole K-12 spectrum (Clark, 2001, p. 4). In Canada, there is also evidence of growing demand for virtual schools. The two-year cumulative growth rate for Alberta virtual schools was 125 percent (SAEE, 2002).

Collectively, the implication of these trends is that there will be increased attention devoted to those problems that arise from virtual schooling across the K-12 range. When virtual schools made their first appearance, it would have been possible for some educators to dismiss them because they were experimental, or ignore their existence because they catered only for a niche market of high school students. In some cases, this suggestion may still be valid, but support for virtual schooling is increasing rather decreasing, and the nature of what is offered is becoming more comprehensive.

Virtual schools profoundly reshape the custodial functions of schools. One of the continuing assumptions of school education is that the school accepts responsibility for the students in its charge during school hours, and parents are free to earn a living or pursue their own interests. Where the students are in the post-compulsory years of schooling, the problem of parental supervision is of reduced importance. Students can earn money at a job during the daytime, and learn through a virtual school in the evening. By this means, they can increase their opportunities for University entrance or a better career.

The compulsory years of schooling, however, require a responsible adult to supervise students. If students are to spend much of their time at home, then a parent or guardian must be available to care for them. Not all parents will have the opportunity to work from home, and economic necessity may well mean that some parents are unable to choose virtual schooling for their children. In this sense, they will be disadvantaged in comparison to those families that can afford for one parent to remain home to help with their child's education. The quality of the supervision that parents can offer is also likely to vary. If much of the responsibility for a student's education is returned to parents, then it is important that parents provide appropriate support to enable the timely completion of schoolwork, using an online computer at home or elsewhere.

Virtual Schools: The Next Generation

The characteristics of the next generation of virtual schools will be largely determined by the related imperatives of globalisation and information technology developments. Increasingly, geographic boundaries and physical walls are becoming less important as markets interact across the world. Information technology makes this process possible, and it shapes cultural meanings, ethical values, and educational perspectives. In the U.S., the Web-Based Education Commission (Kerrey, 2000) has commented that:

The promise of high-quality web-based education is made possible by technological and communication trends that could lead to important applications over the next two to three years. These include greater bandwidth, expansion of broadband and wireless computing opportunities provided by digital convergence and lowering costs of connectivity (p. iii).

Increasingly, students will have access to computers that are more powerful than they are today. By 2007, it is predicted that more than 80 percent of those online in U.S. households will access the Internet through a high bandwidth connection (OECD, 2001). Interactive lessons with movies, sound and access to the Internet will provide an educational experience that will motivate students and increase demand for virtual schooling. Advances in wireless technologies will stimulate the development of mobile computing. This will mean that students who once had to be at home or at school in order to obtain a reliable Internet connection could complete their work wherever they were—including the local shopping centre or the beach. Although such changes might be technically possible, they are likely to be greeted cautiously by parents, because supervision will become more difficult.

As virtual schools become a more attractive option, they will compete with conventional schools for funding, teachers and students. It is likely that there will be heated debates over issues such as teacher training for virtual schools, course certification and accreditation, authentication of student work, and academic rigor and teaching practices. There will be resistance to virtual schools from some schools or interests that see virtual schooling as a threat. The result is likely to be an increased focus on evaluations, and an overall improvement in the choice of education offered to students.

Conclusion

Virtual schools continue the tradition whereby students learn at a distance from their teachers. Students who lived in remote areas or those who have been unable to attend school because of an illness or disability have been able to use predecessor technologies including mail, telephone, radio, and television in order to complete their education. The availability of online courses through the Internet has simultaneously reduced the emphasis given to older forms of distance education, while increasing the opportunities for students to explore alternatives to traditional school education. It is likely that there will be an increase in the number of virtual schools, and that they will continue to attract students.

The expected increase in the number and type of virtual schools is likely to provide both exciting possibilities and daunting challenges. Changes in technology and society will continue to shape the nature of virtual schools, and it is likely that continued interest in the alternative that they provide to traditional education will help to match them more closely with students' needs. Virtual schools have both advantages and disadvantages, but the radical nature of the alternative that they offer may yet lead to reconsideration of the nature of school education. From this perspective, virtual schools are indeed valuable.

References

Bigum, C. & Kenway, J. (1998). New information technologies and the ambiguous future of schooling: Some possible scenarios. In A. Hargreaves, A. Lieberman, M. Fullan, & D. Hopkins (Eds.), *International Handbook of Educational Change*, Part 1 (pp. 375-395). Dordrecht: Kluwer Academic.

Bikson, T.K. & Paris, C.W.A. (1999). Citizens, computers and connectivity: A review of trends. Available on the World Wide Web: http://www.rand.org/publications/MR/MR1109/mr1109.pdf.

California Virtual School Report. (2000). *The California Virtual High School Report: A National Survey of Virtual Education Practice and Policy with Recommendations for the State of California*. Available on the World Wide Web: http://www.uccp.org/docs/VHS_Report_lowres.pdf.

Cavanaugh, C.S. (2001). The effectiveness of interactive distance education technologies in K-12 learning: A meta-analysis. *International Journal of Educational Telecommunications, 7*(1), 73-88.

Clark, T. (2001). *Virtual Schools: Trends and Issues — A Study of Virtual Schools in the United States.* Available on the World Wide Web: http://www.WestEd.org/online_pubs/virtualschools.pdf.

Cooper, L. (ed.). (1932). *The Rhetoric of Aristotle: An Expanded Translation with Supplementary Examples for Students of Composition and Public Speaking.* New York: D. Appleton and Company.

Correspondence School. (1978). *Report and Minority Report of the Committee of Enquiry into the Future of the Correspondence School.* Melbourne, Australia: Government Printer.

Daft, R.L. & Lengel, R.H. (1984). Information richness: A new approach to managerial behaviour and organizational design. In B. Staw & L.L Cummings (Eds.), *Research in Organizational Behaviour* (Vol. 6, pp. 191-233). Greenwich, CT: JAI Press.

DECV. (2002). Distance Education Centre Victoria - DECV Delivery Options. Available on the World Wide Web: http://www.distance.vic.edu.au/services/servdel.htm.

Dede, C.J. (1991). Emerging technologies: Impacts on distance learning. *Annals of the American Academy for Political and Social Science, 514*(1), 146-158.

Del Litke, C. (1998). Virtual schooling in the middle grades: A case study. *Journal of Distance Education, 13*(2), 33-50.

Dunn, S.L. (2000, March/April). The virtualizing of education. *The Futurist.* Available from the World Wide Web: http://proquest.umi/pqdweb.

ECOT. (2002). Electronic classroom of tomorrow. Available from the World Wide Web: http://ecotohio.org/About.htm.

Elliott, D.S, Hamburg, B., & Williams, K.R. (1998). Violence in American schools: An overview. In D.S. Elliott, B.A Hamburg, & K.R Williams (Eds.), *Violence in American Schools: A New Perspective* (pp. 3-28). New York: Cambridge University Press.

Epp, J.R. (1996). Complicity and sources of violence. In J.R Epp & A.M Williamson (Eds.), *Systemic Violence: How Schools Hurt Children* (pp. 1-23). London: Falmer Press.

Evans, T. (1997). (En)countering globalisation: Issues for open and distance education. In L. Rowan, L. Bartlett & T. Evans (Eds.), *Shifting Borders: Globalisation, Localisation and Open and Distance Education* (pp. 11-22). Deakin University, Geelong: Deakin University Press.

Falling through the Net. (2000). *Falling through the Net: Towards Digital Inclusion — A Report on American's Access to Technology Tools.* Available from the World Wide Web: http://www.ntia.doc.gov/ntiahome/fttn00/Falling.htm#2.

Florida High School Evaluation. (2002). *The Florida High School Evaluation: 1999-2000 year-end report for the Orange County School Board.* Tallahassee, FL: Center for the Study of Teaching and Learning, Florida State University. Available from the World Wide Web: http://www.flvs.net/_about_us/pdf_au/fhseval_99-00.pdf.

Fraser Valley Distance Education Centre. (2002). Available from the World Wide Web: http://www.fvrcs.gov.bc.ca/.

Hume, D. (1898). *A Treatise on Human Nature, being an Attempt to Introduce the Experimental Method of Reasoning into Moral Subjects and Dialogues Concerning Natural Religion* (Vol. 2). London: Longman's Green & Co.

Isenhour, P.L., Carroll, J.M., Neale, D.C., Rosson, M.B., & Dunlap, D.R. (2000). The virtual school: An integrated collaborative environment for the classroom. *Educational Technology and Society, 3*(3). Available from the World Wide Web: http:// ifets.gmd.de/periodical/vol_3_2000/a03.html.

Jansz, C. (2001). Why I support the integration of online technology. *Curriculum Perspectives, 27*(1), 53-55.

Katz, E.J. & Aspden, P. (1997). A nation of strangers? *Communications of the ACM, 40*(12), 81-86.

Kerry, B. (2000). *The power of the Internet for learning: Moving from promise to practice — Report of the Web-based Education Commission to the President and Congress of the United States.* Available from the World Wide Web: http://www.ed.gov/offices/AC/WBEC/Final Report/WBECReport.pdf.

Kozma, R., Zucker, A., Espinoza, C., McGee, R., Yarnell, L., Zalles, D., & Lewis, A. (2000). *The online course experience: Evaluation of the Virtual High School's third year of implementation, 1999-2000.* Available from the World Wide Web: http://www.sri.com/policy/ctl/html/vhs.html.

Kraut, R., Kiesler, S., Boneva, B., Cummings, J., Helgeson, V., & Crawford, C. (2002). Internet paradox revisited. *Journal of Social Issues, 58*(1), 49-74.

Kraut, R., Patterson, M., Lundmark, V., Kiesler, S., Mukopadhyay, T., & Scherlis, W. (1998). Internet paradox: A social technology that reduces social involvement and psychological well-being? *American Psychologist, 53*(9), 1017-1031.

Louisiana Virtual School. (2002). Available from the World Wide Web: http://www.icet.doc.state.la.us/distance.

Marrou, H.I. (1956). *A History of Education in Antiquity*. (G. Lamb, Trans.) New York: Sheed and Ward.

Martinez, M. (1994). Access to information technologies among school-age children: Implications for a democratic society. *Journal of the American Society for Information Science, 45*(6), 395-400.

McLuhan, M. (1994). *Understanding Media: The Extensions of Man*. Cambridge, MA: MIT Press.

Moll, M. (1998). No more teachers, no more schools: Information Technology and the "deschooled" society. *Technology in Society*, 20, 357-369.

NEA. (2002). *Guide to Online High School Courses*. Washington, DC: National Education Association. Available from the World Wide Web: http://www.nea.org/technology/images/02onlinecourses.pdf.

Noam, E.M. (1995). Electronics and the dim future of the University. *Science*, 270, 247-249.

Odyssey Charter School. (2002). Available from the World Wide Web: http://www.odyssey.org/about_faq.htm.

OECD. (2001). *E-Learning: The Partnership Challenge*. Paris: OECD.

Open School. (2002). Open School in British Columbia, Canada. Available from the World Wide Web: http://openschool.bc.ca.

Outreach. (2001). *Is online schooling for you?* Available from the World Wide Web: http://www.rdpsd.ab.ca/osc/online/for.html.

Parks, M.R. (1996). Making friends in cyberspace. *Journal of Communication, 46*(1), 80-97.

Perelman. L. (1992). *School's Out: Hyperlearning, the New Technology and the End of Education*. New York: William Morrow and Company.

PEW. (2002). *The Internet goes to college: How students are living in the future with today's technology* (PEW Internet and American Life Project). Available from the World Wide Web: http://www.pewinternet.org/reports/toc.asp?Report=71.

Putnam, R.D. (1995, January). Bowling alone. America's declining social capital. *Journal of Democracy,* 6, 65-78.

Russell, G. (2002). Ethical concerns about virtual schools. *Journal of Religious and Theological Information, 5*(1), 31-47.

Russell, G. & Holkner, B. (2000). Virtual schools. *Futures,* 32, 887-897.

Russell, G. & Russell, N. (2001). Virtualisation and the late age of schools. *Melbourne Studies in Education, 42*(1), 25-44.

Rutherford, T. (1993). Democracy, markets and Australian schools. In C. James, C. Jones & A. Norton (Eds.), *A Defence of Economic Rationalism* (pp. 151-159). St. Leonards: Allen and Unwin.

SAEE. (2002). Executive summary of E-Learning: Studying Canada's virtual secondary schools. Available from the World Wide Web:http://www.saee.bc.ca/vschoolsum.html.

Schnitz, J. & Young, J.E. (2002). Models of virtual schooling. Available from the World Wide Web:http://www.can.ibm.com/k12/pdf/Virtualschool.pdf.

School of the Air. (2002). *Alice Springs School of the Air: History.* Available from the World Wide Web: http://www.assoa.nt.edu.au/history.html.

Segaller, S. (1998). *Nerds 2.01: A Brief History of the Internet.* New York: TV Books.

Simonson, M., Smaldino, S., Albright, M., & Zvacek, S. (2000). *Teaching and Learning at a Distance: Foundations of Distance Education.* Upper Saddle River, NJ: Merrill.

Smith, R. & Sachs, J. (1995). Academic work intensification: Beyond postmodernism. In R. Smith & P. Wexler (Eds.), *After Postmodernism: Education, Politics and Identity* (pp. 225-240). London: Falmer Press.

Tiffin, J. & Rajasingham, L. (1995). *In Search of the Virtual Class: Education in an Information Society.* London: Routledge.

Virtual Schooling Service. (2002). Available from the World Wide Web:http://www.education.qld.gov.au/curriculum/service/virtual/index.html.

Wellens, R.A. (1986). Use of a psychological distancing model to assess differences in telecommunication media. In L.A. Parker & O.H. Olgren (Eds.), *Teleconferencing and Electronic Communication* (pp. 347-361). Madison, WI: University of Wisconsin Extension.

Chapter II

Administering a Virtual School

Gaye Lang

Houston Independent School District, USA

Abstract

Why build a Virtual School? The rationale for the virtual school project arose from the need to address the shortage of teachers, especially in the area of advanced placement (AP) classes that school districts experience from time to time. Houston Independent School District was interested in providing a cost-effective model of instructional delivery that would positively affect student transportation issues and related expenses. In addition, there was a need to improve middle school students' academic skills in preparation for high school and college. Reclaiming the home school market in the greater Houston area was another benefit that was anticipated. In addition, a virtual school would prepare students for a 21st century learning environment.

Introduction

In Texas, during the latter part of the twentieth century, the superintendent of the Houston Independent School District (HISD) envisioned the implementation of a distance learning vehicle, a "virtual school." The Superintendent, Dr. Rod Paige, now U.S. Secretary of Education, recognized the potential of technology to revolutionize education in the new millennium. After much deliberation, research, consultation and contacts with professionals from Houston universities, he was given the approval by the HISD Board for the Virtual School Project in the fall of 1999.

Dr. Gaye Lang, an administrator in HISD, was chosen by the School Board to serve as project manager. Dr. Lang had demonstrated considerable skills in leadership and other characteristics in the inner-city school she headed while also serving as a part-time instructor at the University of Houston main campus. Additionally, she had acquired training and experience in various technologies while working with Region IV of the Texas Education Agency. Therefore, she was quite knowledgeable of possible contributions technology can make to positively affect the pedagogy essential for maximizing achievement.

The project manager was expected to assume roles including the completion of the design and creation of the final virtual school proposal, acquisition of approval of competent staff, and then administration of the futuristic method of education delivery for the HISD Virtual School. These tasks became quite a challenge since there were no other public schools in the state which had initiated such a program. It became apparent that no other public school in this country had developed a distance learning instructional tool for middle school students (grades six to eight). Therefore, the realization surfaced that perhaps the project manager's task could be compared with some early explorers and astronauts who had experienced "going where no one else had gone before."

Purposes

The purposes of this chapter are as follows:
1. Describe demographic data concerning HISD and its efforts to maximize learning through the implementation of technology.

2.   Identify the rationale for the virtual programs, including the mission and goals.

3.   Present literature concerned with perceptions regarding the effects of technology in education.

4.   Describe the development and implementation of the virtual program in HISD and some problems encountered.

5.   Identify budgetary and evaluation issues addressed, as well as perceptions of staff.

6.   Identify future trends in technology which may result in new pedagogy.

The goals of the HISD Virtual School Program include the following:

1.   To provide opportunities for high school and middle school students to acquire some course credits online that can foster preparation for special college entrance exams.

2.   To enable students to acquire enrichment courses online that can foster preparation for special college entrance exams.

3.   To permit students to participate in advanced placement (AP) classes which will permit them to increase skills in specific areas.

4.   To assist students with special needs, such as skill weaknesses due to deprivations encountered, in order to achieve greater success.

5.   To permit homebound instruction in order to accommodate students with medical problems.

6.   To permit students from our districts and others to acquire skills desired to enhance their technology skills.

7.   To enable students to experience different types of teaching styles which enhance their learning style.

8.   To provide activities which are interesting, motivational and meaningful and foster critical thinking.

9.   To expose participants to audio and visual experiences online which help to clarify particular concepts and skills.

10.   To enable students to become skillful in using email to communicate with other students and teachers.

Overview of the HISD and its Virtual Computer Program

The Houston Independent School District is the largest district in Texas and has often served as a model in the implementation of new methods, materials and strategies to enhance learning. The district has often utilized input from a number of higher educational institutions in the city to not only assist in the training of employees, but in the research to implement and measure the effectiveness of teachers and programs on various levels. Therefore, a number of professionals from colleges and universities, not only from the Houston area, but also in various parts of the country, provided consultation during the planning process for the HISD Virtual School.

Rationale for Virtual Schools and Mission of Our Virtual Program

The rationale for the virtual school project arose from the need to address the shortage of teachers, especially in the area of advanced placement (AP) classes, that school districts experience from time to time. Also, HISD was interested in providing a cost-effective mode of instructional delivery that would positively affect student transportation issues and related expenses. In addition, there was a need to improve middle school students' academic skills in preparation for high school and college. Reclaiming the home school market in the greater Houston area was another benefit that was anticipated.

The reason for the major emphasis on middle school is the fact that research findings document many middle school student skills are deficient. Too many students are leaving the middle grades intellectually unprepared; deficient in basic academic and critical reasoning skills; and lacking the strong sense of social and ethical obligation essential to their own growth, let alone to a viable democracy.

It has been found that if students do not have the necessary skills when they leave middle school, the dropout rate in high school increases. Middle school students tend to do less well on national exams than they did in elementary school, and the inequities between high-achieving and low-achieving students deepen during the middle school grades.

The mission of the HISD Virtual School is to provide HISD students with state-of-the-art online secondary courses through the use of Web-based interactive audio and video technologies in real time. The students can become involved in the interactive learning anytime, anywhere and at their own assessment level.

Realizing this vision, accomplishing the mission began with an assessment of the district's current computing resources and how best to turn those resources into a virtual school. The planning effort involved starting from square one. No virtual school project had ever been implemented prior to the current project approval. Initially, a considerable amount of time and effort was spent in doing research to study the information that was available on schools currently delivering instruction via the Internet. Working without staff also presented quite a challenge because the initial workload could not be delegated. Strict adherence to timelines was mandatory. Direct reporting to the superintendent of the district on a weekly basis was required during the embryonic planning stages. This method of monitoring was necessary throughout the virtual school's implementation phases.

Review of Related Literature

Nieto (1992, p. 77) expressed the belief that traditionally, in most schools, particularly secondary schools, subject matter dominates pedagogy and there is a need for making learning more fun and interesting. Pedagogy refers to how teachers perceive the nature of learning and what they do to create conditions that motivate students to learn and become critical thinkers. This belief was kept in mind as other research concerning new technologies to enhance learning was reviewed for the HISD Virtual School Program.

A continuous growth of literature and results of successful studies are being made in regard to virtual school programs. Jones (1998) describes a virtual classroom as one within a computer-mediated communication system where interaction between teachers and students take place by typing and reading from computer terminals. The software used has the ability to administer and grade tests on assignments. Virtual classrooms offer a powerful tool for teaching most skills and academic subjects. Kafka and Frank (1999) reported on a study, which involved the initiation of a partnership between a private technical college and a high school in Wisconsin. The college offered technical courses to junior and senior high school students for one year. The results revealed that partnering with the school and college yielded a great benefit, not only for students, but also for the teachers and the institution involved. The test results revealed students' growth in technical skills. Danham (1999) expressed the belief that information literacy, which is computer mediated, enables students to acquire knowledge and skills from various sources independently. Information literacy involves collaboration that enables students to access information efficiently, discern quality and authority, and to apply it to decision making and problem solving. Information literacy holds the keys to success in the rapidly growing technological world society. Students must access these keys to cope and compete in the global society of the millennium.

The information technology revolution is challenging every institution in our society. The capabilities of online communications and the Internet are changing the ways students learn, businesses operate, customers make purchases, and even how people socialize (Henderson, 1999, p. 14).

In schools, computers and online resources offer a new and powerful tool for teaching most skills and academic subjects. How best to use this tool is still a matter of debate. To rely too heavily on a new and unproven technology may work against the best interests of students who, regardless of the excitement over the new technology, still need well-rounded education to succeed. To ignore this new technology, on the other hand, or to waste it on outdated ideas about teaching, is to ensure that students will be unprepared for their futures.

According to Henderson (1999, p. 21), if there is ever any doubt about the importance of preparing the nation's young people for life in the information age, it has long since faded. Politicians, as well as educators, have proclaimed that Americans must prepare for the 21st century by connecting everyone to the information superhighway, the Internet and World Wide Web with its torrent of information, resources, and services.

Winters (1998, p. 58) identified the following advantages of the computer environment.

1.   They have the potential to stimulate learning.

2.   They are pervasive in society.

3.   Computer-based skills must be taught to children.

4.   The speed at which the computer can support change is significant.

5.   The expanded vision that the computer gives to students and teachers is important.

Winters (1997, p. 57) expresses the belief that it is difficult to understand why curriculum planners exclude computer-based learning environments from curriculum development. Instead of being integral to curriculum development, and completely integrating into it, the computer environment remains peripheral, an "add-on" in space and time that many teachers and administrators can reject. This "add-on" is often provided in laboratory settings, where scheduled periods allow students to "do" computing. In such settings, everything positive and creative about the computer environment is destroyed. Moreover, individual teachers who would like to embrace a computerized learning environment are forced by these arrangements to compete with other teachers for access to these sporadically used "tools."

Because of the rapid rise in literacy and education levels in many countries, there is an ongoing debate in our country over the quality of our education institutions, but others have no such concern. Many students from other countries come to our universities and obtain the U.S. brand on their university diplomas. The demand for electronic delivery of college courses should mushroom as we move into the 21st century. Our global society's rate of technological adaptation is both driving the demand and providing the tools to present education via electronic media (Jones, 1998).

According to Jones, the knowledge revolution now in progress is much more rapid than other evolutions because its principal resource is information. The tools of the information society drive the creation, storage, delivery, manipulation, and transformation of that information. The principal characteristic of the knowledge revolution is that it allows us to dramatically extend the human mind by introducing a new model of learning.

We are embedded in this evolution, and education has an important part to play. Education is a process because it is how information becomes meaningful. It converts information into knowledge.

It was reported by Winters (1997, pp. 136-137) that the idea of linking schools to the computer network known as the Internet was one of the hottest education topics of the 1990s. President Clinton stated that the United States should set a national goal of connecting every school to the information superhighway by the year 2000. He expressed the belief that we must make technology literacy a standard.

Clinton's networking goal was almost certainly beyond reach. Reports during that time revealed that only 3% of the nation's elementary, middle and high school classrooms had Internet connection, and only about 16% of the teachers used the Internet or computer-based communication services. These services include America Online, Compu Serve, or Prodigy, according to the research from Quality Education Data, Inc. They reported that linking the remaining classrooms could cost $30 billion or more plus at least $5 billion in annual operating expenses.

Some critics question whether the current fascination with computer networking is blinding us to more pressing needs. These critics believe that our schools face serious problems, including overcrowded classrooms, teacher incompetence and lack of security. Computers address none of these problems. Other criticisms of computer networking involve kinds of information available to children and youth, such as pornographic materials and dating services. A number of critics recommend censorship to limit information available to students.

Gay (1996, p. 2) reported on the findings of the president's National Information Infrastructure Advisory Council (NIIAC) as provided by Bonnie Bracey, education representative of the council. The findings revealed the following:

1. The digital pathway to the future is more than the Internet. It is a series of components, including the collection of private and public high-speed interactive, narrow and broadband networks that exist today and will emerge tomorrow.

2. The digital pathway is the satellite, terrestrial and wireless technologies that deliver content to homes, businesses, and other public and private institutions.

3. It is the information and content that flow over the infrastructure, whether in the form of a database, the written word, a film, a piece of music, a sound recording, a picture, or computer software.

4. It is computers, televisions, telephones, radios, and other products that people will employ to access the infrastructure.

5. It is the people who will provide, manage and generate new information and those who will help others to do the same.

6. It is the individual Americans who will use and benefit from the information superhighway.

7. Information superhighway is a term that encompasses all of these components and captures the visions of a nationwide, invisible, dynamic web of transmissions, mechanisms, information, appliances, content and people.

According to Porter (1997, p. 1), distance learning is educational or training information, including the instruction and experience that learners gain, although they are physically distant from the source of that information and instruction. It involves the use of new technologies, innovative materials and interactive methods. Distance learning is not a cure for all educational or training ills, but it does offer additional possibilities for educating and training more people than can be easily and efficiently accommodated in more traditional settings.

Porter (1997) expresses the belief that the starting points for distance learning should be the mechanics of establishing where the information is to be transmitted, transmitting the information, and leading activities which match educators/trainers with the interest and desire to teach a distance learning course. The learning requires educators and trainers, as well as learners, administrators, executives and others who play any role in a course or program, to take the best of in-person educational and training technologies and methods. They must find innovative ways to bridge the distance between the learner and the source of information. The most effective distance-learning professionals are working not only to provide highly interesting and effective courses and programs, but also to help their colleagues, learners, and society in general reconceptualize education and training.

Luhn (2000, p. 4) identifies some advantages and disadvantages of email (electronic mail). He expresses the belief that email is as important to some people as their automobile. It is often considered as the background of communications. It enables individuals to send messages internally on the office network or flash to distant countries. It permits day-to-day departmental communication with other institutions.

Some disadvantages of email involve permitting messages to be sent that are cold, sarcastic, or crushing, which are delivered at the speed of light. Individuals who use email negatively can avoid suffering the recipients' pain, look, glances or human interactions.

McCarthy (2000, p. 22) reports on a program being initiated in schools located in minority areas to help to reduce the gap between the number of computers available to students in high and middle-income families. The program has involved the passage of a law, which will permit tax credits for corporations donating their old computers to schools, to bridge the digital divide. The report indicated that despite the rapid growth of the Internet and plummeting computer prices, the gaps between technology haves and have-nots have actually widened along racial and economic lines in recent years. The New Millennium

Classroom Act is expected to help bring more computers to classrooms to foster greater computer literacy among minority students.

According to Gore (2000, pp. 35-36), the days of using home computers to play games are long gone. It's about e-commerce. This involves high-speed trade to build new businesses, provide new jobs, and pump new money into national, state and local economics.

Gore (2000) stated that the Lieutenant Governor of Texas, Rick Perry, in an address concerning the new economy, reported that access to computers and the Internet will be required in schools. He stated that Texas must bridge the so-called digital divide to get technology to people of every color, income level, and every corner of this big, diverse land.

It is the belief of Mosley (1999, pp. 36-37) that this is the age of information, and the ability of technology to pull together disparate bits of data puts pressure on companies and institutions to find people competent enough to operate specific machines and products. Too few people, it seems, can bridge the gaps between business and technology, communication, and world knowledge.

Many so-called experts clamor to restructure our education system to meet our future needs. Mosley expresses the belief that the coming tech-saturated world will need content engineers and knowledge managers to evaluate its effectiveness.

Winters (1998, pp. 22-23) identifies the following list of negatives concerning the information revolution:

1. Having much more information is bad for our heads because it leads to information overload. It has been estimated that scientific information doubles every twelve years and general information doubles every two and a half years. Ironically, the most important knowledge that should steer society, communities, enterprises and individual lives is increasingly in short supply relative to other information devoted to entertainment and commercial interests.

2. It is bad for the future. There seems to be a decline in the quantity and quality of serious future thinking.

3. It is bad for law and order. Computer crime is a major cost for business and government, and much of it is not recorded.

4. It's bad for national security.

5. It's bad for jobs. As the new software becomes more widespread, we can expect more unemployment and under-employment.

6.   It's bad for the environment. The information society is a distraction from the necessity of building a sustainable society.

7.   It's bad for democracy. As a society becomes more complex, people are turned off of politics and turned on to an expanding variety of electronic entertainment.

8.   It's bad for privacy. Interlinked databases have individual's names, numbers, and much more personal information.

9.   It's bad for quality of life. It speeds the pace of life and makes time increasingly scarce.

10.   The information revolution is bad for equality, creating ever-greater social gaps within and between gaps.

Jones (1998, p. 165) expressed the belief that the technology and communications revolutions are propelling us into a new Renaissance, the knowledge age. This age will accelerate as the private side of our world economy and cultural life.

In a domino-like fashion the media called for demonstrations of the product. These presentations were conducted at local, state and national venues. The idea of a virtual school began to gain acceptance and received a great deal of positive publicity. As we move through the 21st century, personal computers will become a part of the instructional tools used to educate students.

In 1959, children were entertained by Lincoln Logs, Barbie dolls and black and white television. Today's children are captivated by Nintendos, X-Boxes and computers (although Barbie is also still around). To grab the attention of these children and educate them will take a lot more than text online. Educators must deliver courseware to them that will compete with the flash of the video game, yet still provide them with a valuable learning experience. A new educational paradigm is upon us and everyone must embrace it or risk losing, as a society, intellectual footing with other industrialized countries of the world. America must "leave no child behind" and, with that as our mantra, we shall continue to develop and refine online courseware until every computer in every home, library, Internet café and office can be looked upon as a virtual school.

In today's world, the idea of a traditional "little red schoolhouse" is quickly becoming antiquated. Projections have been made that by the year 2010 nearly 65% of all students (young and adult) will take some part, if not all, of their courses online. This being the case, it is important for educators to form partnerships with high-tech businesses, universities and governmental entities that will work with them to continuously improve courseware delivered via the Internet. With these partners, educators can more fully explore the potential of "online distance learning." They can refine their courseware until it meets the needs of not only the "typical" student but also those of the non-traditional (home schooled), home bound or disabled student. The classroom is no longer a fixed geographic location, but rather it is a dynamic and virtual place that exists as much in the minds of the users as it does in the swiftly flowing bits and bytes of data packets moving between computers on the World Wide Web. In this new millennium there are no walls, no buildings and no limits to the possibilities the future holds.

Steps in the Development of the HISD Virtual Program

After an extensive review of related literature, communication with professionals and experts in the computer technology field, and visits to sites, the time had come to form an advisory board to begin our monumental task of developing and implementing our Virtual School Program. The Virtual School Advisory Board is a group of professionals drawn from the community in the areas of business, government and education. This board is tasked with oversight and guidance responsibilities for the virtual school. At first the board met on a monthly basis to help assure that the virtual school stayed on course with its development goals. Several months into the process, the board altered its meeting schedule to quarterly gatherings or as needed.

In addition to the Advisory Board, there was "outside" review from state universities and colleges. This review was for the purpose of validating the design and structure of the courseware so that it would meet industry standards expected in online learning products. The university reviewers were enlisted to gather baseline data for monitoring purposes. Some staff members were then assigned to assist in the preliminary processes. Staff positions were advertised in the HISD Employment Bulletin. Some technical personnel were recruited from industries. Requirements for staff varied but all were certified. Most were teachers who had acquired specific technology skills from special institutions, in-services provided by HISD and special consultants, and some were self-taught. All were skilled in at least two areas of expertise.

The staff members involved in the HISD Virtual School program included the following positions:

- Project Managers
- Instructional Evaluation Supervisor
- Senior Secretary
- Program Specialist
- Educational Technologist
- Content Area Specialists in: language arts, math, science, and social studies
- Courseware Development Specialists in: language arts and social studies
- Online Teachers for: language arts, science, math and social studies
- Graphic Designer
- Virtual School Partners
- Curriculum Writers
- Technology Support

We began by researching those virtual schools' projects that were up and running whether purchased, co-developed or completely out-sourced. The Florida Virtual School, the Concord Consortium and Texas Tech University Distance Learning program were some of the preliminary resources. Please note these were high school programs (there were no middle school programs at the time of research), and interactive courseware was limited. Over several discussions via the phone and in person, these organizations provided suggestions and guidelines as to how their projects were implemented.

The Virtual School Department scheduled meetings with district personnel in the area of technology. The meetings ensured that the current network infrastructure had the capability to facilitate the connectivity required to support a potentially large client base and media rich courseware. During these discussions, it was determined that the hardware presently in place would more than adequately accommodate our courseware and client load.

The district operated a multi-domain server configuration. From each of the respective schools a T1 line ran back to a central location. The T1 lines were then bundled into groups of 16, thereby producing a single T3 line. The T3 lines were connected to the Internet proper. At the heart of the network are multiple clusters of Windows NT 4 and Windows 2000 servers. These very robust

Compaq Proliant servers were the repositories for files and the platforms from which applications were served. Network cabling within the schools consisted of category five cable with a throughput of 10 to 100 megabits per second, depending upon speed of the network interface card. Hubs and routers were also in place to extend the signal and add more connections. All workstations were certified to run basic multimedia applications, and therefore were able to support our planned courseware.

Once it was validated that the infrastructure was in place and ready for courseware delivery via the Internet, the development could begin. The Virtual School Department project manager and the general superintendent contacted the curriculum department personnel so that the district and state curriculum could be used to provide content for the online courses. The focus was primarily on the middle school grades in the areas of language arts/writing, math, science and social studies.

The project began moving by offering preparation for the Advanced Placement Exam Review to high school students. The instruction was offered in spring 2000, which led to summer 2000 implementation of three Advanced Placement one-semester courses. In fall 2000, a full array of Advanced Placement classes were added to address the shortage of course offerings, student scheduling problems and insufficient student interest. These course offerings were out-sourced to a select vendor. This system served to meet the requirements of course delivery services online to students in a short period of time. The advanced placement courses served the purpose of piquing the interest of school administrators and community leaders. This interest then paved the way for continuing support and development of a virtual school.

After the high school program was in operation, the next step was to implement the middle school program. The HISD Virtual School online courses for middle school are based on HISD's curriculum. The curriculum is aligned with state mandated testing requirements. During the first year of operation, four sixth grade core courses were developed. These core subjects included language arts/writing, math, science and social studies. In addition, seventh and eighth grade level versions of these courses had also been developed and were ready for student participation. With the meetings and research completed, the priority became hiring a staff that was not only knowledgeable and capable, but had the energy to take on a project of this magnitude.

The course development process involved the selection of staff that included curriculum writers who prepared course lesson plans based on the district's approved curriculum. This group passed along the plans to the content area specialist (one per discipline) who made storyboards of the content. Then the courseware development specialist (also one per discipline) posted the content to a custom template. After this step, the graphic artist rendered the content and added images, animation and video as needed. The instructional evaluation specialist reviewed the quality of the content. The entire course development team edited the content and student activities, after which it was uploaded to the Web server for delivery via the Internet. In addition to these checks, the curriculum department reviewed the courseware via the Internet for quality control.

A virtual school requires expertise beyond that found in the traditional "bricks and mortar" school. It is important to assemble a team of individuals who are as comfortable with educational subject matters as they are with technology. They would receive training in specialized software that would allow them to convert the turn of a textbook page to the click of a mouse. In the online courses, students engage in a variety of interactive activities, including audio-led instruction, assigned reading, follow-up comprehension questions for feedback, video presentations, URL links for research, self-check exams, and chat room/email. Students log on through a course entry page with user names and passwords. Students then click on the course content icon to access interactive Web lessons. Other tools that serve as course resources are available on the entry page. Mentor teachers are available at schools to assist students and monitor their progress. E-teachers are on staff with HISD Virtual School and are assigned to be online during the instructional day with all students who are in their respective classes.

The Virtual School staff received a crash course on how to use Macromedia's Dreamweaver software. The training format provided the specialists with the knowledge and hands-on practice they needed to build and manage professional Web sites. The Dreamweaver fast track training modules included: Adding Content to a Site, Working with Graphics, Cascading Style Sheets, Page Design, and Creating Forms. The training objectives included: (1) Working with Dreamweaver Effectively; (2) Creating Pages with Well-structured HTML Content; (3) Creating Hyperlinks Between and Within Documents; (4) Adding Images and Image Maps to Web Pages; (5) Formatting Page Contents using Cascading Style Sheets; (6) Creating Page Designs and Templates using Tracing Images; (7) Testing and Deploying a Web Site; and (8) Working with HTML Forms.

The staff-training component also included instruction on Macromedia's Flash, Fireworks and Coursebuilder. Development specialists and content specialists integrated these applications into Dreamweaver pages to enhance the multimedia effects. Although the developers received extensive training, they continued to improve the product with a "hands on," on-the-job training approach.

For the assessment, it was decided to use Blackboard's System Administration Tool, which would be the front-end and assessment component for our courseware. The application provides students with course materials, discussion boards, virtual chat, Web-based email, online assessments, and a dedicated academic resource on the Web. Training was arranged for the entire Virtual School staff to learn the fundamentals of Blackboard in order to deliver the online curriculum to the Web in a format that conforms to the online education industry standards. The Blackboard system administrator position was established to ensure that the Web-based courses were administered and accessible twenty-four hours a day, seven days a week by developers and students. Blackboard is a comprehensive and flexible e-learning software platform that delivers a course management system. It also offers a customizable institution-wide portal for online communities.

There was a very steep learning curve required for staff to become proficient in the use of the Virtual School software applications. In spite of this challenge, course developers learned to use the software immediately after training in order to begin creating the templates for online courses. Upon completion of the template design, content specialists were directed to adhere strictly to the Houston Independent School District's approved curriculum to author interactive course material that would then be transferred into the newly designed online courseware. After the staff selection and the training had been completed, the concern was none of these were free. Therefore, budgetary and other concerns required special consideration.

Budgetary and Evaluation Issues

One might think that the personnel in the Virtual School had put the "cart before the horse" by discussing the Virtual School plans, stages of development and connecting it to the Internet before outlining the costs. When the proposal for the program was first approved, a projected budget was set. However, since the program was so new, the costs for specific requirements could only be estimated. After a thorough investigation of the existing equipment, technologies, and skills of the present department of technology personnel, it was found that some projected needs were already available. In addition, before compiling the review of the literature, visiting virtual schools, and communicating with various software and Web site developers, we learned to economize. Therefore, while conducting discussions about development, infrastructure and acquiring staff, the question "What are the costs?" was used frequently. Some of the major costs included:

- Start up process
- Web Server
- Consultants
- Hardware (including computers and printers)

Figure 1: Budget

HISD VIRTUAL SCHOOL: ACTUAL BUDGET 2000-2001

Start-up...$	68,083
Consultants to assist with courseware development.........	25,000
Acquire existing, applicable high school courseware........	168,000
Internet Access...	1,140
Hosted Environment including	41,000
Web Server................................20,000	
Blackboard Inc. Software License.......15,000	
Macromedia Software Site License.......6,000	
Hardware including:..	20,000
Computers (15 desktops, one laptop)	
Printers (two black and white, two color)	
Personnel...	869,071
Project Manager and Supervisor – 2	
Support Staff – 1	
Educational Technologist – 1	
Program Specialist – 1	
Course Developers – 6	
Online Teachers – 2	
Graphic Designer – 1	
Total...	$1,192,294

Note: This budget includes the development of four middle school courses and license negotiations with a vendor for five advanced placement high school courses. HISD's budget also accounts for training on the Blackboard and Macromedia products. Most importantly, in-house development grants HISD full product ownership.

- Courseware
- Software Licensee
- Internet Access
- Site Licensee
- Salaries of Personnel (including full-time, consultants, specialists, writers, online teachers and graphic designers)

Unlike the vendor model presented to us, HISD does not face large recurring implementation costs every year. It only pays a small annual license fee for its hosting software. Furthermore, HISD owns its Web server and only incurs software costs upon upgrade or for a new purchase.

There are certain *sunk costs* that every start-up department must bear that should be categorized as an initial investment and that are never recouped. Therefore, they should not be counted as a loss. HISD's *sunk costs* include office space and supplies, initial hardware and software applications and training for the staff.

Early in the planning process of the virtual program, the issue of building or buying courseware for middle schools was discussed. Pros and cons were identified and the decision was made to develop our own courseware. This choice was also a means to reduce some expenses, since some pros of building courseware would include:

1. It would belong to the district.
2. It can be updated, adapted or modified when needed.
3. It can become an economic asset if bought by other districts in Texas as well as others in the nation.
4. Our technical personnel can make adjustments or other services when needed.

HISD moved forward with developing its own product at a cost of $900,000 during the first year. For this amount, four middle school courses were developed and 12 employees were hired and trained during year one. As a result, HISD owns the product and solely controls all future profit margins, if any. In year two, $1 million was spent to develop eight middle school courses and maintain the departmental staffing requirements. So, at least for HISD, the conclusion was obvious that it was far better for the district to spend the funds necessary to create its own courseware rather than to contract with a vendor to do so. The advantages are that any changes, updates or upgrades to the product are at nominal cost.

Another issue, which arose after the Virtual Program was online, was to assess its operation and to evaluate students' and adults' perceptions in regards to its capabilities to foster independent learning. A decision was made to conduct a pilot study of the middle school virtual program. The issue arose concerning who we would use for the beta testing and how we would select them. After some deliberation, it was agreed that communications would be made with middle school principals in our district, describe the pilot program and invite them to participate. A form was enclosed for them to sign and return along with the name of the person who would be in charge of the program at their school. There were twelve middle school teachers who participated in the study and 400 students. A survey was designed for teachers and students to evaluate aspects of the lessons provided. The surveys for students were also concerned, to a great extent, with their perceptions concerning their ability to navigate through the lessons, whether they were competent in the use of computers and the Internet, and the peripherals included to operate the lessons. The surveys also proposed to determine whether students were learning independently. Additionally, the surveys requested their perception of whether the lessons were too difficult, too easy, or challenging, and whether they enjoyed the experiences. Comments from principals revealed that they were very pleased to have been a part of the implementation of the first public virtual school in our district and state. They were very impressed to find out that students who participated had made considerable progress, were attending school more regularly, and there was some evidence of greater interest in setting higher goals for their future.

The teachers' survey requested similar information, in addition to their perceptions of the value of the graphics, pictures, charts and variations for responding to specific activities. Since each student was enrolled in only one of the four subjects which the program offered, and some schools had different schedules of time spent on the programs, the number of variables hampered the measurement of specific progress made. Some teachers made comments about students' improvement in academic achievement, attitudes toward school and in their self-esteem. Additionally, some teachers reported that there was improvement in attendance as well as self-motivation. The survey results revealed an overwhelming number of positive responses made by the students and teachers. These results revealed that both groups were supportive of the Virtual School Program.

In addition to the pilot study of the Virtual Program, some HISD administrators, department heads, advisory council members and retired teachers who were serving at schools as volunteers, tutors or substitutes expressed special interest in going online to view some of the lessons. Some made special requests and were provided temporary passwords to access aspects of the programs. Some requested surveys to evaluate the program, and their comments and suggestions were also very positive and supportive. Some of these educators indicated that they would have liked to have had the technologies available when they were in school or teaching. They expressed a belief that students today and in the future will have many opportunities to broaden their knowledge and achieve higher goals as a result of learning experiences which technologies provide.

The media provided coverage, and our Virtual School received nationwide attention. The program has expanded considerably since its beginning.

Implications

The experiences encountered during the planning, development and implementation of the HISD Virtual School have resulted in the realization that what may appear as impossible can be achieved. Using the analogy of Lewis and Clark as well as the achievements of astronauts, inventors, explorers and others who have faced many new challenges, we accomplished the goal of implementing our Virtual School Program. Our greatest challenges involved the development of our own courseware for middle school students. This experience may help to serve as a guide to others who want to ensure that courseware is consistent with their own curriculum, the needs of their population, and the limitations their district may face regarding economic possibilities.

The related literature reviewed, in addition to communication with technologists as well as vendors and other specialists, assisted greatly in our awareness of the value of distance learning, another name for virtual schools. These experiences have brought about greater awareness of how our educational systems can be revolutionized through the use of virtual programs.

This venture has not diminished the continuous need for teachers, as some may think, but has brought about greater awareness of the use of distance learning as an essential tool. Teachers are still needed to develop courseware which utilizes teaching techniques that are considered as being most effective in increasing achievement. Online teachers are needed to assist students who may be experiencing some difficulties. Teachers are also needed to keep up with the records of students' responses to lessons to ensure they have fulfilled requirements. Teachers can be accessed in some lessons for audio and visual assistance, in addition to being contacted by email.

Virtual schools offer promise for closing gaps between the "haves" and "have-nots," as well as increasing knowledge and understanding between many people in various parts of our world. It offers promise of increasing relation-ships, health knowledge and skills, as well as improving life for many in undeveloped countries and those deprived in our own country.

Some of the situations or experiences, which could be avoided in order to reduce problems, expenses or excessive time use, include the following:

1. Avoid setting a specific deadline for implementation of the program before consideration of steps involved in the process and considerable consulta-tion, visitations to existing programs, and some staff members have been acquired.

2. Do not wait until budgetary concerns are tentatively set before surveying existing technologies or equipment that are available.

3. Do not plan for implementation of a specific subject area or grade level before thoroughly determining courseware availability and whether it corresponds with existing curriculum and specific needs of students enrolled.

4. Avoid waiting until a specific need arises to try to schedule specialists for part-time technical work.

5. Do not wait until the plans for implementing a program are final to make the decision to purchase or develop one's own courseware.

Future Trends

There are now many vendors with educational courseware on the market (though courseware specifically for middle school is still very limited), and they run the gamut from very interactive advanced placement courseware to "test online" with CD supplements. The important factor in buying one of these products is to locate a package that allows for a "quick start" or "turn-key" solution (this implies the district has Internet access and multimedia workstations). With courseware of this type it would be relatively easy to have it in place, for use by students, within a matter of weeks.

There are advantages to buying a package in that the overhead is substantially reduced. There is no need to have servers or staff to maintain the courseware as the burden for that support falls onto the shoulders of the vendor. The cost can vary, depending on the number of users and the interactivity of the courses purchased, and it would be a continuing cost that would most likely rise each year. So, though buying courseware from a vendor is an attractive option (and even HISD used some vendor courseware during its initial phases and currently), it does not place a huge burden on the organization in terms of infrastructure and staffing requirements. In the end, purchasing courseware is not a perfect solution due to issues of cost and product ownership.

In-house design and development of courseware can provide a 10-to-one return on the district's investment over time. Research supports these figures and demonstrates that internal courseware creation and development will improve the quality of course delivery while helping to implement and refine cost-effective online courses.

One of the final key elements in delivery of a good online course is that of technical support. Having established the client market the courseware is to be delivered to, it is important to have a technical support team that can maintain the servers, troubleshoot hardware/software issues, and work with the clients and developers in resolving any problems originating either at the workstation, at the server, or somewhere in between.

The courseware is delivered from an Internet Information Server. It is this software which makes the courseware accessible to Internet users. So it becomes necessary to have on staff an individual who is adept in managing not only IIS servers but has a working knowledge of database language (SQL) and management. Though it would be great if the person who manages the Web server and database could also support the developers and the end-users, it was not feasible. Also, it is doubtful one could find someone who is a database specialist and who had expertise in the hardware/software functionality of the network and workstation. For this area of support, it is necessary to have on staff a network engineer/administrator who has a good deal of "hands-on" hardware and software experience. These days it is smart to acquire people who have gained certification (such as Microsoft, Novell or A+) in their special area of systems support. Certification is an indication that the person has received training and passed examinations guaranteeing a level of competency that is necessary in any technology-oriented endeavor. By acquiring people who are certified as your support staff, you have the comfort of knowing you will have individuals who already have a strong technology background and who have the skills and knowledge to face the challenges of supporting an online learning product.

A certified database specialist along with a certified network engineer/administrator should be able to address just about any problem that may arise for a small to mid-sized technology group. These two individuals would be responsible for helping to perform these functions: maintain the server, configure the workstations, assist the developers with hardware/software matters, update and maintain software, as well as software libraries, perform routine backups of "mission critical" data, help clients with problems that may occur when connecting to courseware and train staff and clients in the use of the courseware. While all of these are absolutely, positively necessary, it is equally important to know about the product.

Making the virtual school a reality that others can reach out and touch should become one of the primary goals. The journey should begin with small presentations in the local school district then at other districts and locations throughout the state. During the presentations, "live" access to the courseware should be facilitated as a "hands on" activity. These "road shows" should prove to be beneficial towards getting the word out about the virtual school. In time, the local media become aware of the Virtual School Program and therein began the television and print marketing of the virtual school concept.

Conclusion

As a result of this report of the challenges faced in the development and administration of the Virtual School in the Houston Independent School District, it is believed that other districts across the nation may have an easier task to implement their own programs. With the expansion of distance learning, many students who are handicapped, residing in hospital facilities, incarcerated in juvenile facilities or have other special needs may be able to prepare for their futures and reach their fullest potential. Additionally, students who have special talents can complete courses quickly and achieve their goals early to make our global society a better place in which to live.

References

Donham, J. (1999). Collaboration in the media center: Building partnerships for learning. *NASSP Bulletin, 605,* 20-26.

Gay, M. (1996). *The New Information Revolution.* Santa Barbara, CA: Contemporary World Issues.

Gore, C. (2000, April). Bridging the digital divide. *Texas Technology,* 35-36.

Henderson, H. (1999). *Issues in the Information Age.* San Diego, CA: Lucent Books, Inc.

Jones, G. (1998). *Cyberschools, an Education in Renaissance.* Englewood: Jones Digital Century, Inc.

Kafka, K. & Frank, L. (1999). Wiring a tech school partnership. *The High School Magazine, 6*(4), 42-44.

Killion, J. & Hirsch, S. (1998, March 18) A crack in the middle. *Education Week on the Web.*

Lipsitz, J., Mizell, M., Jackson, A., & Austin, L. (1997, March). *Speaking with one voice. A manifesto for middle grades reform.* Kappan.

Luhn, R. (2000, May 4). My e-mail, my bodyguard. *Computer User Technology, Solutions for Today's Businesses.*

McCarthy, J. (2000, April 22). Subtracting the divide – New act helps bring computers to the classroom. *Texas Technology.*

Mosley, K. (1999, November). The y2001 problem. *Texas Technology,* 36-37.

Nieto, S. (n.d.). *Affirming diversity.* New York: Longman.

Porter, L. (1997). *Creating the Virtual Classroom – Distance Learning with the Internet.* New York: John Wiley & Sons, Inc.

Winters, P. (Ed.). (1997). *Computers in Society.* San Diego, CA: Greenhorn Press.

Winters, P. (Ed). (1998). *The Information Revolution.* San Diego, CA: Greenhorn Press, Inc.

Chapter III

Managing Virtual Schools: The Canadian Experience

Margaret Haughey
University of Alberta, Canada

William Muirhead
University of Ontario Institute of Technology, Canada

Abstract

Although Canada has offered alternative forms of schooling through distance education for over a century, the advent of online schooling options has helped overcome two of the major obstacles: lack of sufficient current resources and lack of regular interaction. Today across Canada, online schooling options tend to be focused at the high school sector. However, in Alberta there are more than 19 schools, most of which offer elementary and secondary courses. The schools mainly serve their local population, and the issues administrators face include marketing and obtaining infrastructure support and facilities, as well as ensuring quality of curricula and student-teacher interaction, meeting parental concerns, and provision of professional development.

Introduction

Virtual schooling in Canada is a growing phenomenon. A virtual program refers to a series of courses that are offered via the Internet to students in grades 1-12, usually by their local school jurisdiction. It meets the needs of parents who want their children to be involved with the school program but not their peers, and the needs of students who cannot access sufficient credits to complete a high school diploma. It provides opportunities for students who wish to accelerate their programs, and for those who cannot attend a school regularly (due to travelling, illness, incarceration, or activities such as sports, music, etc.). In this chapter, we describe the Canadian experience with virtual schooling, discuss administrative issues and outline trends. We begin with a brief overview of the development of virtual schooling in Canada from its initial development in Alberta in 1996, with more than 20 schooling programs, to its rapid expansion across Canada. Then, we will focus more directly on the virtual schools in Alberta. In particular, we identify the administrative issues that have arisen, that are in some ways unique to online schooling, from admission requirements to course development, and from parent support to funding. We have also included ongoing issues related to educational leadership, such as issues of supervision of teachers, quality of instruction, and provision of professional development. Finally, we outline likely trends and their implications.

The History of Virtual Schooling in Canada

Geography and demographics have combined to make Canada a country where distance is an integral aspect of life. Canada is larger in area than the continental United States, but with only a fraction of its population, the majority of whom live within 100km of the United States border. Perhaps for those reasons, Canadian educators have always employed technologies to bring together those students who were unable to access courses with teachers who provided schooling at a distance. Since the 1920s, most Canadian provinces have provided distance education as one schooling option (Haughey, 1990). Once, that schooling depended on print and the mail; now virtual schooling uses networked computers to provide similar options to today's students. While initially distance education was provided to students who were unable to attend a school, over the years it became the option of choice for students whose small schools did not provide the courses necessary for high school completion or further education. Unfortunately, the dropout rate from these courses was relatively high, at almost 80%. Researchers (Balay, 1978) pointed out that the independent model of providing print materials to students who would do their work in school without much supervision or guidance led most often to low commitment on the part of the student and a high likelihood of non-completion. An alternative model, which employed local facilitators to provide student support and guidance, demonstrated that, in the appropriate circumstances, student completion rates could rise to more than 80% (Froese, Harris, Restall, & Witherspoon, 1987; Gee, 1989; Little & McKibbon, 1990). Hence, in the following decade, Canadian jurisdictions were already aware of the importance of student support in ensuring success when employing alternative models of schooling.

In Canada, the development of online schooling had its impetus in the requests of Alberta parents to home-school their children. Coupled with the economic downturn of the 1990s, when 141 school jurisdictions were amalgamated and reduced to 63 and smaller schools were forced to close, were concerns about the long distances and length of time students had to spend on school buses during the winter months. Parents were also concerned about changes in the provincial language arts curriculum, and they wanted more control over what and how their children learned. As a result, provincial legislation was changed to allow parents to undertake the education of their children under the general supervision of a willing school board. Parents could receive advice and assistance from a local teacher, but could choose the curriculum to follow and the materials to use, as long as the objectives of the required provincial program of studies were kept in mind, and their children took a yearly assessment test or similar procedure to determine their progress. In addition, funding was restructured to reflect this change and parents could offset the costs of instructional materials and curriculum guides against a provincially designated amount for each student.

As children progressed through the primary grades, many home-schooling parents found instruction in some subjects to be quite challenging. These parents began to seek other alternatives to ensure that their children received a quality program. At the same time, jurisdictions were concerned that if sufficient numbers of parents withdrew their children, decreases in funding would increase pressures on the system at a time when the province was announcing annual reductions in educational spending. The advent of the Internet and the World Wide Web provided both system administrators and parents with another option. For the parents, their children could remain at home but part or all of their schooling could be provided by certificated teachers in a virtual school. For the school administrators, virtual school programs could provide a way to meet these parents' needs and the funding per child could help underwrite the operation.

For many parents and students virtual schooling provided the flexibility they desired. Virtual schooling gave flexibility to parents and students who, for a variety of reasons, wanted free from the restrictions of in-school attendance. These reasons included children who were involved in elite sports or fine arts activities with demanding schedules which made regular attendance impossible, as well as those in families whose work (missionary, oil industries, ranching) took them to other countries for periods of time. Other reasons included students who fared better when they were not attending a school, whether for social, learning or medical reasons. Virtual schooling also provided opportunities for those students who wanted a more interactive experience than traditional distance education was able to provide, and for those students in regular school attendance who wanted to obtain additional courses to expand or accelerate their programs.

The development of virtual schooling owes much to the province's involvement in distance learning. Like other Canadian provinces, Alberta had a provincial Distance Learning Centre that developed appropriate learning materials and also provided distance learning opportunities for students throughout the province. In 1992/1993, for example, 628 elementary students and 7,586 secondary school-age students registered for courses. In all, over 18,000 students were registered for secondary courses (Haughey & Muirhead, 1999). In addition, approximately 12,000 course enrolments were funded through jurisdictions, indicating that the number of distance learning enrolments was even more extensive. These students used distance learning courses, but their instructors were hired by the local jurisdiction in order to decentralize provision, to enable faster feedback and to provide more local support. In 1995, the

Distance Learning Centre School began offering an email option to its students and, by 1997, when the school was relocated under a school division, more than 100 students were registered online (www.adlc.ca).

Today, all provinces and territories offer online education. In Canada, education and its funding are under the mandate of individual provinces and territories and there is no national body at the federal level. Instead, each province and territory identifies its own issues and chooses what is most appropriate for its own context. In the Atlantic Provinces (Newfoundland and Labrador, Nova Scotia, New Brunswick, Prince Edward Island) —those bordering the east coast — the issues concerned declining populations and the need to enhance the educational attainment of early school leavers. Therefore, in Newfoundland, the provincial network, STEM-Net (www.stemnet.nf.ca), which had used audio and video-conferencing to provide Advanced Placement courses to students in small rural communities (Brown, Sheppard, & Stevens, 2001), has recently decided to provide a much broader variety of courses through the Internet. This will expand both the numbers of students who can avail themselves of courses and the range of options available (W. Sheppard, personal communication, February, 2002). In Nova Scotia, the emphasis is on helping early school leavers return to school to complete their high school qualifications. In many small communities, this is being done through local adult high schools, but the largest centre, Halifax, recognizing that many students are also working or looking after young families and cannot attend evening school on a regular basis, now offers courses entirely online through its Flexible Learning and Education Centres (www.glooscap.ednet.ns.ca/~margie.hopkins/index.html. Last accessed 17.10.02).

In Quebec, the issue is also one of providing sufficient courses to pupils in small communities. The commission of school superintendents has decided to focus on students in elementary grades, not only to enhance courses, but also to help provide a broader social base for students (T. Laferrière, personal communication, June 2002). In Ontario, there are pressures from rural schools for course options, especially at the secondary level, but there are also pressures from students in urban areas for greater flexibility in obtaining courses. Many jurisdictions have developed a virtual school program for their students. Examples include Durham, (www.durhamvc.org/), Peel (www.school-online.ca/) and District School Board Ontario North East (http://205.150.219.183/home/welcome.html). Another model is the use of partnerships between school boards and a private virtual school, such as those with www.virtual highschool.com. A number of rural jurisdictions have formed a virtual portal that will handle offerings from schools in any of the participating jurisdictions. One example is the Avon Maitland Distance Learning Centre (www.virtuallearning.on.ca/fmain.htm). Alternatively, the Toronto School Board, which is the largest school board in Canada, has opened a virtual school that offers the mathematics and science curriculum to students in grades 8-12 (www.goschool.org/overview/inderx/htm).

Across the prairies, in Manitoba and Saskatchewan, the need to provide options for students in small rural schools has resulted in a number of models. There are consortia of school boards who combined to offer courses, such as Inform Net in Manitoba (www.inform-net.mb.ca), single boards who have chosen to confine course offerings to students within their own jurisdiction, such as Saskatoon Catholic Cyber School (www.scs.sk.ca/cyber/home.htm), and government agencies who have coordinated options for their province. One example of the latter is Central I-School (www.centralischool.ca), which is coordinated by the Saskatchewan government. Teachers are seconded to the provincial department to write the I-school courses and students from any jurisdiction in the province can sign up within the appropriate regulations. The student's home school assigns the credits. One of the differences about the Saskatchewan initiative is that the multi-media course development is for the provincial network rather than for individual schools.

In Alberta, there is also a variety of models. In 2002/2003, there are 19 virtual school programs operating in the province. All are attached to local school boards. Some serve students in their jurisdiction only, and so tend to have small enrolments of approximately 100 to 250 students. Some serve students throughout Alberta and tend to have larger enrolments of approximately 4 to 600 students; the largest schools also register national and international students and have enrolments in excess of 2,000 students.

On Canada's Pacific coast, in British Columbia, only the nine provincially funded distance education schools could offer distance learning courses, and in 1995/1996 they were serving over 23,000 secondary and 2,200 elementary students. In 1994, they began putting their courses online and subsequently formed a consortium of distance learning schools CONNECT (www.deconnect. com). Recently, the legislation has been changed and local school jurisdictions have begun to advertise their own online courses, such as the Vancouver School Board (www.vsb.bc.ca/VSBLN/), or a consortium of school districts called COOL SCHOOL, the Consortium of Online Schooling, Vernon, BC (www.coolschool.bc.ca).

On Canada's northern coast, in Yukon, Northwest Territories, and Nunavut, schools have arrangements with provinces to the south both in terms of provision of online options and also in the development of courses particular to Canada's Arctic coast. For example, a multimedia online version of *Northern Studies 10*, a mandatory course in the culture, history and languages of the Northwest Territories was developed in cooperation with Chinook College (www.chinookcollege.com/online/), a virtual school in Calgary, Alberta.

Virtual Schooling in Alberta

Because of its funding arrangements, Alberta, in 1995, was the first province to support online learning entirely through virtual schooling. These school programs have continued to develop and adapt with changes in information and communications technologies. The province of Alberta is about the same size as the state of Texas, but has a population of only 3 million. There are 63 school jurisdictions that, together, are responsible for the school education of approximately 590,000 students in 1,900 schools. Outside the large urban areas, these schools are likely to have small populations of about 200 students in grades 1-6, 7-12, or 1-12 schools.

The expansion of Internet services to small towns in Alberta was essential to the development of a telecommunications infrastructure for virtual schooling. In 1994/1995, a government task force examined the extent of use of computers and computer communications technologies in schools. Their report supported the development of a coordinated infrastructure and funding was made available in 1996. A federal initiative, coordinated by SchoolNet (www.schoolnet.ca), and begun in 1993, has ensured that all Canadian schools were hooked up to the Internet by March 1999. However, in Alberta, outside the major corridor linking the two major cities, most of the connections were via a 56 or even 28.8 kb modem. The provincial government, dissatisfied with the quality of the province's telecommunications infrastructure, has been implementing a SuperNet project in which more than 400 communities and all schools will be linked through a broadband network by 2004. For schools, this network will be capable of 10mb per second (approximately downloading 50 pages/second) (www.connect.gc.ca).

Alberta's Virtual Schools

In fall 1995, four schools received permission from their school boards to begin offering virtual programming for their students. Their initiative was immediately replicated by other jurisdictions so that, within two years, 22 virtual school programs were being offered. In an initial analysis of Alberta's virtual school programs (Haughey & Muirhead, 1999; Muirhead, 2000, 2000a), six schools used FirstClass, three used Lotus Notes, three used web pages, seven used a combination of web pages and Adobe files to send assignments, and one had experimented with LearnLinc and WebCT. Some also used a web-based interaction software such as Microsoft's NetMeeting.

At this early stage in their development there were already a variety of instructional formats being offered. We identified four patterns. The independent learner pattern, which was based on the original distance learning model, used email as the main communication source. Materials were either accessed on the web or lessons were sent by email. The student worked on the assignments and contacted the teacher if there were any difficulties. This model stressed autonomy and flexibility for both student and teacher. In contrast, the teacher-mediated pattern stressed interaction as an ongoing aspect of the learning process. Students were required to sign on within a designated time in the morning and provide daily work schedules. Often, teachers provided the actual module only, so students could not work ahead. Students were expected to contact the teacher if they had any difficulties, but the teacher might also ask the student to respond to questions about the work. This model was more frequently used with junior secondary and elementary students. The third pattern involved group interaction. Here synchronous conferencing communications were used to have students and teacher online at the same time. The teacher set the topic for discussion and students participated while the teacher monitored the interactions. The teacher's task was to summarize, clarify, support, explain, and extend the discussion. The fourth pattern, parent-mediated, where the teacher and parent shared in the instructional process, was the basis for the home-schooling programs. We found that because of the short startup time, many teachers were still involved in course development. Appointed to teach in the program, most had only beginning computing skills and lacked design and course development strategies suitable for online learning. Hence, many of the initial programs were still text-based and had been developed by the teachers themselves, often based on materials from the originating jurisdictions or from the provincial technology services branch.

A recent review of online schools (Haughey & Purdy, 2002) identified a number of changes. Almost all schools were now using proprietary course management software, most often WebCT. The course materials were posted on the school's platform, but while some teachers were adding audio and video segments to further enhance students' learning, the previously identified instructional patterns still remained. The independent learner pattern was still important, especially in the senior grades. Students could pace themselves and move through the materials more quickly if they so chose. However, usually student access to the course site was monitored daily, and those who did not access the site for a couple of days were contacted to ascertain if there were difficulties. The teacher-mediated pattern still involved daily sign-ins, but course materials were now on the web, and so teachers tended to monitor student progress through their weekly assignments, which were usually emailed to the teacher. As well, the student in all forms of virtual learning more often used the telephone than email when they were looking for assistance with something that arose during their work, and so online teachers often had regular telephone contact with their students. In these two patterns the emphasis is on the individual's learning with greater or lesser autonomy and flexibility depending on the level of parental support and the grade level of the student. In the third pattern, the emphasis is on learning with one's age group peers while at home. The group interaction pattern was similar to the teacher-mediated pattern, except teachers used some form of synchronous conferencing to pace students. Usually, teachers gave students a timetable with designated times when they were expected to sign onto a synchronous conference, using software such as Elluminate (www.elluminate.com), where students could participate in two-way audio and also share a whiteboard. Frequently, the interactions were teacher-led and involved explanations or group reports from students. These students often had to do daily signing-in and they had sufficient online synchronous conferences scheduled so that they were at their desks for about the same amount of time as if they had attended school. In contrast, students in the independent or teacher-mediated patterns often reported that they could complete their schoolwork in about three hours per day compared to the five and a half hours in a classroom setting.

These instructional patterns are not only reflections of the different learning philosophies of the individual schools, but also of their response to issues of autonomy versus structure, pacing versus flexibility, continuous progress versus traditional grading patterns, and the level of teacher involvement which parents expected. They raise a variety of issues that will continue to need to be addressed: Who are the designated clientele? What is the purpose of regular teacher interaction? How much synchronous conferencing is best? How are different learning styles best accommodated? How can active learning skills be best supported? What are the comparative costs involved in the various models?

Administrative Issues in Alberta's Virtual Schools

In most situations, Alberta's virtual schools began as specific projects under the supervision of a school principal. Teachers were assigned, hired or volunteered to develop and teach specific courses in the virtual program. In a regular school setting, principals are expected to help define and consistently model the purpose for the school, to work with teachers and support staff to provide positive working relationships that focus on teaching and learning, to know the students and their parents and engage the community in the purpose of the school, to ensure adequate resources, to provide adequate time for professional development and opportunities for collaboration, and to meet the public's expectations for accountability. When principals in the virtual school settings began to organize their programs they found themselves faced with a different set of issues within these same requirements.

For the principals, setting a purpose involved understanding their own perspectives on the use of technology in education, but that was only one aspect of setting a philosophy for the program. Some wanted a focus on continuous progress, while a number stressed the importance of students' needs in deciding on the focus or goals for the program. The issues they raised included whether the program should be predominantly synchronous or asynchronous, whether it should be calendar or client-paced, and whether it should be for the traditional year or year-round. While many saw the virtual program as a way to step aside from the traditional structuring of learning, only one principal envisaged an activity-oriented, project-based, interdisciplinary program.

These views were also evident in their discussions of structure. One of the advantages of virtual schooling was that it could occur from any location, and principals wondered about the wisdom of having teachers work from home and what this would involve in terms of computer hardware, Internet costs, fax machines, cell phones and pagers. They worried about specifying the number of hours during which teachers should be available for student contact, and the impact of different models of instruction and their relationship to students' slow dial-up 28.8kb connections. Class size was another issue, since principals and teachers had no clear idea of how numbers and models of instruction interacted. We found that the pupil-teacher ratio varied considerably among the different programs (Haughey & Muirhead, 1999; Haughey & Purdy, 2002; Muirhead, 2000a).

The development of the courses was seen as a crucial aspect of their first years as online school administrators. They varied in their requirements, one noting the need for rules while another stressed the importance of development teams. What we found in a subsequent study (Muirhead, 2000a) was that most teachers had only the summer between being assigned to the virtual school and beginning to teach. This meant that, especially in the first few years, there were issues of teacher motivation and commitment, of the time needed to develop materials, and to discuss the issues involved in teaching online. These required additional teacher support and sufficient time for sharing experiences. Litke (1998), in describing the development of one virtual school, reported that problems with "overworked" teachers was one factor that led to the school's closure. One administrator referred to the human resources issues as involving recruitment and hiring, staff deployment, supervision, and professional development.

In situations where teachers were teaching a combination of site-based and virtual courses, issues around which program got precedence and how to handle student access when the teachers were teaching site-based classes proved problematic. This was not unlike another concern which principals expressed: the teachers they most wanted to hire and the ones who frequently volunteered were experienced teachers with solid reputations as engaging teachers who were seeking a different experience. Unfortunately, especially in smaller jurisdictions, their principal colleagues were unhappy about losing such staff. Principals mentioned teacher supervision, and this often focused on their teachers' ability to interact with students and project a caring, positive tone in text-based communications. The principals knew that there needed to be enhancement of most courses but saw this as a matter of time; when teachers became more competent and comfortable with the technology and cognizant of online resources, this would occur.

Another issue that concerned principals was student evaluation. Students in Alberta are required to write Provincial Achievement Tests in grades 3, 6 and 9, and the grade 12 Diploma Examinations. Scollie (2001) reported the results of a survey of parents and students, and of teachers and administrators in virtual schools. He concluded that almost all surveyed (more than 90%) were generally or very satisfied with the quality of education. He also did an assessment of student grades from achievement tests and diploma examinations for 1998/1999 and 1999/2000, the first two years many of these schools were in operation. His analysis indicated that participation rates were lower (70% as opposed to 95%) and that, while results were improving and score ranges were similar to provincial ranges in language arts and grade 6 social studies, they were much lower in grade 9 mathematics, science and social studies. In a subsequent provincial analysis of the 2000 achievement results (Alberta Learning, 2001), the analysts concluded that students in virtual schooling had similar levels of achievement in grades 6 and 9 English and lower levels of achievement in grades 6 and 9 mathematics than would be predicted given their prior level of achievement. Mathematics, with its use of formulae, diagrams, and specific positioning of information on a page, has been particularly difficult to teach online. Many schools resorted to fax machines to make the transfer of assignments easier for students. These were areas that principals were continuing to monitor.

Most principals found that their time, at least initially, was taken up by other concerns. In practice, administrators spent their time handling student recruitment and answering parental concerns. These involved listening to parents' complaints about their experiences with the public school system without engaging in argument, talking to parents about non-performing students and dealing with situations where the student was not supervised and needed to be disciplined. In most jurisdictions, parents had to sign a form indicating that there would be an adult providing direct supervision of the student while working on school requirements. Although some schools tried to limit student interaction by not distributing email addresses, students quickly developed their own networks and chat forums where they traded software games rather than ideas about school topics. Principals found these situations were ameliorated when schools opted to use a proprietary platform, which then meant that monitoring of student forums was much easier and other chats were the responsibility of the cooperating parent. Smith (2000) noted in her survey of parents that while they had a wide range of reasons for preferring the online environment for their children, they believed their children's academic performance, satisfaction with learning, and personal confidence had all improved.

In terms of technology resources, most principals were more interested in the quality of the services than the actual infrastructure, hardware and software that were usually under the coordination of the district's technology specialist. Instead, the principals commented on the need for consistency in the service offered. Having their own server was seen as an advantage and having parents' email addresses was also helpful. The issue of cost was one where all coordinators had had difficulties. Some were trying to amortize the costs of their hardware and software over time and were envious of those who had managed to obtain corporate sponsorship of their technology services. Because many of these virtual programs were sited in space "surplus to needs" in a regular school, there was an ongoing balancing act between in-school funding and virtual program costs. Some principals with large enrolments were able to fund development while others were looking at deficits. Having small student numbers and controlled growth might be the best advice for site-based schools, but virtual schools needed sufficient enrolment to break even from the beginning.

They focused on planning and supported the need for a year-long planning process prior to opening involving setting target dates, developing an infrastructure needs plan, and doing in-depth research on purchased software and course materials. One area where ongoing planning was essential was in advertising and marketing. This area was relatively new to the principals and many cautioned, "Build slowly," and "Grow over time to become self-supporting." Because these programs developed in a climate of parent choice, principals recognized that some parents would do comparison-shopping. A number of principals were troubled by this system which seemed to encourage competition for students. Others saw that in their situations, having a healthy number of students was a means to providing better services for all their students, and so had a stronger business orientation to the need for a market focus. Of the 22 schools, five schools had opted to have at least a provincial focus, four shared courses between partner jurisdictions, while 13 jurisdictions restricted enrolment to students from that catchment area. What all soon realised, however, was that virtual school students may attend any school as long as the jurisdiction is willing to accept them. Location of the school was irrelevant. Instead, parents were concerned about the amount of money that they could access to support Internet charges and curriculum materials, what hardware and software were provided, and the particular structuring of the student's time.

In a follow-up workshop with administrators (Haughey, 1999) and a recent review of administrative issues (Haughey & Purdy, 2002), we noted that some of these start-up issues have been replaced by new concerns. One continuing concern for those programs which involved "call-back" days or teacher visits was the amount of organization required to hire an appropriate venue (often a church or community hall) and make arrangements for staff, advertising and equipment. In a large program with more than 2,000 students living anywhere in the province, this required almost weekly attention. Teachers made visits to families with elementary children so that the teacher could observe the students' progress and meet the children in their homes. Although these teachers lived in the general vicinity, it still involved planning and coordination to ensure that all students were visited as frequently as promised.

Some schools had, for their elementary and junior high grades, set up call back days to deal with student lab work in science and mathematics. Often these also involved field trips to selected sites. The financial and legal liabilities of these field trips were a specific issue for some administrators.

Another issue was the recognition of the importance of support staff. In virtual schools, each student can be registered in a continuum ranging from a single course to a full-time program. The student is registered for that year only and may decide to attend a different school the following year. In secondary school situations, students are often picking up one or two courses to help them accelerate and complete their programs, so that new enrolments can occur every term. Each student's file has to be stored and then forwarded to the student's next school. All of these complications in registration and record-keeping enlarge the work of the support staff. In addition, support staff are often the first to handle a wide range of telephone queries from calls about the school program to financial disbursements for equipment rentals. Principals spoke about the need to hire a higher proportion of support staff than was usual for site-based school administration.

They also identified the need for additional storage facilities, not only for student files, but also for books and resources that had to be sent out to students each year and returned for summer storage. In addition, some schools asked students to return their hardware to the school before the summer recess. The school usually used this time to check equipment, do maintenance and load upgrades. All of this required a large space with good security. Some schools were trying out laptops and had found that these were as robust as desktop machines.

In most schools, teachers no longer work from home. Instead, schools have set aside work areas where teachers can go online and receive and answer telephone calls. This seems to have resulted from feelings of isolation on the part of the teachers, who found it difficult to separate their professional and home lives, as well as the cost to the school of providing teachers with office furniture, upgraded computer equipment and Internet access in their homes. The practice of what technology resources teachers receive varies widely depending on the particular instructional format. But even where teachers live some distance from the school and are not required to attend, many choose to do so. Schools that use synchronous conferencing for instruction have set aside a space with all the appropriate hardware where a teacher can teach online. Schools who plan to use digital video conferencing once the provincial SuperNet comes online are similarly allocating space. This has resulted in different facility demands.

Finally, principals in the 1999 study identified the benefits to themselves of some form of professional support. This led to the development of an online educational consortium for all those involved in virtual education, whether in K-12 school jurisdictions, post-secondary institutions, or technology companies. The Alberta Online Consortium (www.albertaonline.ab.ca) has been successful in providing workshops, running an annual conference and coordinating policy and course development among Alberta jurisdictions (Muirhead, 1999).

Trends for the Future

Virtual schooling is an alternative learning provision to site-based schooling. It has provided an option for parents who prefer some form of home schooling, but this is only a small proportion of those students in the K-12 sector. The biggest expansion is occurring in the secondary school population, where the trend is for students to take courses in both formats. This blended format is likely to grow and the opportunities for online learning as an alternative to site-based courses are likely to continue to increase.

The latest learning research (Bransford, Brown, & Cocking, 2000) points out that learning should be both active and interactive, involving group work and collaboration, and based on real world or authentic problems in a resource-rich, supported environment with ongoing assessment. New communications technologies provide opportunities for regular interaction as part of learning. They encourage lateral thinking, an integral aspect of creativity, and provide a resource-rich environment, and they give learners control over their own learning. However, the central benefits of ICTs are not likely to be realised unless these aspects are integrated into our designs for learning.

The continuance of virtual schooling is based on the quality of its learning environments. Given costs, students' expectations and the possibilities of technologies, there is likely to be a move to have these designed cooperatively, and possibly at the provincial level, to ensure a quality resource and a range of media options. Learning is designed for learners, not for teachers, so the focus should be on options for students that provide for variety and creativity, as well as structure and support.

The development of new communications technologies has raised many questions about the configuration of schools and schooling. In the future, will schools form networked learning communities? Will communities share teaching and learning among staffs? Will the standard school day and school year disappear? Will students be able to attend a local learning centre for all of their schooling and not have to move into other settings for senior grades? Will secondary school students be given more responsibility for their own learning? How will secondary programs articulate with post-secondary programs? Add to these issues concerns about the declining numbers of teachers entering the profession, and the need for high quality alternative options for learning becomes even more crucial. Illich (1971) in *Descooling Society* commented, "Technology is available to develop either independence and learning or bureaucracy and teaching" (p. 80). Over the last 30 years we have chosen learning, but much remains to be done if we are to shape technology practices around possibilities for learning rather than around replicating the present provision of schooling.

References

Alberta Learning. (2001). Student participation and achievement by type of delivery system, 1996-2000. Retrieved October 17, 2002 on the World Wide Web: http://learning.gov.ab.ca/k_12/testing/.

Balay, E. (1978). *Factors associated with the completion and non-completion of correspondence courses*. Unpublished master's thesis, University of Alberta, Edmonton, AB.

Bransford, J., Brown, A., & Cocking, R. (eds.). (2000). *How People Learn: Brain, Mind, Experience, and School* (expanded edition). Washington, DC: National Academies Press. Retrieved October 15, 2002 from the World Wide Web: http://www.nap.edu/html/howpeople1/.

Brown, J., Sheppard, B., & Stevens, K. (2001). *Effective Schooling in a Telelearning Environment.* St. John's, NF: The Centre for TeleLearning and Rural Education, Memorial University.

Froese, C., Harris, G., Restall, L., & Witherspoon, E. (1987). *Taking the distance out of distance education. A regionalized approach.* Paper presented at Symposium '87: Distance education by design, Edmonton, AB.

Gee, T. (1989). Introduction. In S.J. Thiessen & G. Logan (Eds.), *Networks Policies, Procedures and Technology Manual* (p. 1). Edmonton, AB: Alberta Education.

Haughey, M. (1990). Distance education in schools. *The Canadian Administrator, 29*(8), 1-8.

Haughey, M. (1999). Administrative issues in online schools. Workshop presented at the *Virtual Schools Symposium*, Edmonton, AB (November 24-26).

Haughey, M. & Muirhead, W. (1999). *Online Learning. Best Practices for Alberta School Jurisdictions.* Edmonton, AB: Alberta Education.

Haughey, M. & Purdy, D. (2002). *Online Learning Review.* Edmonton, AB: Alberta Infrastructure and Alberta Learning.

Illich, I. (1971). *Deschooling Society.* London: Penguin.

Litke, D. (1998). *Virtual schooling at middle grades.* Unpublished doctoral dissertation, University of Calgary, Calgary, AB.

Little, G. & McKibbon, M. (1990). *Monitored independent distance learning: An effective use of correspondence courses in secondary schools.* Paper presented at CADE conference, Quebec City, QC.

Muirhead, W. (1999). The benefits of an online education consortium for Alberta. *International Electronic Journal for Leadership and Learning, 3*(4). Retrieved October 17, 2002 on the World Wide Web: http://www.ucalgary.ca/~iejll.

Muirhead, W. (2000). Online education in schools. *International Journal of Educational Management, 14*(6 & 7), 315-324.

Muirhead, W. (2000a). *Teachers' perceptions of online education.* Unpublished doctoral dissertation, University of Alberta, Edmonton, AB.

Scollie, B. (2001). *Student Achievement and Performance Levels in Online Education Research Study.* Edmonton, AB: Alberta Online Consortium.

Smith, R. (2000). *Virtual schools in the K-12 context*. Unpublished doctoral dissertation, University of Calgary, Calgary, AB.

Section II

Standards and Accreditation

Chapter IV

Distance Learning Success Factors in the RPR Cycle and Virtual School Accreditation Standards

Catherine Cavanaugh
University of North Florida, USA

Abstract

Virtual school administrators and course designers can address the needs of virtual school students using established quality guidelines and standards. The development and implementation of effective distance education happens in an iterative cycle. The three stages in the cycle are: (1) procurement and preparation of the resources necessary to meet the distance education goals; (2) delivery of instruction using the best practices from education, business and research; and (3) analysis of the results of distance education to gauge achievement of the goals. Each stage of the Resources - Practices - Results (RPR) cycle continually revisits lessons learned in the other stages and builds upon the successes realized in the other stages. The success of a web-based virtual school program in part relies on the program's adherence to quality benchmarks. This chapter explores the interconnect among the established success factors incorporated into the RPR cycle and standards published by agencies accrediting virtual schools. A survey of 67 virtual schools in the United States in the spring of 2003 resulted in identification of accrediting standards applied at national, regional and state levels. The standards of seven accrediting bodies are examined, and three are compared to the RPR success factors. Because of the differing foci of the agencies producing the standards, there is variation in the degree to which the standards correspond to the RPR success factors.

Quality in Virtual School Distance Education

In its December 2000 report to Congress, the Web-Based Education Commission made high quality online educational content one of its seven critical issues. In order for a student or institution to determine whether quality has been achieved, quality must be defined. Virtual school programs must serve the virtual schools in meeting their goals. A central goal of education is developing independent learners who can capably apply their knowledge to new situations. To ensure that virtual school offerings meet this goal, designers must identify desired learning outcomes, instructional strategies and evaluation methods. Quality indicates that instruction is effective and appropriate. The assessment of quality virtual school programs may include quantitative elements, such as completion rates, student performance and student evaluations of the learning experience. Qualitative dimensions may include ratings of teaching-learning events, materials, learning process, pace, activities, content, usability, accessibility and options offered to students. Performance in each measure of quality depends on the distance education experience being fully appropriate to all users. Seven groups have published accreditation standards that have been adopted by American virtual schools. Three of the groups operate at the national level: the National Private School Accreditation Alliance, also known as the National Private Schools Association; the Accrediting Commission for

Independent Study; and the Accrediting Commission of the Distance Education Training Council. Four groups have regional jurisdiction: the North Central Association on Accreditation and School Improvement, also known as the North Central Association of Colleges and Schools; the Northwest Association of Schools and Colleges and Universities; the Southern Association of Colleges and Schools; and the Western Association of Schools and Colleges.

The Quality Distance Education Cycle

The process of developing and implementing effective virtual school education happens in an iterative cycle. Broadly considered, the three stages in the cycle are: (1) procurement and preparation of the resources necessary to meet the virtual school education goals; (2) delivery of instruction using the best practices from education, business and research; and (3) analysis of the results of virtual school education to gauge achievement of the goals. Each stage of the **Resources - Practices - Results (RPR)** cycle, shown in Figure 1, continually revisits lessons learned in the other stages and builds upon the successes realized in the other stages (Cavanaugh, 2002). Each stage requires participation of all stakeholders, including students, instructors, support and design professionals, administrators and the community. The success factors included in each stage are based on decades of research and experience with learners from professions, higher education and K-12 education (Barker, 1999; Bruce, Fallon, & Horton, 2000; Cavanaugh, 2001; Educational Development Associates, 1998; Fredericksen, Peltz, & Swan, 2000; Institute for Higher Education Policy, 2000; Mantyla, 1999).

This chapter explores the match among the established success factors incorporated into the RPR cycle and the virtual school accreditation standards established by the state, regional and national accrediting bodies.

The Resources Phase of the RPR Cycle. The resources required to sustain a quality virtual school education program exist to support students, faculty and the program or school toward achieving the goal of effective and appropriate learning. Responsive and flexible human resources, knowledge, skills, policies, procedures and technical infrastructure enable quality practices and contribute to quality results. Procurement, development and adaptation of resources are ongoing processes.

Figure 1: Distance Learning Success Factors

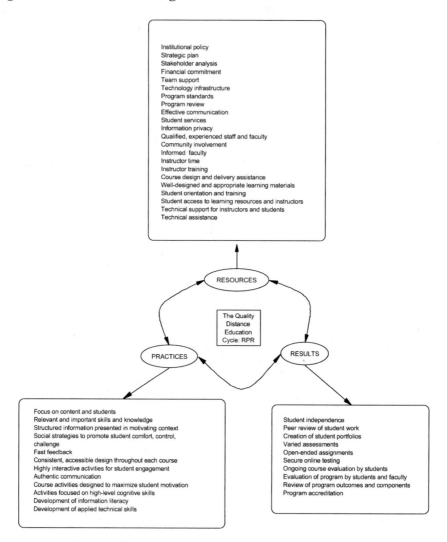

Success Factors for the Resources Phase:

- School policy that values distance education
- Strategic plan for delivering distance education to students
- Stakeholder analysis to determine needs of graduates
- Financial commitment that gives the direction regarding program implementation

- Team support for distance educators and students
- Appropriate technology infrastructure
- Program standards to guide course design and delivery
- Program review to ensure that all components of the program meet standards and to ensure that the standards contribute to program goals
- Effective communication of policies and expectations to students
- Student services: information, advising, orientation and security
- Information privacy
- Qualified, experienced staff and faculty
- Community involvement in the program's goals, policies and outcomes
- Information provided to faculty about teaching in the distance learning environment
- Instructor release time for course development
- Instructor training in distance education pedagogy and technology
- Course design and delivery assistance
- Well-designed and appropriate learning materials
- Student orientation and training
- Student access to learning resources and instructors
- Technical support for instructors and students
- Technology plan to communicate goals to all users

The Practices Phase of the RPR Cycle. With the right resources in place, the stage is set for dramatic virtual school learning performance. At this point the spotlight shifts from the institution to the instructor. Quality virtual school teaching begins with the careful design of courses, materials and learning activities. Next, the practices employed during instruction will aim at developing independent learners with the ability to transfer their learning to novel situations. Throughout the course, effective communication and community building are essential foundations for all events.

Success Factors for the Practices Phase:

- Focus on content and students
- Relevant and important skills and knowledge addressed in courses

- Structured information presented in motivating context
- Social strategies to promote student comfort, control, challenge
- Fast feedback from instructors to students
- Consistent and accessible design throughout each course
- Highly interactive activities for student engagement
- Authentic communication among students, instructors and experts
- Course activities designed to maximize student motivation
- Activities focused on high-level cognitive skills
- Development of information literacy
- Development of applied technical skills

The Results Phase of the RPR Cycle. The only way to know whether a virtual school distance education program has achieved quality is to compare the program results to established quality benchmarks. Measures of quality are tied to school goals, and respond to the specific context of the program. To maintain success, a virtual school program evaluation must account for institutional and instructional factors as well as student factors. Evaluation of course and program results is a continual process that involves all stakeholders and requires a wide range of tools. Success is evaluated by thorough assessment of student learning, program review and program accreditation.

Success Factors for the Results Phase:

- Student independence developed through opportunities for self-assessment
- Peer review of student work as a professional experience
- Creation of student portfolios to showcase accomplishments
- Varied assessments for an accurate view of student abilities
- Open-ended assignments to increase thinking skills and reduce cheating
- Secure online testing
- Ongoing course evaluation by students
- Evaluation of program by students and faculty
- Review of program outcomes and components by all stakeholders
- Program accreditation

Accreditation Standards

Virtual schools are operated by several types of organizations: state governments, colleges and universities, public school districts, state-chartered virtual charter schools, private schools, regional agencies or consortia, or virtual home schools.

State-operated virtual schools are usually operated as public schools, and are accredited by the state board of education and/or the regional educational accrediting body. The virtual schools run by colleges and universities are most often state or regionally accredited. Public school districts that operate virtual schools generally do so as an arm of the public school system, accredited under the public school umbrella. Similarly, state-chartered virtual charter schools also fall under the associated state accreditation. Accredited private virtual schools are either state licensed or regionally accredited. Regional agencies and consortia are cooperating groups of school districts or other organizations, which may be non-profit or for-profit. Schools run by these groups may be accredited by states or regional agencies, if they are accredited. Virtual home schools, for the most part, are not eligible for accreditation, except as correspondence schools.

In the U.S., K-12 school accreditation takes several forms. The websites of 67 virtual schools were examined in spring 2003 to determine whether the schools were accredited, and if so, by which agencies. In 47 cases, a thorough examination of the website resulted in no detection of an accrediting agency outside of the state board of education or accreditation by the local school attended by students. The remaining 20 virtual schools' websites stated that they were accredited. A total of seven different accrediting agencies were named, three of which are national, and four of which are regional. Of the virtual schools not mentioning specific accrediting agencies, 16 are accredited by the state board of education, 12 are accredited in association with a local school board, eight are accredited by the school system in which the students reside, and 17 are undetermined.

The seven regional accrediting agencies associated with virtual schools also accredit traditional public and private schools. One of the national accrediting agencies accredits traditional private schools. One of the national agencies accredits distance learning programs, and one accredits distance learning and correspondence programs.

Of the seven accrediting agencies indicated by the 67 virtual schools that were studied, the standards of three agencies were compared to the distance

Table 1: Virtual School Accreditation Standards, Resulting from Spring 2003 Survey of 67 Virtual Schools

Accrediting agency	Web address	Number of virtual schools accredited of the 67 examined
Accrediting Commission of the Distance Education Training Council	http://www.detc.org/index.html	1
Accrediting Commission for Independent Study	http://www.acisga.com/pages/181839/index.htm	1
National Private School Accreditation Alliance, National Private Schools Association	http://www.npsag.com/	2
North Central Association on Accreditation and School Improvement, North Central Association of Colleges and Schools	http://www.ncacasi.org/	5
Northwest Association of Schools and Colleges and Universities	http://www2.boisestate.edu/nasc/	7
Southern Association of Colleges and Schools	http://www.sacs.org/	2
Western Association of Schools and Colleges	http://www.wascweb.org/	2

education quality success factors of the **Resources - Practices - Results (RPR)** cycle. The three agencies are the Distance Education Training Council, the North Central Association of Colleges and Schools, and the Southern Association of Colleges and Schools.

The Distance Education Training Council developed a set of standards used to evaluate distance learning programs. The standards, published in 2003, were developed "with the advice and cooperation of outstanding authorities on education and accreditation" (DETC, 2003). The 46 standards are organized into 12 areas:

- Institutional mission and objectives
- Educational program objectives, curricula and materials
- Educational services
- Student services
- Student achievement and satisfaction
- Qualifications of owners, governing board members, administrators, instructors/faculty and staff

- Admission practices and enrollment agreements
- Advertising, promotional literature and recruitment personnel
- Tuition policies, collection procedures and refunds
- Plant, equipment and record protection
- Research and self-improvement

The RPR cycle has 22 success factors in the Resources phase, 16 of which were addressed in full or in part by DETC standards. Those not addressed related to instructor support, course design and technology. Three of the 12 success factors in the Practices Phase were addressed by the DETC standards, and they were the more general practices. Five of the 10 Results Phase success factors were addressed by the DETC standards, mainly the ones related to program-level concerns. Overall, the DETC standards addressed 24 of the 44 RPR success factors, more than the other agencies, and the factors not addressed were those specifying course-level practices.

The North Central Association Commission on Accreditation and School Improvement (NCA CASI) is a regional accrediting agency that has developed 98 standards organized into five areas:

- Process of schooling
- Information system
- Vision, leadership-governance and school community
- School improvement plan
- Resources and allocation

The NCA CASI standards addressed eight of the 22 Resources success factors, those concerned with institution or program issues rather than those concerned with technical, distance learning or course issues. The standards corresponded with six of the 12 Practices success factors, and four of the 10 Results success factors. The standards addressed the factors that focused on broad issues and practices rather than those focused on specific course and teaching practices. Eighteen of the 44 success factors were addressed by NCA CASI standards.

The standards of the Southern Association of Colleges and Schools (SACS), published in 2000, are grouped into nine categories:

- Beliefs and mission
- Governance and leadership
- Resources
- Support services for student learning
- Curriculum
- Instructional design
- Library media services
- Assessment
- Standards for specific types of schools, such as middle schools or nonpublic schools

Ninety of the standards apply to all schools. The SACS standards corresponded to 18 of the 44 Success factors: 11 of the 22 Resources factors, eight of the 12 Practices factors, and two of the 10 Results factors. The factors not addressed by the standards are those related to distance learning, uses of technology, specific teaching practices, and student assessment.

Because the DETC standards are specifically designed for distance education programs, it would be expected that they would address more of the accepted success factors related to distance education than would standards designed for traditional schools. Even so, the DETC standards addressed only 54 percent of the success factors. The success factors of the RPR cycle include practices at the instruction, program and instructor levels. Together, the accreditation standards and the success factors identified in the literature provide a comprehensive instructional resource for virtual school administrators. Instructional developers and instructors are encouraged to continue to review the literature to add their own standards of practice to the standards provided by accrediting agencies. Implemented in tandem, the RPR success factors and the accreditation standards provide a comprehensive set of design and implementation guidelines for virtual schools.

Conclusion

One strength of distance education is its potential to focus the learning process on the student, regardless of the student's unique needs and abilities. Virtual

Table 2: Correspondence of Accreditation Standards to Success Factors

Accrediting agency	Number of standards	Number of standards corresponding to the 44 RPR success factors
Distance Education Training Council (DETC)	46	24
North Central Association Commission on Accreditation and School Improvement (NCA CASI)	98	18
Southern Association of Colleges and Schools (SACS)	90	18

schools that emphasize their focus on the student's strengths and needs will succeed in attracting students. In order to build their reputations and retain students, virtual schools must reach quality goals. With increased need for new career skills and improvement in delivery technology, distance education students will demand full accessibility and evidence of quality and authenticity in distance courses. It is imperative that distance education developers implement and review quality benchmarks regarding **Resources - Practices - Results (RPR)** success factors and accreditation standards in response to the needs of students, employers and the community. Virtual schools must continue to develop and maintain standards, and they must clearly communicate those standards to the public. When students benefit from an education program that meets their needs, the community benefits as well.

References

Barker, K. (1999). *Quality Guidelines for Technology-Assisted Distance Education*. Washington, DC: U.S. Department of Education Office of Learning Technologies.

Bruce, B., Fallon, C., & Horton, W. (2000). Getting started with online learning. Macromedia, Inc. Available online at http://www.macromedia.com/learning/online_learning_guide.pdf.

Cavanaugh, C. (2001). The effectiveness of interactive distance education technologies in K-12 learning: A meta-analysis. *International Journal of Educational Telecommunications, 7*(1), 73-88.

Cavanaugh, C. (2002). Distance education quality: Success factors for resources, practices and results. In R. Discenza, C. Howard, & K. Schenk

(Eds.), *The Design and Management of Effective Distance Learning Programs.* Hershey, PA: Idea Group Publication.

Distance Education and Training Council. (2003). Accreditation Standards. Available on the World Wide Web at http://www.detc.org/content/acredditHandbk.html.

Educational Development Associates. (1998). *What Quality Distance Learning Courses for an Institution?* Las Cruces, MN: Author.

Fredericksen, E., Peltz, W., & Swan, K. (2000). Student satisfaction and perceived learning with online courses: Principles and examples from the SUNY learning network. *Journal of Asynchronous Learning Networks, 4*(2).

Institute for Higher Education Policy. (2000). *Quality on the Line: Benchmarks for Success in Internet-Based Distance Education.* Washington, DC: Author.

Mantyla, K. (1999). *Interactive Distance Learning Exercises that Really Work.* Alexandria, VA: American Society for Training and Development.

Appendix A: Virtual Schools Surveyed in the Spring 2003 Study

Virtual School	Web Address	Location	Accrediting Agency
Alabama Online High School	http://www.aohs.state.al.us/index.html	Tuscaloosa, AL	None indicated
Arkansas Virtual High School	http://arkansashigh.k12.ar.us	Dardanelle, AR	By cooperating schools
Basehor-Linwood Virtual Charter School	http://vcs.usd458.k12.ks.us/	Linwood, KS	None indicated
Birdville Virtual School	http://www.birdville.k12.tx.us/cf/Virtual/Virt Schl.htm	Birdville, TX	None indicated
Brigham Young University Independent Study	http://ce.byu.edu/is/site/index.dhtm	Salt Lake City, UT	Northwest Association of Schools and of Colleges and Universities (NASC)
CAL Online	http://www.cusd.com/calonline/Default.htm	Clovis, CA	None indicated
CCS Web Academy	http://www.ccswebacademy.net/	Fayetteville, NC	North Carolina
Choice 2000 Online School	http://www.choice2000.org/	Perris, CA	Western Association of Schools and Colleges
Christa McAuliffe Academy	http://www.cmacademy.org/?source=overture	Yakima, WA	Northwest Association of Schools and Colleges and Universities
Clintondale Virtual High School	http://www.clintondalevhs.org/	Clinton Township, MI	None indicated
CompuHigh	http://www.compuhigh.com/	Morgantown, WV	National Private School Accreditation Alliance
Cool School	http://coolschool.k12.or.us/	Eugene, OR	Northwest Association of Schools and Colleges and Universities
Delta Cyberschool	http://www.dcs.k12.ak.us	Delta Junction, AK	None indicated
Dennison Academy	http://www.dennisononline.com/	Los Angeles, CA	Accreditation Commission for International Internet Education
E School	http://www.eschool.k12.hi.us/	Honolulu, HI	None indicated
E*COT	http://www.ecotohio.org/home.htm	Columbus, OH	None indicated
Eldorado Academy	http://www.eldoradoacademy.org/	Nederland, CO	National Private Schools Association
Electronic Charter School	http://onlineecs.org/	Elkhart, KS	None indicated
Electronic High School	http://ehs.uen.org	Utah	Northwest Association of Schools and Colleges and Universities
Evergreen Internet Academy	http://eia.egreen.wednet.edu/	Vancouver, WA	None indicated
Florida Virtual School	http://www.flvs.net	Orlando, FL	By cooperating schools
Francis School	http://www.francisschool.com/	New York	New York State Department of Education
Gwinnett County Online Campus	http://gwinnettk12online.net/	Lawrenceville, GA	None indicated
Illinois Virtual High School	http://www.ivhs.org/	Springfield, IL	Through institution providing course
Indiana University High School	http://www.indiana.edu/~iuhs/	Bloomington, IN	North Central Association of Colleges and Schools
International High School	http://www.internationalhigh.org/	Oceanside, CA	Accrediting Commission of the Distance Education

Appendix A: Virtual Schools Surveyed in the Spring 2003 Study (continued)

Internet Academy	http://www.iacademy.org/	Federal Way, WA	None indicated
Internet High School	http://www.rmhs.org/Internet.htm	Woodbridge, VA	Southern Association of Colleges and Schools
Internet Home School	http://www.internethomeschool.com/	Prescott, AZ	North Central Association of Colleges and Schools
James Madison High School	http://www.jmhs.com/?code=9941	Norcross, GA	Southern Association of Colleges and Schools
JeffcoNet Academy	http://jeffcoweb.jeffco.k12.co.us/access/academy/index.html	Lakewood, CO	None indicated
Juneau CyberSchool	http://jcs.jsd.k12.ak.us/	Juneau, AK	None indicated
Kentucky Virtual High School	http://www.kvhs.org/	Frankfort, KY	By cooperating schools
Keystone High School	http://www.keystonehighschool.com	Bloomsburg, PA	Commission on Schools and Colleges of the Northwest Association of Schools and Colleges and Universities
Laurel Springs School	http://www.laurelsprings.com/default.asp	Ojai, CA	Western Association of Schools and Colleges
Louisiana Virtual School	http://lvhs.doe.apexvs.com/	Baton Rouge, LA	By cooperating schools
Michigan Virtual High School	http://www.mivhs.org/	Lansing, MI	Northwest Association of Schools and Colleges
Mindquest	http://www.mindquest.org/	Bloomington, MN	None indicated
Missouri Virtual School	http://mvs.smsu.edu/	Springfield, MO	None indicated
Monte Vista Online Academy	http://monte.k12.co.us/	Monte Vista, CO	Colorado Dept of Education
Nevada Virtual High School	http://www.nvhs.org/	Ely, NV	None indicated
New Mexico Virtual School	http://www.intelligented.com/nmvs/	Georgia	Taught by Intelligent Education: Accrediting Commission for Independent Study
North Dakota Division of Independent Study	http://www.dis.dpi.state.nd.us/	Fargo, ND	North Central Association Commission on Accreditation and School Improvement
Northwest WebSchool	http://www.nwwebschool.org/	Hillsboro, OR	Nebraska and Northwest Association of Schools and Colleges and Universities
Oakland Virtual School	http://www.oakland.k12.mi.us/ovconnect/index.html	Oakland, MI	None indicated
Odyssey Charter School	http://www.odysseycs.org/	Las Vegas, NV	None indicated
Oklahoma State University Extension	http://extension.okstate.edu/k12.htm	Stillwater, OK	None indicated
Plano eSchool	http://planoisdeschool.net/home.htm	Plano, TX	Nebraska and Northwest Association of Schools and Colleges and Universities
Rock Hill Virtual High School	http://www.rock-hill.k12.sc.us/departments/vhs/	Rock Hill, SC	None indicated
seeUonline	http://www.seeuonline.org/	Palmer, AK	None indicated

Appendix A: Virtual Schools Surveyed in the Spring 2003 Study (continued)

SK Online	http://skonline.org/	Salem, OR	None indicated
Southern Oregon Online School	http://www.soesd.k12.or.us/it/soos/	OR	None indicated
Stanford University Education Program for Gifted Youth	http://www-epgy.stanford.edu/	Stanford, CA	None indicated
TEACH: The Einstein Academy Charter School	http://www.einsteinacademycharterschool.org/	Morrisville, PA	None indicated
Texas Virtual School	http://www.texasvirtualschool.org	Houston, TX	By cooperating schools
The BabbageNet School	http://www.babbagenetschool.com/	Port Jefferson, NY	By cooperating school
University of California College Prep Initiative	http://uccp.ucsc.edu/	Santa Cruz, CA	None indicated
University of Missouri-Columbia High School	http://cdis.missouri.edu/MUHighSchool/HShome.htm	Columbia, MO	North Central Association Commission on Accreditation and School Improvement
University of Nebraska High School	http://dcs.unl.edu/ishs/	Lincoln, NE	North Central Association Commission on Accreditation and School Improvement
University of Texas Austin Continuing Education	http://www.utexas.edu/cee/dec/uths/index.shtml	Austin, TX	Texas Education Agency
VILAS	http://www.vilas.k12.co.us/vilas/vilas.htm	Vilas, CO	None indicated
Virtual Greenbush	http://www.virtualgreenbush.org/	Girard, KS	From class.com: state of Nebraska and Northwest Association of Schools and Colleges and Universities
Virtual High School	http://www.govhs.org/website.nsf	Concord, MA	By cooperating schools
Virtual High School @PWCS	http://www.pwcs.edu/pwcsvirtualhs/	Manassas, VA	State of Virginia
Virtual School @ Liverpool	http://www.liverpool.k12.ny.us/virtual.html	Liverpool, NY	New York State
Western Penn Cyber Charter School	http://www.wpccs.com/	Midland, PA	Yes
Westside Virtual HS	http://wvhs.westside66.org/	Omaha, NE	Nebraska and Northwest Association of Schools and Colleges and Universities

Chapter V

Distance Learning as a Form of Accommodation

Terence W. Cavanaugh
University of North Florida, USA

Abstract

Over the recent past, the population in schools and the options for education have changed. Recently, the number of students identified as special needs has increased, as has the number of special needs students included in "regular" classrooms. Specific laws pertain to their education, including the U.S. Individuals with Disabilities Act (IDEA), which requires that students with disabilities each have Individual Education Plans (IEP). An aspect of the IEP is the possibility of using assistive technology to assist in the student's education or in accommodation or modifications needed for disabled access. The web-based learning environment itself can be considered an accommodation or modification of instruction to meet the needs of special needs students. Opportunities are increasing in the online distance learning environment for colleges and universities, and the increase is expanding to the high school and middle school programs. When creating online instruction, it is important to follow the accessibility standards such as the Section 508 and W3C accessibility standards to enable persons with disabilities access to the educational material. Within the U.S., more than 26,000 K-12 students classified as IDEA hospital/homebound, received education through some form of "distance education" as of 1999. While the methods of instruction do not commonly include online delivery, it is an option that should be investigated. In-depth examples of a school system's hospital/homebound program, online programs being used by a school for students with disabilities, and a state public online school and its interactions with students with disabilities are presented. The results of a survey of online schools and their services for students with disabilities are also reported.

Introduction

Special education programs or resources are offered through schools to assist in educating children with special needs. In addition, they provide resources for the rehabilitation for those with disabilities. Disability rights leaders have said that the application of technology will be the equalizer of the 21st century (Flippo, Inge, & Barcus, 1995). Through the use of assistive technology (AT) devices, many students can decrease their isolation and become a part of a regular classroom, even if they are physically not in the actual classroom at all. Assistive technology is a tool that can provide a method for an individual who is experiencing a disability to participate in a classroom. Screen readers that read aloud the text on the screen or web page can overcome barriers to accessing electronic information encountered by students who have vision disabilities. Captions can overcome barriers for students who have hearing disabilities. Some access solutions that use principles of universal design are built into the hardware or software of computers and programs (RESNA, 2001). The design of a distance learning course, or the participation in a course through distance learning, is in itself the application of assistive technology, and is an accommodation to instruction that can meet many of the special needs of learners in today's schools.

According to the Half the Planet Foundation (2001), an organization that supports the application of technology to promote the values of the Americans with Disabilities Act, an estimated three billion people (or half of the entire planet's population) are in some way affected by disabilities. It is estimated that in the U.S. alone there are more than 150 million people affected by disabilities.

Consider some of the following population statistics on disabilities:

- 750 million people worldwide are challenged by disabilities.
- More than 8 million Americans have visual impairments.
- 500,000 visually impaired Americans use assistive technology devices.
- 13.5 million Americans consider themselves visually impaired to some degree.
- Nearly 3 million Americans are colorblind.
- 2.7 million Americans have speech impairments.
- 22 million Americans are deaf or hard-of-hearing.
- 4.6 million Americans use assistive technology devices for hearing impairments.
- Dyslexia affects more than 40 million Americans.
- 54 million Americans report some level of disability, equaling about 15% of the population.
- 5% of school children are reported as Learning Disabled (LD), but as many as 15% of people are believed to have some form of learning disability.
- Fewer than 15% of people with disabilities were born with them.
- Americans with hearing impairments equal the population of California.
- More than 6% of entering college students identify themselves as having a disability. (IBM, 2001; New York State Council on the Arts, 2001; National Center on Educational Statistics, 1999)

As the inclusive education of all students occurs more frequently within the standard classroom and through the electronic environment, incorporating assistive technology approaches and accommodations becomes more important. The changes in population that have occurred in schools in recent years will have a major impact of changing the learning goals, the teaching methods, and the means of assessment for all students. Distance learning as a form of assistive technology is an educational option for students classified with a disability. As teachers now design educational environments either for in-class or distance learning, they "…need to be focused on classroom-wide and building-wide contexts, reflecting an alignment within special education as well as between special and general education" (McGregor & Vogelsbert, 1998). Educational environments need to be designed for all students, even those students who may need modifications and accommodations.

Laws and Legal Aspects of Disability Education

The percentage of special needs students served in an inclusive setting along with non-disabled students is rising. As educational professionals we are charged by law to make accommodations to the process of education to allow all students access to the educational situation. At the K-12 level, these accommodations usually take place as part of a student's IEP (Individual Education Plan), and at the post secondary level, an office of student services usually handles the student's needs. Educators must be able to adapt, make accommodations, or adjust the educational material to make it work for the student, allowing access to the material.

Federal support for special education in the U.S. dates back to 1975. In that year, Congress passed Public Law 94-142, The Education for All Handicapped Children Act (EHA), to ensure equal access by children with disabilities, ages five through 21, to publicly funded educational opportunities and programs from which many of them had, until then, been excluded. Then, in 1986, Public Law 99-457 reauthorized the EHA, and changed its name to the Individuals with Disabilities Education Act (IDEA). This statute required states to serve children, ages three to five, who require special education by 1991. It also established the Infants and Toddlers with Disabilities Program by offering states financial assistance to serve children from birth to age three with disabilities. The Federal Individuals with Disabilities Education Act (IDEA), and its 1997 amendments, make it a requirement that schools educate children who have disabilities, in general education classrooms whenever possible. With this charge came a requirement that all students classified as having any form of disability have an individual education plan (IEP) developed specifically for that student. The IEP will be developed by a team of people including teachers, administrators, counselors, parents, outside experts (as needed), and often the student. As part of the Federal IDEA amendments, statements now require assistive technology devices and services to be considered on an individualized basis and become a part of the individual education plan if the child needs the assistive technology or services to benefit from his educational program.

Assistive technology is "…any item, piece of equipment, or product system, whether acquired commercially off the shelf, modified, or customized, that is used to increase, maintain, or improve functional capabilities of individuals with disabilities…." 20 U.S.C. 1401 (33)(250)

The IDEA regulation states: "Each State must establish procedures to assure that, to the maximum extent appropriate, children with disabilities ... are educated with children who are not disabled, and that special education, separate schooling, or other removal of children with disabilities from the regular educational environment occurs only when the nature or severity of the disability is such that education in regular classes with the use of supplementary aids and services cannot be achieved satisfactorily." 20 U.S.C. 1412(5)(B)

At the same time as the education population is changing, so are the possibilities of the educational setting, which now include forms of interactive telecommunication, such as the Internet and two-way video communication, as options for the delivery of instruction. Many state university systems are under the directive to encourage institutions and their faculty to embrace electronic and distance learning (Hurst, 1997) and, while the state universities were expanding into the distance learning environment, K-12 schools were experimenting with it as an educational option. While K-12 schools, colleges and universities may not have been planning and creating distance learning courses to meet the needs of students with disabilities, it was still accomplished. Electronic learning in and of itself is a form of accommodation, and there is a range of assistive technology that can support the student in the distance learning environment. The online class becomes an assistive technology tool that students can use who would otherwise not be able to participate in a classroom due to physical, health or other issues.

IEP: Individualized Education Plan/ Program

Individualized Education Program. *The term 'individualized education program' or 'IEP' means a written statement for each child with a disability that is developed, reviewed, and revised in accordance with this section. 20 U.S.C. 1414 (d)(1)(A) (IDEA, 1997)*

The IEP is a very important document for children with disabilities and for those who are involved in educating them. Each child's IEP describes, among other things, the educational program that has been designed to meet that child's unique needs and necessary assistive technology and/or services. The Tech Act and IDEA have a major impact on how and where students with disabilities are assisted and placed. The IDEA statements concerning the need and application of assistive technology require that the IEP team ask a series of questions about assistive technology devices and/or services:

- Will assistive technology enable the student to meet the goals set for the education program that cannot be met otherwise because of his/her disability?
- Does the student need assistive technology to be involved in the general curriculum, including participation in state and district wide assessments?
- Does the student need assistive technology for augmentative communication?
- Does the student need to use the device at home or in the community to achieve the goals of the IEP?

If the IEP team finds that the answer to any of the questions is yes, then the team must ensure that the needed assistive technology devices and/or services are made available to the student (Florida Department of Education, 2000). Assistive technology can then include the option of taking courses through distance learning as a form of accommodation or educational modification.

By law, the IEP must include certain information about the child and the educational program designed to meet his or her unique needs. Basically, this information is about a student's:

- Current performance;
- Annual goals;
- Needed special education and related services;
- Participation with non-disabled children;
- Participation in state and district-wide tests;
- Service dates and locations;

- Transition service needs; and
- Means of measuring progress.

By law, certain individuals must be involved in writing a child's Individualized Education Program. It is possible for an IEP team member to fill more than one of the team positions, if that person is properly qualified and designated. For example, the school system representative may also be the person who can interpret the child's evaluation results. These people must work together as a team to write the child's IEP. A meeting to write the IEP must be held within 30 calendar days of deciding that the child is eligible for special education and related services. Each team member brings important information to the IEP meeting. Members share their information and work together to write the

Figure 1: The Members of a Student's IEP Team

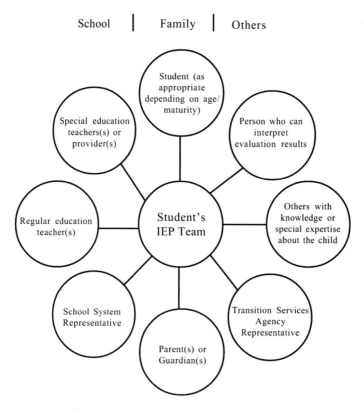

Source: Florida Department of Education (2000). Developing Quality Individual Education Plans: A Guide for Instructional Personnel and Families.

child's Individualized Education Program. Each person's information adds to the team's understanding of the child and the services the child needs.

A standard IEP team will be composed of parents, teachers (regular and special education), other focused individuals and possibly the student (see Figure 1). The other focused individuals include persons who can interpret the child's evaluation results, represent the school system and its services, transition service agencies (when the student is old enough), and any other individual who has knowledge or special expertise about the student.

Assistive Technology (AT)

The Technology-Related Assistance for Individual with Disabilities Act of 1998 (PL 100-407) gave us the first legal definition of assistive technology devices as any item, piece of equipment, or product system, whether acquired commercially off the shelf, modified, or customized, used to increase, maintain, or improve functional capabilities of individuals with disabilities. An assistive technology service was described as: any service that directly assists an individual with a disability in selection, acquisition or use of an assistive technology. Distance learning can be considered an adapted form of instruction that, through the use of telecommunication technology (usually the Internet), allows a student to participate in a class, meeting the classification of assistive technology.

The Levels of Assistive Technology Use

In applying assistive technology (AT) for a student, the environment, the individual and the characteristics and levels of the technology all must be considered (Gitlow, 2000). Assistive technology may be classified as high tech, middle tech or low tech. The concept of a high technology device usually includes items that require computers, electronics or microchips to perform a function. In addition to the level of the technology, it is important to consider the levels of how the assistive technology item will be applied. The levels in applying the assistive technology application include whether the item is personally, developmentally or instructionally necessary (Judd-Wall, 1999). The personally necessary level is concerned with assistive technology devices that are for the use of an individual student, such as a screen enlarger to enable a learner to more effectively interact with online or computer based materials. Developmentally necessary devices may be shared among individuals. These devices help meet an educational need based on a developmental delay, which ideally would be improved, eliminating the need for the item in an individual's future. Lastly, instructionally necessary devices are ones that modify the instructional process at a course or grade level, and this level has important implications concerning Internet-based distance learning. It is important to design the online environment so that all students, including those with disabilities, have full access to the instruction.

According to David Rose and Anne Meyer (CAST, 2000), AT tools can make a significant difference for students with disabilities. AT tools can allow access to information and activities that otherwise are inaccessible. Another side of AT application is that the tools can make information and resources more available to those who don't have a disability or have not yet been identified as having a disability. Exceptional education teachers are not the only ones who need awareness of AT applications. All teachers are likely to teach mainstreamed students, and the purpose of the AT is to support the student with disabilities in the general population. Professional organizations including the International Society for Technology in Education (ISTE, 2000) and National Council for Accreditation of Teacher Education (NCATE, 2000, 2002) have standards for all teachers and administrators regarding AT. The standards require teachers and administrators to use technology to support learner-centered strategies that address the diverse needs of students and apply technology resources to enable and empower learners with diverse backgrounds, characteristics and abilities.

AT, including distance learning, increases student independence while advancing academic standing, because it can increase participation in classroom activities by students with special needs. Rehabilitation Engineering and Assistive Technology Society of North America (RESNA, 2000) has identified twelve different application areas of AT, four of which would have a major impact in any school situation: Work Site Modifications, Instructional Material Aids, Seating and Positioning Aids, and Sensory Aids. The application of asynchronous distance learning as a form of assistive technology could be thought of as an Instructional Material Aid for the student, if it allowed the student to access the class material that he/she would otherwise not access.

508/W3C Accessibility Standards and Distance Learning

Currently there are two major "players" in the structuring of accessibility guidelines for web-based materials in the U.S. The United States government passed section 508 of the 1998 Rehabilitation Act, and the World Wide Web Consortium developed the Web Accessibility Initiative . Other countries have developed guidelines, such as the United Kingdom's Disability Discrimination Act, the open.gov guidelines, and Australia's Disability Rights policy. Some are in the process of development, and some countries have not yet addressed online access issues.

Section 508 of the Rehabilitation Act was put into place to help eliminate the barriers in accessing information technology, specifically to make web-based information available for people with disabilities (ATBCB, 2000; Section 208, 2002; Web Able Inc., 2002). While this law currently only applies to Federal agencies when they develop, procure, maintain, or use electronic and information technology, it is to a school's advantage to make information about the school as accessible as possible. While not currently required, it is reasonable to expect that in the near future, state governments may make Section 508 guidelines a requirement for state web sites as well as those of public schools, colleges and universities. A website will be in compliance with the Section 508 standards if it meets paragraphs (a) through (p) of Section 1194.22. Similar to the U.S. Section 508 standards are the World Wide Web Consortium (W3C, 1999) guidelines. The W3C guidelines are much more extensive, with each guideline containing levels of priorities. The World Wide Web Consortium's fourteen guidelines concern web accessibility. Within each guideline are a number of checkpoints, and each checkpoint has a priority rating from one to three assigned by the W3C Working Group based on the checkpoint's impact on accessibility. According to the W3C, at a minimum for accessibility, a web site *must* be designed to meet all Priority One elements; otherwise some groups of people will find the site impossible to access. Satisfying all Priority Two elements *should* be done to remove the most significant barriers to accessing a web site. The Priority Three elements are an optional set that *may* be addressed to ensure improved access to the web documents. By following the W3C web accessibility guidelines, sites can earn an accessibility rating of "A," "AA," or "AAA," which is based on the level of conformance that the site achieves. A conformance level of "A" indicates that all Priority One elements are satisfied, "AA" shows that the site is satisfying all Priority One and Two elements, and "AAA," being the highest level, with all Priority One, Two, and Three checkpoints in compliance.

The accessibility guidelines should be kept in mind by distance learning course designers and instructors when creating or teaching courses through distance learning. Instructors should be aware that they must provide accommodations, and know the accommodations that are possible for the instructional methodology to aid students with a disability who are participating in the electronic learning.

Accommodations or Modifications Needed for Disabled Access

Teachers must be prepared in the instructional setting to adapt instruction for an individual by changing one or more aspects of the material being taught, such as:

- The method by which the instruction is delivered to the student

- The amount of content material to be covered

- The evaluation method or criteria

- The level of assistance provided in the learning situation

- The learning environment and/or the instructional materials that are used by the student. (Beninghof & Singer, 1995)

The Council for Exceptional Children (CEC) supports the use of appropriate applications and educational modifications, including technologies, to improve the education of exceptional persons. To the CEC, equal access to technology and supports provides equal educational opportunities and technology utilization by all individuals, and includes electronic tools, devices, media, and techniques (CEC, 1997).

There is a difference between accommodations and modifications for students of special needs. Accommodations are considered to be provisions made in how a student accesses and/or demonstrates learning. The term accommodations focuses on changes in the instruction, or how students are expected to learn, along with changes in methods of assessment that demonstrate or document what has been learned. The use of an accommodation does not change the educational goals, standards or objectives, the instructional level, or the content, and provides the student with equal access and equal opportunity to demonstrate his or her skills and knowledge (State of Florida Department of State, 2000). Accommodations assist students in working around the limitations that are related to their disabilities and allow a student with a disability to participate with other students in the general curriculum program. Accommodations can be provided for instructional methods and materials, assignments and assessments, learning environment, time demands and scheduling, and special communication systems. By comparison, a modification is a change in what a student is expected to learn and demonstrate. The use of a modification for a student changes the standard, the instructional level or the content to be learned by the student (Beech, 2000).

Some schools and organizations have taken steps concerning access to distance learning for students with disabilities. For example, the California Community Colleges have developed their own set of eleven access guidelines (California Community Colleges, 1999) that describe principles that should be followed to allow students educational access in a variety of distance learning situations. Recently, a collaboration was developed among a number of international participants in online learning working to produce a set of guidelines, called the IMS guidelines, to educate the electronic and distance learning community concerning challenges and situations that people with disabilities face in accessing online education. This collaboration is also working to provide solutions and resources to solve the problems. The IMS Guidelines are available online at http://ncam.wgbh.org/salt and are being designed as a resource for online education materials development. While the group expects to soon provide a variety of development tools and materials, the current site is excellent for assisting in the identification of current problems in the distance learning environment that a school is using, along with suggestions for applications to assist in overcoming access difficulties (NCAM, 2002).

Changes in the Population of Schools

The inclusion model, in which a special needs student participates in the "regular" classroom, has become the current classroom education standard.

Increasing numbers of students are being classified or identified as special needs students. Today, special needs students have increasing impact on the general education teacher. During the past 10 years, the percentage of students with disabilities served in schools and classes with their nondisabled peers has gradually grown. In Florida alone, over a single school year period, the number of students with disabilities served, as classified by Individuals with Disabilities Education Act (IDEA), increased more than 11,000, from more than 345,000 for the 1998-1999 school year to more than 356,000 for 1999-2000 (U.S. Department of Education, 2002; U.S. Department of Education, 2000; U.S. Department of Education, 1996). In the U.S., for the 1999-2000 school year, the number of students with disabilities served was 588,300 preschool children and 5,683,707 students ages six through 21, an increase of 2.6% over the previous year (U.S. Department of Education, 2002).

Because of the large and increasing number of special needs students, assistive educational technology is growing in importance. The percentage of students with disabilities served in schools and classes with their nondisabled peers has gradually increased. In the 1997-1998 school year, U.S. states reported that 97.8% of students ages six through 11 with disabilities were served in schools with their nondisabled peers, as were 94.7% of students ages 12 through 17 with disabilities, and 87.2% of students ages 18 through 21 with disabilities (see Figure 2). These figures represent a large increase when compared to just four years before, when in 1993-1994, the states served 43.4% of students with disabilities ages six through 21 in a regular classroom situation (U.S. Department of Education, 2000; U.S. Department of Education, 1996). As the percentage of special needs students served in an inclusive setting along with nondisabled students rises, the educational situations prepared to provide an inclusive environment must also increase.

It has been proposed that laws that ensure equal access to education for individuals with disabilities, such as IDEA, the Rehabilitation Act, and the Americans with Disabilities Act, have been largely responsible for the changes in the population of postsecondary students. The population of postsecondary students with disabilities has increased over the past two decades, and currently there are approximately one million people in postsecondary institutions who are classified as having some form of disability (U.S. Department of Education, 2000). In 1994, approximately 45% of the adult population who reported having a disability had either attended some college or had completed a bachelor's degree or higher, as compared to only 29% in 1986 (NCES, 1999).

Figure 2: Percentage of Students Ages Six through 21 in Different Education Environments During 1988-1989 through 1997-1998

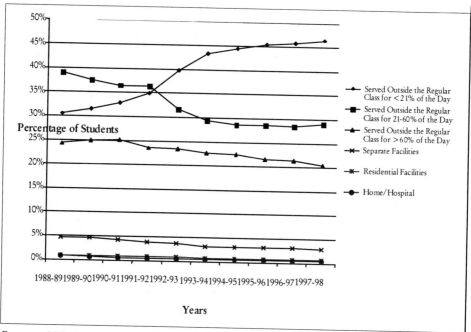

Source: *U.S. Department of Education, Office of Special Education Programs, Data Analysis System (DANS).*

Distance Learning and Students with Disabilities

According to a National Center for Education Statistics Report (2002), a survey of more than 3,500 institutions in 1999 found that 78% of four-year and 62% of two-year public colleges and universities used distance learning. This trend displays an overall increase for all higher institutions of learning concerning distance education, with an increase of 11% over a two-year period, from 33% to 44% (see Table 1) (NCES, 1999b). The growth in electronic learning was mostly at the individual course level, rather than in complete academic programs. An estimated 1.6 million students across the nation took at least one course through distance learning in 1999 (U.S. Department of Education, 2000a). Of the electronic learning courses, the presentation format of asynchronous computer-based instruction was on the rise, going from 58% to approximately 83% of all electronic distance learning courses offered between

Table 1: Percentage Distribution of Two-Year and Four-Year Higher Education Institutions According to Distance Education Courses, by Institutional Characteristics: Fall 1995 and 1997-1998

Institutional characteristic	Offered distance education	
	1995	1997–98
All institutions	33	44
Public two-year	58	72
Private two-year	2	6
Public four-year	62	79
Private four-year	12	22

Sources: U.S. Department of Education, National Center for Education Statistics, Postsecondary Education Quick Information System, Survey on Distance Education Courses Offered by Higher Education Institutions, 1995, and Survey on Distance Education at Postsecondary Education Institutions, 1998-1999.

1997 and 2001 (see Table 2) (NSES, 2002). As the trend continues, it is reasonable to expect it will be reflected in the K-12 educational setting.

The web-based learning environment can itself be an accommodation. As most web-based courses are asynchronous, they provide accommodations that many students with special needs require. Assistive technology specialists from the Florida Assistive Technology Education Network (ATEN) stated that to accommodate students with special needs, instructors should expect the students to communicate, and they should provide students with opportunities to interact with others, varied models of print use, choices, wait time for them to respond, and opportunities to communicate (2002). All of these accommodations are inherent in most asynchronous distance learning environments. Asynchronous learning structure inherently includes a number of effective special education strategies. It is important to use these strategies and considerations as well as the accessibility guidelines when designing any form of electronic learning. Unfortunately some of today's most used online course environment packages are not fully W3C or 508 compliant for full accessibility.

The numbers of students with disabilities are growing in the online education environment. A 1999 Canadian study of students with disabilities (n = 725)

Table 2: The Percentage of Undergraduates who took any Distance Education Courses in 1999-2000, and, among those who did, the Percentage Reporting Various Ways in which the Courses were Delivered

Institutional and student characteristics	Took any courses	Mode of delivery if participated		
		Live, interactive	Internet	Pre-recorded
Total	8.4	37.0	59.0	39.1
Institution type[1]				
Public	8.6	38.1	57.4	39.2
two-year	9.6	39.0	55.7	43.3
four-year nondoctorate-granting	7.8	36.2	64.9	30.1
four-year doctorate-granting	7.1	37.1	57.1	33.1
Private not-for-profit	6.6	28.2	69.3	37.1
Less-than-four-year	6.0	47.0	70.0	44.6
four-year nondoctorate-granting	7.3	27.9	68.8	35.6
four-year doctorate-granting	5.6	26.2	70.3	38.9

Source: U.S. Department of Education, National Center for Education Statistics, 1999–2000 National Postsecondary Student Aid Study (NPSAS, 2000).

attending community colleges and universities found that an overwhelming majority of respondents (95%) indicated that they used a computer in their education situation. The students in the study had a variety of impairments/disabilities, with the largest group (37%) indicating that they had a learning disability, which is consistent with the rest of the North American disabled population. Of the students in the study, 87% had Internet access, and the most noted reason for using the Internet was in doing research (Fichten et al., 2000). Thompson's (1998) summarizing report states that approximately 5,000 of the undergraduates (about 5%) of the Open University of the United Kingdom have disabilities, with their population increasing at a rate of approximately 10% per year. This growth is ascribed to the convenience of home study and the ability of information technology to overcome barriers to learning for students with disabilities. According to the U.S. Department of Education's (2002) National Postsecondary Student Aid Study of 1999-2000, more than

Table 3: Percentage of College Undergraduates Taking Distance Learning Courses (1999-2000), with Percentages Concerning Modes of Delivery, and Students with a Disability Taking Distance Learning

Institutional and student characteristics	Took any courses	Mode of delivery if participated		
		Live, interactive	Internet	Pre-recorded
Total	8.4	37.0	59.0	39.1
Disability status				
No disability reported	8.2	37.5	58.4	39.2
Some type of disability reported	9.9	33.1	63.6	38.5

The percentage of undergraduates who took any distance education courses in 1999–2000, and among those who did, the percentage reporting various ways in which the courses were delivered

Source: U.S. Department of Education, National Center for Education Statistics, 1999– 2000 National Postsecondary Student Aid Study (NPSAS 2000). (US DOE 2002b)

8% (8.4%) of all undergraduates took at least one distance learning course and approximately 10% (9.9%) of those students identified themselves as having some form of disability (see Table 3). Unfortunately, the area of distance learning concerning students with disabilities in the K-12 situation is in need of further research, including tracking or documentation.

Hospital/Homebound Students

According to U.S. government statistics, there are more than 26,000 students classified as hospital/homebound students across the nation (U.S. Department of Education, 2002a). How these students are being served at a distance from their "home" school is a distance learning strategy question. The classic hospital/homebound program has a visiting teacher who acts as intermediary between a student's regular teacher and the student. The hospital/homebound teacher contacts the student's classroom teacher or teachers to collect assignments and directions to deliver to the hospital/homebound student, and visits the student to provide instruction and assistance. In a communication with Instructional Support and Community Service department, from the Florida Department of Education, a program specialist indicated that the services provided to the hospital/homebound students vary by school district. The department indicated that a number of districts use a "teleclass" phone model, but other districts may also use online instruction, audio/video taped instruction or CD-ROMs. The districts provide the needed hardware and software, and some school systems have even placed fax machines in students' homes for receiving and submitting assignments (Personal email communication with C. Bishop, January 2003).

In multiple contacts across the nation, including states that are well known for their assistive technology programs, this author was unable to discover any information concerning whether asynchronous internet based distance learning strategies were being applied to students in hospital/homebound situations. As an example, Florida has the Florida Information Resource Network (FIRN), which provides networking for educational administrative data as well as resources and Internet connectivity and web space for schools, teachers and classrooms. The FIRN network is free to schools throughout Florida and approximately 95% of the instructional use is at the K-12 level under the direction and guidance of a teacher (FIRN, 2002). While student use usually occurs at an educational institution, and most students cannot independently acquire an account, teachers can request classroom accounts for student use, and hospital/homebound students could classify as exceptions. FIRN representatives stated that the FIRN organization has no information concerning whether they provide Internet access to hospital/homebound students. FIRN indicated that a hospital/homebound student's teacher could sign up for the accounts, and then assign classroom accounts to the student, meaning hospital/homebound students could be using the service, but FIRN would be uninformed of the account purpose (FIRN Help Desk, personal email communication, September 27, 2002).

A local school system was questioned about the applications and delivery methods used for homebound or hospital bound students. The school system has a population of approximately one million persons and 160 schools serving more than 126,000 students (103 elementary schools, 24 middle schools, 17 high schools, two academies of technology, three exceptional student centers, five special schools and six charter schools) (Duval County Public Schools,

2002). The school system is technology equipped, and is currently in the last year of placing a minimum of four Internet connected multimedia computers in every classroom for student use, and an additional computer for teacher applications. In interviewing the hospital/homebound program, this author found that, on average, the program serves approximately 400 students throughout the year with students regularly entering and leaving the program. The current methods of instruction used with this hospital/homebound program include:

- Elementary program. At this level, a visiting teacher does drop-in teaching for approximately an hour on a weekly basis with each student.
- Middle and high school. Here, students participate through phone-based instruction (teleclass), in which teachers teach through a conference call system.

In phone-based or teleclass instruction, all students taking a course dial into a common number, and a teacher provides instruction by speaking. Students have the opportunity to ask questions and interact through voice (G. A. Ball, personal phone communication, October 2, 2002). This instruction by phone service qualifies as a true distance learning program, as education is provided to the students through a telecommunication system. There are educational and distance learning issues with this form of instruction. Consider the case of a parent who described the situation of a secondary student who had experienced the hospital/homebound program through phone instruction. In this case, the student participated with the hospital/homebound program at the secondary level through phone instruction. The parent indicated that she found the system design to be disruptive, ineffective and inadequate and had chosen to withdraw her child from the school system to be home schooled instead. The parent felt that the phone delivery method of instruction was too difficult for her child to follow, and that there were constant interruptions from other students, some of who were not interested in learning and were disruptive. She indicated that because the teacher could not identify individual students, unless they first identified themselves, students' disruptive behavior, which included the use of foul and abusive language, created a classroom management situation that was impossible for a teacher to effectively control.

The hospital/homebound situation is an area that could be easily served by the range distance learning approaches, but for the most part does not employ much variety in its methods. Perhaps this is due to the relatively small numbers of students who participate; therefore it is not a priority. Nationally, for the U.S. and its outlying areas in the 1998-1999 school year, of the students who qualified under IDEA, the hospital/homebound students totaled 26,318 students, which was only 0.47% of the total U.S. IDEA student population (U.S. Department of Education, 2002b). In the school system that was interviewed, the 400 students being served by the hospital/homebound department only represents 0.32% of the total student population of the school district. But if, as teachers, we believe in the "no child left behind" concept, then sufficient services, options and approaches need to be used to assist in the instruction of these special needs students.

K-12 Distance Learning Schools and Students with Disabilities

To determine the current population of K-12 students who have a disability taking either synchronous or asynchronous Internet-based distance learning courses a brief survey was developed. A group of virtual schools to be surveyed were identified from a variety of sources including a list of virtual schools produced by the Wisconsin Department of Public Instruction's Academic Excellence program (2002), recommended programs and open searching. Forty-five K-12 distance learning or virtual schools across the North American continent were selected for participation in the survey because they were open enrollment Internet-based distance learning schools (state, public or private, or college/university). The survey was sent by email to representatives at the schools. The survey was composed of 10 questions asking the number of students, number of students with special needs, methods of identifying students, IEP participation, staffing concerning counselors and special education teachers, teacher training, and web accessibility compliance (see Appendix A).

Of the 45 institutions surveyed, seven responded. While an in-depth analysis may not be possible, the information may indicate trends and the current status of distance learning programs and special needs students. The distance learning population of the responding schools ranged from 300 to 5,000 full or part-time students, and the most common size was approximately 1,000 students. While most schools indicated that they did not have records or tracking methods for identifying students with disabilities, schools that did identify them indicated that special needs populations ranged from 2% to 10% of the school enrollment. The methods of identifying the student usually involved the student self-identifying, commonly during the registration process, but a school or parent could also identify students with special needs. With the exception of the responding university school, all of the K-12 distance learning schools indicated that their teachers have participated in IEPs for students. Half of the respondent schools indicated that they currently had students taking distance learning courses as part of the IEP, as recommended or required by the student's home school IEP team. The schools also indicated that they did not participate as IEP team members but that the school, or distance learning environment, can be written in as a service in the student's IEP. Some of the schools have participated by maintaining contact with the home IEP team, providing weekly reports and needed accommodations. A consistent thread in the responses was that the distance education schools were sure that they had special needs students, but the students were not identified. The student, the student's home school, the student's counselor, or the IEP team may contact the distance learning course teacher, but the virtual school was not involved in the process, and therefore did not keep records concerning students with disabilities. When identifying their accommodations for students with special needs, all of the schools responded that they were willing to make accommodations, and the most common accommodation occurring in their programs was extending the required time on tests and assignments.

When questioned about the virtual school's faculty, only half of the respondents indicated that they had both counselors and exceptional education teachers on staff. Others indicated that they depended on counselors or other support personnel to work with the student's home school. Interestingly, all responding virtual schools did indicate that distance learning instructors have already had, or currently have access to, training concerning accommodations for educating special needs students.

Only two of the responding distance learning schools indicated that their web-based instruction pages were compliant with either Section 508 or W3C. One additional school indicated that it was not currently compliant, but was in the process of becoming so.

While the responding population was not large enough for significant analysis, it does provide a glimpse at the current situation. Students, for the most part, are not being identified by virtual schools as having special needs, but virtual schools are willing to work with the students and their IEP teams to provide the necessary accommodations or provide an instructional accommodation. Some of the schools have support staff to assist the special needs students or their teachers, and all of the schools provide resources in the form of training for their instructors. While the majority of the schools' websites are not currently "handicapped" accessible, it is encouraging finding that some of the schools are accessible, and that others are aware of their shortcomings and are in the process of repair.

One Virtual School's Disability Situation

The Florida Virtual School (FLVS), once known as the Florida Online High School, is a statewide, Internet-based, grade eight through 12 public high school offering its curriculum online. Started in 1997, the virtual school currently offers 65 courses to a student population surpassing 8,200, and enrollment projections exceed 10,000 for 2002-2003. FLVS students receive their diplomas from local high schools in local school districts. The courses are free to Florida students, and non-Florida students must pay tuition. The current faculty of the school includes more than 100 teachers residing throughout the state. All of the teachers possess a state teaching certificate and are certified in the subject they teach, with 14 teachers having National Board Certification (FLVS, 2002).

One of the school's counselors stated that the current enrollment of students with disabilities was approximately 10% of the total population. When questioned about how the school participates in the IEP process, the counselor stated that the actual IEPs are handled at the student's "home" school and the directives are then reported to FLVS, which relays the information on to the course teachers. She stated that there could be more special needs students attending, but IEP teams may not know that the services are available, and therefore the opportunity for distance learning as an option is not reaching as many students as possible. The counselors and teachers are willing to become members of the IEP team, participating at a distance through methods such as conference calling. The school is working with the State School for Deaf and Blind. From the school's experiences, the distance learning environment works well with attention deficit disorder (ADD) students, students with school anxiety and students with low self esteem. The school has provided consultation with IEP teams and suggested to the teams that certain students not attend courses online, usually because the student's reading level was not sufficiently high enough. The FLVS current standard provides instruction with written material starting at the ninth grade reading level (Personal communication with R. Dorocher, March 2001).

FLVS is working to be as accessible as possible. The school recently switched to a new delivery system, which is cascading style sheet (CSS) based, and the switch occurred after a six-month bid and evaluation process, in which accessibility compliance was a basic component. The school chose the new system based on the software company's willingness to work with the school by sending programmers to the school to work with teachers to design effective interfaces (Personal communication with J. Murphy, August 7, 2002).

A School for Students with Disabilities and its Online Instruction

A series of interviews occurred with faculty from the Florida School for the Deaf and Blind (FSDB) concerning student use of distance learning. Located in St. Augustine, FSDB is a state-supported boarding school for hearing-impaired and visually-impaired students pre-school through 12th grade providing both regular and special diplomas. The school has two departments: the Department for the Deaf and the Department for the Blind and Special Needs. The school has students whose abilities range from learning disabled to gifted, and a number of FSDB students participate as mainstreamed students for part of their day in classes in the local school district. Today, the Florida School for the Deaf and the Blind is the largest school of its type in the United States, and in 2001 it had a student population of 730 students from 57 counties, with 65% of the school population having a hearing disability, 19% having a vision disability and 16% having other special needs situations such as hearing or vision disability and an additional handicap (FSDB, 2002).

Faculty stated that while they were not currently using the Florida Virtual School, they were using online instruction with a number of their students on campus. The school has a Learning Opportunity Center, which uses an online instructional environment that allows student to receive remediation or take self-contained, independent classes. They had students taking courses online in geometry, calculus and history, and other students taking online preparation classes for state assessments (FCAT, HSCT, GED). The center teacher stated that students choose the online program for additional remediation, because of course time conflicts, or because there was no course teacher available. The program has had added benefits in its interaction with the school's curriculum, in part because it requires that students master standard English. There is extra support for the students participating in the online program, in the form of resource and interpreting teachers, and the online program actually provides extra teachers for the school. The current online course environment cannot currently be run totally independently by students, such as from home, because it requires teacher participation or interaction. For example, when a student misses too many questions, the student/lesson is "red flagged," which requires a teacher to clear the flag before the student can continue (Personal communication with J. Witerhose, October 2002).

Another faculty member from the Department for the Deaf stated that instructors from the school found the virtual school program to be excellent, but it did not work for the group of students that they had. In her words, distance learning, "is a wonderful tool but it still needs a teaching support system." The students had response issues and there may have also been issues with the dependence upon print and reading level of print information. While the opportunity lab's distance learning provides a level of onsite support, the system is individualized, self-paced, and can be prescriptive and diagnostic. In expressing her findings on the program's effectiveness, the FSDB faculty member described the current situation, where the online distance education and technology program is used with ninth grade students creating associated courses in intensive reading, intensive language arts and intensive math. Students participating in the program were initially identified as reading at the fourth to sixth grade level while in the ninth grade. At the end of a year, 90% of the students experienced at least a single year of growth in reading, 81% showed more than a year's growth, 63% experienced more than two years growth, 45% had more than three years growth, and 18% had experienced six to eight years growth in reading. The mathematics situation was quite similar, with 90% of the students growing at least one year, 72% showing more than a year's growth, 54% had more than two years growth, 36% demonstrated more than three years growth, and 18% had more than six years of educational growth (Personal communication with D. Schuler, October 2002).

Conclusion

As the education of all students occurs more frequently within the standard inclusion classroom, teaching and learning that incorporate assistive technology approaches and accommodations become more important. The change in classroom population will have the impact of changing the learning goals, the teaching methods and the means of assessment for all students. Assistive technology, which can include distance learning, is a wide-ranging educational tool, the use of which is growing along with its importance, and it is required for consideration for all students classified with any form of disability as a component of a student's individual education plan (IEP). Teacher education programs need to restructure themselves to include content for all teachers in special education methodology and pedagogy, along with student modifications, accommodations and assistive technology. A cadre of teachers at the K-12 level must be developed that can effectively teach through distance learning, and the supporting tools and accommodations must also be identified and provided.

As the inclusive education of all students occurs more frequently within the standard K-12 classroom, and through the electronic environment at the college level, then it is reasonable to expect that more K-12 students with disabilities will participate in online education. While many accommodations are already available online, designers and instructors should adhere to accessibility guidelines as proposed by state, national or international organizations. Educational environments should be designed for all students, even those students who may need modifications, accommodations and assistive technology. To ensure that the needs of these students are met, additional research and documentation is needed concerning K-12 students with disabilities who are participating in distance learning.

References

Architectural and Transportation Barriers Compliance Board (ATBCB). (2000, December 21). *Electronic and Information Technology Accessibility Standards, including Section 508* [Published in the Federal Register]. Retrieved from the World Wide Web: http://www.access-board.gov/sec508/508standards.htm, last accessed 5/29/03.

Assistive Technology Education Network (ATEN). (2002). *Assistive Technology: Unlocking Human Potential.* Seminole County Public Schools.

Beech, M. (2000). *Accommodations and modifications: What parents need to know.* Florida Developmental Disabilities Council, Inc.

Beninghof, A. M. & Singer, A. L. (1995). *Ideas for Inclusion. The School Administrator's Guide.* Longmont, CO: Sopris West.

California Community Colleges Chancellor's Office. (1999, August) *Distance education: Access guidelines for students with disabilities.* Retrieved from the World Wide Web: http://www.htctu.fhda.edu/dlguidelines/final%20dl%20guidelines.htm, last accessed 5/29/03.

Council for Exceptional Children (CEC). (1997). *Basic commitments and responsibilities to exceptional children.* Retrieved March 1, 2001, from the World Wide Web: http://www.cec.sped.org/pp/policies/ch3.htm#322.

Duval County Public Schools (DCPS). (n.d.). Retrieved October 2002 from the World Wide Web: http://www.educationcentral.org/SBA/super.htm.

Fichten, C. S., Asuncion, J. V., Barile, M., Fossey, M., & De Simone, C. (April 2000). *Access to educational and instructional computer technologies for postsecondary students with disabilities: Lessons from three empirical studies* (EvNet Working Paper). Retrieved from the World Wide Web: http://evnet-nt1.mcmaster.ca/network/workingpapers/jemdis/jemdis.htm, last accessed 10/3/02.

Flippo, K.F., Inge, K.J., & Barcus, J.M. (1995). *Assistive Technology: A Resource for School Work and Community.* Baltimore, MD: Paul H Brookes.

Florida Department of Education (FL DOE). (2000). *Developing Quality Individual Education Plans: A Guide for Instructional Personnel and Families.* Tallahassee, FL: Author.

Florida Information Resource Network (FIRN). (n.d.). Retrieved October 2002 from the World Wide Web: http://www.firn.edu/about/, last accessed 5/29/03.

Florida School for the Deaf and Blind (FSDB). (n.d.). Retrieved October 2002 from the World Wide Web: http://www.fsdb.k12.fl.us/, last accessed 5/29/03.

Florida Virtual School (FLVS). (n.d.). Retrieved October 2002 from the World Wide Web: http://www.flvs.net, last accessed 5/29/03.

Gitlow, L. (2000). *Assistive technology.* Retrieved from the World Wide Web: http://www.ume.maine.edu/cci/FACTSFC/articles/assistec.html, last accessed 5/29/03.

Half the Planet. (2001). *Half the Planet Foundation Information.* Retrieved from the World Wide Web: http://www.halftheplanet.com.

Hurst, F. M., et al. (1997). *Assuring equitable access: A distance learning vision for Florida.* Available on the World Wide Web: http://www.state.fl.us/institute/finvis.htm, last accessed 1/2001.

IBM. (2000). *About human resources.* Retrieved from the World Wide Web: http://www-1.ibm.com/businesscenter/za/sb3zapub.nsf/detailcontacts/Industry+Solutions600E, last accessed 12/2000.

Individuals with Disabilities Education Act (IDEA). (1992). Pub. L. No. 101-476. Retrieved from the World Wide Web: http://frwebgate.access.gpo.gov/cgi-bin/getdoc.cgi?dbname=105_cong_public_la, last accessed 5/29/03.

International Society for Technology in Education (ISTE). (2000). *Teacher technology standards.* Retrieved from the World Wide Web: http://www.iste.org/, last accessed 5/29/03.

Judd-Wall, J. (1999). *Necessary categorizations.* Retrieved September 1999 from the World Wide Web: http://www.aten.scps.k12.fl.us/.

McGregor, G. & Vogelsberg, R. T. (1998). *Inclusive Schooling Practices: Pedagogical and Research Foundations: A Synthesis of the Literature that Informs Best Practices about Inclusive Schooling.* Baltimore, MD: Paul H. Brookes Publishing Co.

National Center for Accessible Media (NCAM). (2002). Specifications for Accessible Learning Technologies (SALT), (Dec. 2000 - Sept. 2004). Retrieved from the World Wide Web: http://ncam.wgbh.org/salt/, last accessed 5/29/03.

National Center for Educational Statistics (NCES). (1999). *Students with disabilities in postsecondary education: A profile of preparation, participation, and outcomes.* Retrieved from the World Wide Web: http://nces.ed.gov/pubs99/1999187.pdf, last accessed 5/29/03.

National Center for Educational Statistics (NCES), & Phipps, R. A. (1999b). *Distance education at postsecondary education institutions, 1997-98: Statistical analysis report.* Retrieved from the World Wide Web: http://nces.ed.gov/pubs2000/2000013.pdf, last accessed 5/29/03.

National Center for Educational Statistics (NSES), & Phipps, R. A. (2002). *Access to postsecondary education: What is the role of technology? Report written for the National Postsecondary Education Cooperative (NPEC)*. Retrieved from the World Wide Web: http://nces.ed.gov/npec/papers/PDF/WhatRoleTechnology.pdf, last accessed 2/2003.

National Council for the Accreditation of Teacher Education (NCATE). (2000). Educational computing and technology leadership standards In *NCATE guidelines for educational computing and technology leadership*. Retrieved from the World Wide Web: http://www.ncate.org/, last accessed 5/29/03.

National Council for the Accreditation of Teacher Education (NCATE). (2002). *Professional standards for the accreditation of schools, colleges, and Departments of Education (2002 ed.)*. Retrieved from the World Wide Web: http://www.ncate.org/2000/unit_stnds_2002.pdf, last accessed 5/29/03.

New York State Council on the Arts. (2001). *A universal environment: Beyond access to opportunity*. Retrieved from the World Wide Web: http://www.nysca.org/UniversalPlanning.html, last accessed 2/2003.

Rehabilitation Engineering and Assistive Technology Society of North America (RESNA). (2000). *Assistive technology categories*. Retrieved from the World Wide Web: http://www.resna.org/, last accessed 5/29/03.

Rose D. & Meyer A. (2000). *The future is in the margins: The role of technology and disability in educational reform*. Retrieved from the World Wide Web: http://www.cast.org/udl/index.cfm?i=542, last accessed 5/29/03.

Sivin-Kachala, J. P. & Bialo, E. R. (1992, October). *Using computer-based, telecommunications services to serve educational purposes at home* (Report prepared for the Alfred P. Sloan Foundation by Interactive Educational Systems Design, Inc.). Retrieved from the World Wide Web: http://www.wnydf.bfn.org/library/compedu.text, last accessed 5/29/03.

State of Florida, Department of State. (2000). *Developing quality Individual Educational Plans (Document ESE9413)*. Florida Department of Education, Bureau of Instructional Support and Community Services, last accessed 5/29/03.

Thompson, M. M. (1998). *Distance learners in higher education (Global Distance Education Net)*. Retrieved from the World Wide Web: http://wbweb5.worldbank.org/disted/Teaching/Design/kn-02.html, last accessed 5/29/03.

U.S. Department of Education (US DOE). (1996). To assure the free appropriate public education of all children with disabilities. In *Eighteenth Annual Report to Congress on the Implementation of IDEA*. Washington, DC: Author. Retrieved from the World Wide Web: http://www.ed.gov/pubs/OSEP96AnlRpt/, last accessed 5/29/03.

U.S. Department of Education (US DOE). (2000a). *Getting ready pays off: A report for National College Week*. Retrieved from the World Wide Web: http://www.ed.gov/offices/OPE/News/collegeweek/collegeweek pdf.pdf, last accessed 5/29/03.

U.S. Department of Education (US DOE). (2000b). To assure the free appropriate public education of all children with disabilities. In *Twenty-Second Annual Report to Congress on the Implementation of IDEA*. Washington, DC: author. Retrieved from the World Wide Web: http://www.ed.gov/offices/OSERS/OSEP/Products/OSEP2000AnlRpt/index.html, last accessed 5/29/03.

U.S. Department of Education (US DOE). (2002a). *Twenty-third annual report to Congress on the implementation of the Individuals with Disabilities Education Act*. Retrieved from the World Wide Web: http://www.ed.gov/offices/OSERS/OSEP/Products/OSEP2001AnlRpt/index.html, last accessed 5/29/03.

U.S. Department of Education (US DOE). (2002b). The percentage of undergraduates who took any distance education courses in 1999-2000, and among those who did, the percentage reporting various ways in which the courses were delivered. In *1999-2000 National Postsecondary Student Aid Study* (NEDRC Table Library). Retrieved from the World Wide Web: http://nces.ed.gov/surveys/npsas/table_library/tables/npsas22.asp (number of disabled students taking distance learning), last accessed 5/29/03.

U.S. Federal Register. (1994). *Technology-related assistance for Individuals with Disabilities Act Amendments, 1994* (P.L. 103-218). Retrieved from the World Wide Web: http://www.section508.gov/, last accessed 5/29/03.

U.S. Federal Register. (1997). *Technology-related assistance for Individuals with Disabilities Act, 1988* (PL 100-407). Retrieved from the World Wide Web: http://www.resna.org/taproject/library/laws/techact94.htm, last accessed 5/29/03.

U.S. General Services Administration's Office. (2002). *Section 508*. Retrieved October 2002 from the World Wide Web: http://www.section508.gov/.

U.S. Government. (2000). *Electronic and information technology accessibility standards*. Retrieved from the World Wide Web: http://www.access-board.gov/sec508/508standards.htm, last accessed 5/29/03.

Web Able Inc. (2002). *Section 508 accessibility requirements for web sites*. Retrieved from the World Wide Web: http://www.webable.com/508_guidelines.html, last accessed 2/2002.

Wisconsin Department of Public Instruction (WDPI). (2002). *Virtual schools and programs online*. Retrieved from the World Wide Web: http://www.dpi.state.wi.us/dpi/dlsis/vischname.html, last accessed 5/29/03.

World Wide Web Consortium (W3C). (1999). Web Content Accessibility Guidelines 1.0 (WCAG 1.0). Web Accessibility Initiative of the World Wide Web Consortium. Retrieved from the World Wide Web: http://www.w3.org/TR/WCAG10/full-checklist.html, last accessed 5/29/03.

Appendix A: Survey Sent by Email to Internet-Based Distance Learning Schools

1. How many students attend your high school program through distance learning?

2. How many of those are classified as special needs students?

3. What is your method of determining if a student is classified as a special needs student?

4. Do your online teachers participate in a student's IEP (individualized education plan)?

5. Are any of your students taking distance-learning courses as required or recommended by the IEP team from the local school?

6. What kind of accommodations do your teachers make for special needs students?

7. Does your school have school counselors serving students?

8. Do you have any Special Education personnel on staff?

9. Do you give your instructors training concerning accommodations for special needs students, and if so what kind?

10. Are your web pages ADA (section 508) or W3C compliant for accessibility?

Section III

Virtual School Educators

Chapter VI

Teaching Any Time, Any Place, Any Pace

Sharon Johnston
Florida Virtual School, USA

Abstract

With the launch of six courses in January 1997, Florida Virtual School (FLVS) became a new resource for all students in Florida. FLVS teachers, developers of the online curriculum, experimented with innovative ways of encouraging students to be responsible learners. In the virtual classroom, teachers soon discovered that frequent communication with students and parents reaped tremendous rewards. In this chapter, the reader will see inside the teaching process at Florida Virtual School as the following essential characteristics of online teaching are highlighted: communication, teamwork, flexibility, student-centered learning, and love of students. Using technology as a tool to design and deliver curriculum and instruction, the virtual learning environment mirrors the technological world that students live in today and will work in tomorrow. Virtual education changes the way teachers teach and interact with each other, with students and with parents. Virtual educators are reshaping the routine learning modes of the traditional school day to a dynamic, interactive real-world learning environment that presents choices to parents and students and requires students to take ownership of the learning process.

Teaching Any Time, Any Place, Any Path, Any Pace

Teacher performance is a major reason for the success of Florida Virtual School (FLVS), which was noted as being "the largest and most well-established state-supported virtual school in the nation" in *Education Week's Technology Counts* edition (Doherty, 2002, p. 19). With a mission to give students choices in how they learn, when they learn and where they learn, FLVS provides a learning environment that serves all learners. Home schoolers, athletes, performers, and students with scheduling conflicts or medical problems benefit from the "any time, any place, any path, any pace" motto. FLVS takes full advantage of its electronic environment. A sample page from the website (http://www.flvs.net) showcases our services:

- *Welcome to FLVS* from your Executive Director, Julie Young

- **Attention Students:** Spring 2003 registration is now open. Click here to view the *Spring 2003 course list* (PDF). Please note space in full credit courses is limited.

- Need to know when the next progress report is due out? Check out the *FLVS calendar.*

- Request a copy of your transcript when you receive a final grade in your course using our *Transcript Request Form* (PDF file)

At the website, parents and/or students seeking general information about our school find an intuitive system, allowing them to research curriculum options, see sample lessons, and view a video quiz to see if they are suited to online learning. Students ready to engage in e-learning can register for courses, update their records, read the online student newspaper, "News in a Click," or log in to their course(s).

FLVS is a statewide, internet-based, public high school offering performance-based curriculum online. The Florida Legislature initially funded the FLVS as a pilot project in 1997, at $1.3 million to begin course development. The 2000 Florida Legislature enacted 228.082, a Florida Statute, establishing FLVS as an independent education entity with a separate governing board appointed by the Governor.

In 2001-2002, FLVS served more than 8,200 student enrollments and achieved an 87.5% completion rate. Critical to growth and success is a dedicated teaching staff of 49 full time and 51 adjuncts. The chart in Figure 1 highlights enrollment history.

Figure 1: Course Enrollment Data by School Year

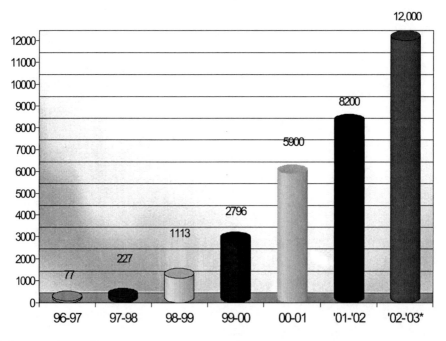

* *Projected enrollment*

The objectives of this chapter are to showcase the following essential characteristics of online teaching:

- Communication
- Teamwork
- Flexibility
- Student-Centered Learning
- Love of Students

Communication

As FLVS educators have discovered, teacher-student interaction is the most important ingredient in student success. Before a student is activated in the FLVS classroom, the teacher conducts a welcome phone call. In that call, the teacher greets the student and begins the important rapport building that continues throughout the course. By the end of the welcome call, the goal is for the teacher and student to know that they will be working together and communicating often via the phone, e-mail, threaded discussions, classroom activities, synchronous or real time chats, and school-sponsored field trips. The teacher also talks with a parent, issuing an invitation for the parent to call or send e-mail anytime a question or concern arises. After the welcome phone call, the teacher sends the student a welcome e-mail to emphasize the student-teacher partnership, to describe the online course, to repeat class expectations outlined in the welcome phone call, provide contact information and to reiterate the class procedures and policies.

Sample e-mail from a ninth-grade biology teacher:

Welcome to Biology and Florida Virtual School. When you receive this message, please send a reply to let me know you have received it. Please keep the same e-mail address for the duration of the course.

Biology is a one-credit course. I certainly hope that you will enjoy the course and that you will enjoy discovering that Biology is all around you. I hope you are ready for an exciting and challenging time.

You will be able to access the "Student Orientation" on August 7, 2001. Usually within four hours of completing the "Student Orientation" you *will have access to your course. Please note that you will be expected to complete the "Student Orientation," within **10** days from the day you start the orientation. The "Student Orientation" must be completed before you have access to your course.*

It is important for you to understand that this course is a REAL high school course and that the grade you earn will become part of your academic record at your home district. In order to be successful, you will need to apply yourself and manage your time carefully. I recommend you set aside time each day to spend on the course. In order to achieve success you should expect to spend four to six hours per week on the Biology course.

There is a 28-day grace period, which begins from the time in which you first have access to the course. (NOT from the time in which you first enter the course.) During this grace period, if you realize that the online learning environment will not work for you, please request to be removed from the course without a grade penalty. However, please understand that if you decide to remain in the course and you do not participate at the minimum level of expectation, you will be removed during this grace period. Remember, my goal is to help you be successful in mastering the course concepts and in completing the course.

I encourage you to take some time to explore our website. It will be of great benefit for you to be familiar with the resources and information provided on the website (http://www.flvs.net).

How to contact your instructor:

Mrs. Mary Madison:

Voice mail:

E-mail:

Pager:

Home phone:

For technical support, please contact: help@flvs.net

I am very excited about sharing this learning adventure with you.

Smiles,

   Mary Madison

Throughout the course, the teacher calls the student and the parent once a month. This monthly call is made to all students and parents, so even a student who is doing a superb job receives that personal contact. Parents, who often become a teaching partner, appreciate the calls and tell us that they have never before had this level of communication with teachers. School policy dictates that instructors respond to student or parent e-mails or voice messages within 24 hours. Students at first are surprised that the teacher is calling home, but soon they become quite accustomed to the calls. One teacher related a humorous response to her calls to a student: the mother called out to her daughter, "Hey, Sue, it's the online lady calling again." Some students tell us that they receive more communication from one online teacher than from all the teachers they see every day. Keeping students and teachers connected is crucial to student success.

Communicating outside of the classroom is another method we use to connect to students. For example, the Science Club plans events and invites parents and students in different parts of the state to meet and participate. A favorite is the yearly turtle watch. Students and their families are invited to meet staff members at beach sites across Florida to participate in the turtle watch.

Often the whole family comes to the Turtle Field Trip:

After the field trip, digital pictures of the event are put online to include the students who cannot travel to the event, and students share their experiences in the club's discussion area. Another annual field trip event is the Latin Club's participation in state competition. To include students who cannot travel to the event, teachers put digital pictures online, and students share their experiences and discoveries in the club's discussion area. Other field trips occur each year when the Latin Club participates in state and national conferences and competitions, from which they always bring home awards. The Computer Science Club also competes annually in state competitions and brings home trophies and computers. The Student Union area of the website hosts the student awards each month. For example, in one month, these awards and recognitions appear:

In the 2001 school year, the student online newspaper, *News in a Click,* launched. Every six weeks a new edition appears in the Student Union at the FLVS website. All students are invited to submit entries to the student editors and the instructor/sponsor. Figure 2 and Figure 3 feature one edition of the student-created virtual newspaper.

While teachers find one-on-one communication with students very rewarding and very successful, they are aware that the virtual school needs to provide settings for conversation and interaction among students. In the 2001 midpoint survey in the courses, only 12% of the students described student-to-student communication as great. After the launch of synchronous chat in the 2001 school year, teachers are experimenting with group lessons and "conversations." Several teachers have hosted "open house" sessions via the chat for parents and/or students. Improving socialization among students is a school-wide goal.

Figure 2: FLVS Student Awards

FLVS Student Awards

Computer Science
Florida Virtual School computer science students took part in the 4th annual high school, Individual Programming Competition held at Embry Riddle University. Stephen Morgan was awarded third place and Paul Adams was awarded fourth place. Read more >

Newspaper
Mary Siegel, an FLVS student, not only writes for the FLVS student newspaper but also writes articles for the *St. Petersburg Times.* Click here to read her most recent article in the St. Pete Times.

Latin
Florida Virtual School Latin Students Win National, State and Regional Awards. The FLVS Latin students have been busy. Students participated in State and Regional Forums and took the National Latin Exam. Read more >

Figure 3: News in a Click Features

Notes from the inside.

Check out our HOMETOWN section. Our students and faculty know how to have fun while working! If you need some **CHEMISTRY HELP**, you'll want to check out HOMETOWN!

Features across the state

Animal abuse continues to intrigue our readers. And don't forget about Jibber Jabber and Dear Kassie! We have it all.

Just for Seniors

Look at our senior planning guide and find out the importance of choosing a major. All of this and more in our **Senior Section!** It's just for you!

Expressions

Take a look at some fantastic art from our students! Read some poetry and short stories.

Instructors at FLVS view communication as the key ingredient to student success. Teachers interact with parents and students as part of each day's work routine. In student midpoint surveys conducted in the courses during the 2001-2002 school year, 85% of FLVS students described the communication with teachers as great or good. By utilizing every possible communication method, especially e-mail and phone, to interact with students and parents, FLVS teachers comment that they have a stronger relationship with students and their families than they did when they taught in the brick and mortar schools. Effective communication is a challenge and a benefit of the online delivery system. Virtual educators know the value of the one-on-one connection with students to determine what motivates them and what action plans to implement to ensure their academic success.

Teamwork

The instructors use a variety of methods to work together even though they do not share the same physical workspace. To ensure that the communication channels are open, FLVS has established specific expectations that are outlined in the staff online handbook that is accessible anytime, anyplace. For example, one policy requires that each morning before 9:00 a.m., staff checks voice mail to hear the latest school news or requests from administrators. As they check voice mail, they update their own voice mail, so callers will know staff members' location and availability for the day. Another method for accessing staff information within our system is a staff log that each staff member completes before 9:00 a.m. on weekdays. If a call for a teacher comes into the office, the office staff first checks the staff log to see the teacher's work location and phone number.

To reinforce teamwork and communication, FLVS's administration gives each new teacher a copy of the official team book, Pat Williams' *The Magic of Teamwork*, which is used in staff development activities each year. To build and maintain the team spirit, the administration hosts staff meetings every other month and a staff overnight retreat once a year. During this face-to-face time, we enjoy our Executive Director's presentation on FLVS' "state of the union," hear marketing summaries, discuss strategies that promote student success and engage in staff development studies.

Teamwork is essential in creating and reviewing curriculum that provides students the opportunity to demonstrate state and national standards. Instructors, who are the subject matter experts, collaborate with web development specialists, project managers, and external instructional designers to develop, review and update courses. As developers of online courses, instructors focus on what students need to learn and be able to do within our courses. To keep the curriculum relevant, the team designs activities that immerse students in real life situations. The development team also considers the varied learning styles of students as they create performance-based choices that allow students to demonstrate proficiency. Working in teams to read and discuss selected texts, to engage in staff development workshops, to review and establish school policy, and to create curriculum is a new and exciting experience for instructors who previously planned lessons and taught students within four walls.

Communicating on issues other than school policy and staff development also keeps the team united. For example, as administrators receive parent and student e-mails, commenting on our excellent service or our outstanding curriculum, they share these responses with the entire staff through e-mail or voice mail. Sharing success stories immediately gives the staff a sense of team and a sense of community pride. A staff motto is "the success of one of us affects the success of the entire school." What one teacher does to impact student success affects the success of everyone.

Flexibility

To be successful in a virtual environment, instructors need to exhibit open-mindedness and flexibility, soft skills that are not typically part of the teacher education program. Teachers must be flexible in creating and utilizing new delivery and teaching approaches that transcend the traditional. In the virtual school, the classroom is always open. Students have access to the "classroom" 24 hours a day, seven days a week. Instructors must balance family life with the open classroom, with the pager and the cell phone that allow students to call with a question, and with the e-mail and submitted assignments that are always there. Instructors schedule time to chat with students online or on the phone, to grade and give feedback to students, to collaborate with colleagues on professional development and course revisions, or to make phone calls to parents. Organizing and following a work schedule is a daily task for the virtual teacher; no bells signal them to move to the next area of responsibility.

Another unique and challenging aspect of teaching online that requires flexibility is functioning within a work world characterized by constant change. For example, selecting new course tools, learning new hardware, and experimenting with new software programs are everyday occurrences. Unlike their colleagues in the brick and mortar schools, who face a room with desks filled with students, online instructors expect the "classroom" view to change. Keeping up with technological upgrades is as crucial as keeping up with the subject matter and educational updates. To survive in this dynamic environment, teachers affirm that flexibility is an essential quality.

FLVS's motto, "any time, any place, any path, any pace," fits the needs of today's families in motion. Student athletes and performers receive tournament and scholarship opportunities that require them to travel. These students now have virtual courses to take with them, so academic studies are not interrupted. In a survey conducted by in an external evaluation, 43% of the students reported that the "any time" part of the motto is the most valuable element (Bigbie & McCarroll, 1999, p. 127). Virtual teachers also appreciate the "any time" aspect of the school's environment. They can schedule a doctor's appointment during the workday and "make-up" the work time in the evening when more students are working online.

Providing a flexible avenue for students and teachers to "go to school" corresponds with the lifestyle of the 21st century. According to the SCANS report, "In our current system, time is the constant and achievement the variable. We have it backwards. Achievement should be the constant and time the variable." Within FLVS, time is flexible; therefore, students can vary the length of time needed to learn the course content and decide the best time for working in the course. Instructors monitor and assess student progress and communicate achievement via the virtual classroom and/or phone calls or e-mails. Teachers report achievement immediately. Students no longer have to wait until class time to receive feedback. Achievement is the constant and time is the variable!

Student-Centered Learning

FLVS encourages the online instructor to continually ask: How am I inviting students into my classroom? After lengthy research of curriculum models, FLVS staff selected the late Robert Gagne's "Nine Events of Instruction" as guidelines for developing curriculum that allows students to problem solve and create meaning. Gagne's Events of Instruction are well known in educational research and provide a solid basis for designing instruction. These events include:

- Gaining learners' attention
- Informing learners of the objectives
- Stimulating learners' recall of prior knowledge
- Presenting the stimulus to the learner
- Providing learning guidance to the learner
- Eliciting performance from the learner
- Providing feedback to the learner
- Assessing the performance of the learner
- Enhancing the learners' retention of the information and transfer of the information to other ideas and contexts

These "events" are closely tied to cognitive theory and research on how the brain uses and stores information. Gagne's theory provides the necessary conditions for learning and serves as the basis for designing instruction and selecting appropriate media (Gagne, Briggs, & Wager, 1992).

To develop student-centered curriculum online that addresses the nine events of instruction, educators must be characterized by a solid understanding of how to organize learning activities in a meaningful and engaging manner. The challenge of the online educational frontier is to ensure that faculty keep the focus on student-centered learning and avoid the temptation of allowing technological capacity to determine curriculum development. Administrators must provide these trailblazers with a high level of technological expertise while keeping the focus on student learning. As Steven Gilbert (2001) recently noted, "Acquiring the knowledge and skill necessary to improve teaching and learning with technology requires faculty, support professionals and administrators to think and behave in new ways — deep learning" (p. 14). At FLVS, administrators and staff continually keep student learning as a focal point while searching constantly for innovative technological implementations. Given these prerequisites, selection of faculty is a key to a school's success.

Course developers, with national and state standards, and Gagne's nine events of instruction as a guide, follow the constructivist approach as they design activities that allow students to show the application of concepts. According to educator Bernie Dodge (1996), "A constructivist use of technology presents information to the learner in multiple forms from multiple sources and invites the learner to make sense of it" (p. 225). The learner can acquire the information needed from several sources via the computer, and from off-line sources including his or her own prior experience, from information gathered while collaborating with other learners, and from references and other sources of expertise found somewhere far away from the computer screen. In general, a constructivist approach is more learner-focused and less teacher-focused. The emphasis is on making a set of tasks and resources available to learners, and creating an environment in which the learners can actively create their own meaning in that context, rather than to passively absorb knowledge structures created by the instructor. In this approach, the instructor is no longer the sole source of information; the instructor's role moves toward being a coach and orchestrator of resources.

Often, current educational systems ignore the fact that curriculum and teaching style play a major role in whether students are successful (Pollak, 1999). What is missing in some classrooms is "learning through doing." A student-centered classroom is not an "incidental pedagogical choice but a choice that shapes how and what students learn and, crucially, how they learn to learn" (Katz, 1993, pp. 2-3). By only asking students to "give us right answers without asking how they arrive at them, make correct choices on multiple-choice questions, or distinguish true from false, . . . they will never see the value of working hard" (Glasser, 1992, p. 208). FLVS instructors provide a caring learning environment that gives students choices in how they learn and in how they show what they have learned.

By establishing high expectations and curriculum choices (projects) for demonstrating proficiency and for constructing meaning, teachers engage students in learning. Within the course design process, instructors are guided to develop coursework with a minimum of 60% Bloom's Level II: analysis, synthesis and evaluation. The evaluators of FLVS's self-initiated study stated: "An impressive finding is that all of the courses reviewed to date address most of the Goal Three Standards and most of the Levels of Bloom's Taxonomy. Essentially, this means that the courses appear to integrate higher order thinking and successful workplace skills throughout the curriculum. This finding is in vast contrast to most of the teaching occurring in Florida and the United States today" (Bigbie & McCarroll, 1999, p. 19). Teachers create problem-solving activities that allow students to make hypotheses, gather information, and apply information to test hypotheses. For example, in the ninth grade English course, students analyze the effectiveness of advertisements to discover what people buy and what strategies cause them to buy. After researching products online at sites provided by the teacher, students create a chart to determine the target audience, the type of delivery, and the effectiveness of the advertisement. Finally, students create their own product and an accompanying marketing strategy. In the practical computer and business skills course, students keep an Internet log as they progress through the course and create a database from this research log. In all courses, students are encouraged to submit assignments for review. Teachers give feedback, and then students revise, if needed, and submit the assignment for grading again. Assessment is an integral part of the learning process, so students have the choice of resubmitting assignments until mastery of the specified standard is achieved.

Creating an integrated, constructivist learning environment is a major goal in curriculum development. As noted in NASSP's *Breaking Ranks*, "Educators should more readily venture beyond the boundaries of their own disciplines to grow familiar and comfortable with the neighboring intellectual terrain" (NASSP, 1996, p. 14). One integrated lesson that puts students in the role of decision-makers occurs in the biology course. With *SCION Image Processing* software, a highly interactive software program, the instructor guides students in analyzing images in a mathematical and scientific manner. For example, the students examine cells of normal and diseased heart tissue.

Figure 4: Screen Shot of the Heart Cell Comparison Image (It has been opened in the SCION Image Processing program. There is a 10um scale bar at the bottom of the image. This is used to set a scale in order to take measurements.)

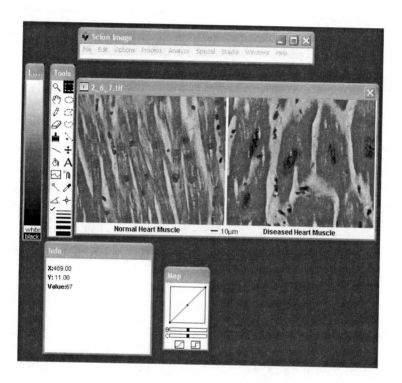

By manipulating the SCION image processing software, students set scales, take measurements, and analyze data. Students move beyond simply viewing and labeling cells as they gather and chart scientific data and conduct an analysis of factors that affect heart tissue. Integrated learning of this type permits students to discover how concepts researched in the classroom relate to their lives. In developing and facilitating this integrated learning activity, using this software and mathematical applications, the teacher and the students become comfortable with "neighboring intellectual terrain."

Based on Susan Kovalic's research on organizing curricula via a theme, instructors design courses that begin with a real-world motif or metaphoric construct, which places students in a specific role within the course. Linda Allison states: "In Kovalic's Integrated Thematic Instruction (ITI) model, theme acts as a pattern for organizing ideas, materials, and actions for both teacher and students. The purpose of the theme is to enhance the pattern-seeking operation of the brain" (Allison, 1998, p. 22). From this approach, students gain a conceptual understanding of content. For example, in the American government course, through a virtual tour of Washington, D.C., students connect to American government concepts as they journey to different monuments and buildings. The course goal allows students to become politically active and learn how to access the governmental system while learning the importance of doing so. Projects include writing letters to senators, researching interest groups, and creating a persuasive product to support a political issue.

In the chemistry course, the industrial plant motif allows students to investigate chemistry concepts as they are utilized in industrial facilities. For example, to investigate gas laws, students create a product for a beginning SCUBA diver, explaining how the gas laws apply. In biology, project-based curriculum also engages students in collaborative learning activities. The motif, BioScope Adventures, sends students traveling through Cellular City, Gene Jungle, Nano World, Fungus Farm and Animal Safari. In these adventures, students experience biological science through real-life applications. For example, in the Create-A-Teen activity the students become gene researchers (geneticists) and work with another classmate to create a new teenager.

The real-world motif or metaphoric construct of a dinner party places the AP literature and composition students in a specific role as a dinner party guest. As members of a dinner party, students examine entrees (classic literature), engage in table talk about language, and create a dinner party for classmates. To involve the students in the learning process, students are given models and choices for ways to demonstrate learning in an independent project. The AP instructor models for students how to design a dinner party, and then students become the creators, selecting the novel or play and the "menu" or theme for the dinner party they design. Figure 5 is the Mystery Dinner menu from the AP course.

The student-centered approach also guides the structure of the learning activities. Instructors give explicit guidelines, including grading rubrics to assist students in making decisions about how to demonstrate mastery of concepts. Students become problem solvers, finding the answers and explaining how they arrive at them. From the beginning of the virtual experience, instructors invite students to have an active role. Through threaded discussions, synchronous chats and conference calls, students and teacher interact on course concepts. The instructor's goal is to continually place learners at the center of the learning environment. Through continuous communication, instructors create caring learning environments that show genuine interest in students' achievement. In

Figure 5: Mystery Dinner Party

the virtual environment, instructors continually challenge students by outlining high expectations that put the student in the center of the learning process. To be successful in the online course, the student must assume responsibility for learning.

Love of Students

When interviewing candidates for a teaching position, a major goal is to ascertain how they relate to young people. A key interview question: describe a time that you were successful in turning a student around. In other words, what interventions have you utilized to help a student who is not performing at an acceptable level? From the responses to this question, the interview team can gauge the interviewee's love and concern for students. It is essential that online instructors care about and know how to move students from one level of achievement to the next. In the virtual environment, the instructor receives immediate data on student performance and uses the data in determining strategies to improve student achievement. Instructors who are dedicated to students will take the time to review data and communicate with students and parents in establishing action plans that will move students to the next level of achievement.

In the traditional school as well as the virtual, instructors' love of students has a major role in determining student success. In a virtual school, though, the instructors' love of students and the instructors' desire for students to achieve determine the school's success, a success that is verified by the completion rate and the student grade reports. With instructors who care about student achievement, the data will be reviewed, the phone calls will be made, and students will receive personal attention and feedback that will ensure mastery of learning and course completion.

Summary

The United States Secretary of Education, Richard Riley, asking Congress for assistance in preparing America's youth for our technologically-driven global society, stated, "Over the last decade, the use of technology in American life has exploded. Yet most schools are still unable to provide the powerful learning opportunities afforded by technology, placing our children at a competitive disadvantage in the new, international marketplace of jobs, commerce, and trade." FLVS is one solution for the type of education Secretary Riley describes.

The Web-based Education Commission (2000) confirms that web technologies are effective educational tools. Based on the growth and successes of FLVS and other virtual schools across the nation, online learning opportunities will continue to increase. Business community members, legislators and parents call for education reform, demanding choices that address the needs of the in-motion families and the ever-changing technological world. Online learning is a viable solution to these public demands. However, the popularity of the online environment raises important questions for the future of education. Here are a few of the looming questions for virtual educators:

- What about the psychological and social aspects of online learning?
- Will virtual education replace traditional teaching or traditional teachers?
- Will virtual instruction be a requirement in pre-service teacher education?
- Will teachers earn certification in virtual education?
- Will virtual education be a solution for overcrowded schools or class size issues?
- Does virtual learning limit student-teacher communication?

The summary of the 1992 SCANS Report, published by the Florida Department of Education, urges educators to implement a constructivist curriculum that includes "applied learning, discovery learning introspection, reflective learning and student-centered applications" (p. 11). The demands of the SCANS Report and of the business community require that educators create a learning environment that parallels that of the real world.

Using technology as a tool to design and deliver curriculum and instruction, the virtual learning environment mirrors the technological world that students live in today and will work in tomorrow. Virtual education changes the way teachers teach and interact with each other, with students, and with parents. Virtual educators are reshaping the routine learning modes of the traditional school day to a dynamic, interactive real-world learning environment that presents choices to parents and students and requires students to take ownership of the learning process.

References

Allison, L. (1998). The status of computer technology in classrooms using the Integrated Thematic Instruction Model. *International Journal of Instructional Media, 22*, 33.

Bigbie, C. & McCarroll, W. (1999). *The Florida High School Evaluation.* Tallahassee, FL: Center for the Study of Teaching and Learning.

Dodge, B. (1996). In B. Brandon (Ed.), *The Computer Trainer's Personal Training Guide (p. 225).* NJ: Prentice Hall.

Doherty, K. M. (2002, May). Students speak out. *Technology Counts/ Education Week, 21*(35), 19.

Gagne, R., Briggs, L., & Wagner, W. (1992). *Principles of Instructional Design* (4th ed.). Ft. Worth, TX: HBJ College Publishers.

Gilbert, S.W. (2001, May). Changing education is lifelong learning. *Syllabus, 14*(10), 22.

Glasser, W. (1992). *The Quality School* (2nd, expanded ed.). New York: Harper Collins.

Katz, S. (1993). The humanities and public education. *The Humanities in the Schools, ACLS Occasional Paper, 20,* 2-3.

National Association of Secondary School Principals. (1996). *Breaking Ranks: Changing an American Institution.* Reston, VA: Author.

Negroponte, N. (1996). *Being Digital.* New York: Vintage Books.

Pollak, M. (1999, June 30). Let's talk curriculum: Predictor of success. *New York Times,* p. 8.

Riley, R. (1996, June 26). *Getting America's Students Ready for the 21ˢᵗ Century: Meeting the Technology Literacy Challenge.* Washington, DC: U.S. Department of Education.

U.S. Department of Labor. (1992). *Learning a Living: A Blueprint for High Performance.* Secretary's Commission on Achieving Necessary Skills (SCANS). Washington, DC: U.S. Government Printing Office.

Chapter VII

Professional Development Recommendations for Online Course Designers

Janice M. Hinson
Louisiana State University, USA

Rachel Sellers Bordelon
Walden University, USA

Abstract

The Internet is redesigning the delivery of instruction, and, consequently, time, space and distance are no longer constraints to teachers and students. Harrison and Berge (2000) state that "Internet access is becoming more widespread and its capabilities for delivering multimedia lessons are improving daily; the Internet is becoming the vehicle of choice for distributing learning across distances" (p. 57). However, teaching online is a relatively new concept and effective professional development is needed to help educators learn to organize content for online delivery, convert instructional materials to online formats, use advanced multimedia tools, and integrate technology resources in online learning environments. This chapter addresses standards for technology-supported instruction and staff development; models of effective face-to-face professional development, along with adaptations for online educators; and professional development programs currently available to online educators. Recommendations for effective professional development have also been provided.

Vignette: Case Study of the Louisiana Virtual High School Project

During the 2000-2001 school year, the Louisiana Center for Educational Technology (a division of the Louisiana Department of Education) developed the Louisiana Virtual High School because some rural high schools in Louisiana were not able to offer certain advanced courses due to a lack of qualified teachers. In the first year, 11 Louisiana high school teachers were selected to teach online. All were certified in their content areas and had five to 10 years of teaching experience in their respective fields. All of the teachers received a $6,000 stipend to design and teach one online course for a year, and each had one hour of unencumbered time during the day to devote to the course. Every teacher had taken a distance education course, and they attended a two-day seminar on how to adapt their course materials to an online format. Once the school year began, however, the teachers had little instructional or technical support as they organized their content, adjusted the curriculum, changed their teaching practices, and struggled with technical problems. At the end of the first year, teachers recommended that for the program to be successful, they and their students needed on-going instructional and technical support.

Despite some attempts to provide professional development training, in the first year of the Louisiana Virtual High School Project, teachers were on their own. As a result, each instructor implemented his/her own version of an online course. Unfortunately, this seems to be a common occurrence. Authors of *The Power of the Internet: Moving from Promise to Practice* (Web-Based

Education Commission, 2000) suggest that more needs to be done to assure that educators have the skills and knowledge they need to deliver online instruction successfully.

Standards for Technology-Supported Learning Environments

The International Society for Technology in Education (ISTE) has developed standards for technology-supported learning environments as part of National Educational Technology Standards (NETS) Project. ISTE supports creating new learning environments through the use of technology by K-12 administrators, teachers and students. According to Thomas and Knezek (2002), traditional learning environments embrace teacher-centered instruction, single-path progression, isolated work, factual knowledge, and passive learning, while technology-supported environments incorporate student-centered learning, collaborative work, multi-path progression, critical thinking and problem solving, and authentic real world contexts (p. 16). To support technology-supported learning environments, ISTE has developed the National Educational Technology Standards for Students (NETS-S), the National Educational Technology Standards for Teachers (NETS-T), and the Educational Technology Standards for Administrators (NETS-A). The ISTE Website (www.iste.org) contains information about these standards and their corresponding publications.

E-Learning Standards for Educators

In addition to the ISTE standards, the National Staff Development Council (NSDC) has developed general standards for staff development (2001), and later revised these to encompass e-learning (2001). Although the purpose of NSDC's e-learning standards is to support online staff development, it may be useful for online course developers to be aware of these standards for possible adaptation to their situations. The entire guide, *E-Learning for Educators: Implementing the Standards for Staff Development* can be found and downloaded from the NSDC Web page (under Standards on the cross bar): http://www.nsdc.org/educatorindex.htm. The standards are discussed.

1. *Learning Communities*: Staff development that improves the learning of all students organizes adults into learning communities whose goals are aligned with those of the school and district.

2. *Leadership*: Staff development that improves the learning of all students requires skillful school and district leaders who guide continuous instructional improvement.

3. *Resources*: Staff development that improves the learning of all students requires resources to support adult learning and collaboration.

4. *Design*: Staff development that improves the learning of all students uses learning strategies appropriate to the intended goal.

5. *Learning*: Staff development that improves the learning of all students applies knowledge about human learning and change.

6. *Collaboration*: Staff development that improves the learning of all students provides educators with the knowledge and skills to collaborate.

7. *Data-Driven*: Staff development that improves the learning of all students uses disaggregated student data to determine adult learning priorities, monitor progress and help sustain continuous improvement.

8. *Evaluation*: Staff development that improves the learning of all students uses multiple sources of information to guide improvement and demonstrate its impact.

9. *Research-Based*: Staff development that improves the learning of all students prepares educators to apply research to decision making.

10. *Equity*: Staff development that improves the learning of all students prepares educators to understand and appreciate all students, create safe, orderly, and supportive learning environments, and hold high expectations for their academic achievement.

11. *Quality Teaching*: Staff development that improves the learning of all students deepens educators' content knowledge, provides them with research-based instructional strategies to assist students in meeting rigorous academic standards, and prepares them to use various types of classroom assessments appropriately.

12. *Family Involvement*: Staff development that improves the learning of all students provides educators with knowledge and skills to involve families and other stakeholders appropriately.

Some helpful professional development resources are listed in Table 1.

Table 1: Professional Development Resource Databases

Site	URL	Content
Association for Supervision and Curriculum Development (ASCD)	http://www.ascd.org/index.html	Journals, newsletters and books on various educational topics
Mid-Continent Research for Education and Learning (MCREL)	http://www.mcrel.org/about/sitemap.asp	Readings on standards, school improvement and evaluation
National Staff Development Council (NSDC)	http://www.nsdc.org/ed	Resources for staff development
North Central Regional Educational Laboratory (NCREL)	http://www.ncrel.org/tech/tpd/index.html	Designing, planning, implementing, professional development technology initiatives
Phi Delta Kappan	http://www.pdkintl.org/kappan/khpartic.htm	Debate on current topics in education

A Professional Development Paradigm Shift

The standards developed by ISTE and NSDC reflect a paradigm shift for teaching, learning and staff development. In the past, professional development often consisted of required workshops where educators would passively receive information from experts (Sparks, 2002). Sometimes, these sessions were not a part of a cohesive professional development improvement plan, but rather were provided so that the participants could earn continuing education units (Sparks, 2002). Even worse, the objectives may not have been obvious or relevant to the participants. Julie, a member of the professional development team for a local school district in Louisiana, made these remarks as part of an online discussion:

I reflected on the common attributes of "good" staff development. Not surprisingly, the common attribute is how closely the staff development addressed the needs of the learner. This seems simple and obvious to me now, and it seems absurd that I ever delivered staff development to learners that didn't see the need for what I was employed to teach them. For far too long, we have practiced the "band aide" approach to staff development. We were quick to send in an "expert" to show teachers how to fix everything that is wrong. The next day, the expert is gone and teachers are expected (not really) to put into practice all the miraculous cures. There was no plan for additional help or follow up support. Research has proven that this one shot quick fix does not work. The money that has been spent on this type staff development, for the most part, has been wasted.

Darling Hammond (1998), Sparks and Hirsh (1997), and Sparks (2002) agree that the paradigm is shifting toward developing and implementing relevant and sustainable professional development to cultivate systemic change. It is hoped that changes to professional development programs will result in increased student achievement.

Face-to-Face Professional Development Models

Several face-to-face professional development models (Sparks, 1989; Wood, Killian, McQuarrie, & Thompson, 1993) support the paradigm shift described above. Other professional development models include the Alliance+Model (Friedman, 2000), a large scale national teacher-training model to help teachers transfer "best practices" from a small group of localized teachers to a national or global community of 10,000 teachers, and the Professional Competency Continuum developed by the Milken Exchange on Educational Technology (1999) for professional development for digital-age educators.

One of the most extensive professional models for technology integration has been created by the North Central Regional Educational Laboratory (NCREL) (http://www.ncrel.org/tech/tpd/index.html). Much of the information presented in the NCREL Model can be utilized by online course developers who wish to initiate instructional changes, because the guidelines and resources can be adapted easily for online professional development. For example, the first phase of the NCREL Model is Visualizing. In this step, developers work with participants to formulate an image of what needs to be done to reach intended goals. Sparks and Hirsh (1997) recommend that, when planning for professional development, developers begin with long-range planning that includes long-term goals and objectives. Referring to Stephen Covey's *The Seven*

Habits of Highly Effective People, Sparks (2002) recommends that planners begin with the end in mind, a results-driven plan. During the Visualization Stage, developers should build support for instructional changes by involving stakeholders (administrators, teachers, parents, and community leaders) in the planning process (Wood et al., 1993). Through discussions, a shared vision and a cohesive master plan should emerge and guide all aspects of the stages to follow.

The second stage of the NCREL Model is Current Reality. During this stage, developers and participants work together to assess what is working and what needs to be changed to meet the desired goals. To assist developers, the NCREL Website contains an excellent guideline, The Framework for Reviewing Professional Development Policies and Practices (http://www.ed.gov/pubs/CPRE/t61/framwork.html). This framework asks developers to reflect on current professional development opportunities available to the participants, incentives for participating in professional development activities, and links between professional development and the improvement of teaching. During this stage, the participants should assist in a self-study to decide on specific strategies to be implemented. As Wood et al. (1993) remind us:

...school improvement does not translate into abandoning effective practices simply for the sake of change. In fact, just the opposite is true, team members need to identify current practices that support goals and expand them to include more teachers and students (p. 6).

Wood et al. also suggest that planners refer to current research and best practices to determine what is working best at other institutions; however, Pogrow (1996) and Sykes (1996) caution that care must be taken to find and apply quality research to current situations. Some useful resources for planners are listed in Table 2.

Development is the third stage of the NCREL Model, and one of the activities presented on the NCREL Website is a guideline for a Development Plan for Target Group (http://www.ncrel.org/tech/tpd/res/sdtemplate1.htm). As part of the development process, planners are asked to consider the following:

*   Who will participate?
*   What activities are needed to achieve the outcomes?
*   What models of staff development will be used?

Table 2: Resources for the Planning Stage

Site	URL	Content
Mid-Continent Research for Education and Learning (MCREL)	http://www.mcrel.org/webforum/forums.asp	Team Building Web Discussion Board
North Central Regional Educational Laboratory (NCREL)	http://www.ncrtec.org/capacity/profile/profwww.htm	Learning with technology profile tool
North Central Regional Technology in Education Consortium (NCRTEC)	http://www.ncrel.org/sdrs/areas/issues/content/cntareas/math/ma2tvisi.htm	A Vision for Using Technology

- How are the needs of adult learners being addressed?
- What delivery models will be used?
- How will teachers experience what engaged learning is like within staff development activities?
- What follow-up is necessary? How will it be provided?
- How much will it cost?

During the development stage, planners should also structure the professional development training activities to meet the needs of adult learners. Wood et al. (1993) have found that adults commit to learning when specified goals and objectives are realistic and important to them. Therefore, they recommend the following guidelines for working with adult learners (p. 25):

- Small-group activities or team learning
- Choices or control over learning
- Experiential activities that encourage participants to try out new behaviors and techniques
- Peer and trainer coaching
- Opportunities to develop action plans for implementation.

Implementation is the fourth stage of the NCREL Model. During this stage, of course, teachers implement the courses they have developed. Wood et al.

(1993) recommend that as part of this stage, teachers have opportunities to field test their courses. This way, they can practice under the direction of their mentors and peers and adjust as necessary. Wood et al. compare this to the experiences of a student pilot who has completed all of the training and is preparing to fly solo. During the implementation stage, teachers should continue to be supported by their mentors and have ample opportunities to confer with each other. Unfortunately, once the implementation phase has been completed, educators often are left alone to implement new strategies independently. Wood et al. state, "Unless organized follow-up experiences are provided after training, neither the pilot nor the educator is totally prepared to use the skills, knowledge, and practices acquired during the training activities" (p. 35). Therefore, teachers should continue to work together to refine their coursework in preparation for a second implementation. After all, sustainability is the primary goal of the Implementation Stage.

Darling-Hammond (1998) notes several professional development strategies that lead to sustainability over time. These include job-embedded staff development that is directly connected to teachers' work and extended opportunities for modeling, coaching and problem solving. Sparks and Loucks-Horsley (1989) also make recommendations for sustainability such as observations, collaborative projects, teaming, and focus group discussions. Communication is the key to sustainability, and participants must have opportunities to share ideas, successes and concerns so that they may benefit from the insight and experiences of others who are implementing the same innovations.

Adoption of the innovation and sustainability also hinge on the role of administrators, especially during the Implementation Stage. The National Staff Development Council encourages educational leaders to promote ongoing staff development and collaboration by providing instructors with adequate time to meet and share ideas. Wood et al. (1993) also stress the importance of administrators participating in professional development activities with their teachers so that they understand the program's goals and objectives and their obligations to the program. For staff development programs to succeed, administrators must be active participants from the beginning. Without their support, the strategies presented during the implementation phase may not be adopted by instructors because they do not perceive the activities to be important. Additional resources for the Implementation Stage can be found in Table 3.

Table 3: Resources for Implementation

Site	URL	Content
North Central Regional Educational Laboratory (NCREL)	http://www.ncrel.org/pd/toolkit.htm	A tool kit for schools and districts
SkyLight Professional Development	http://www.skylightedu.com/mentoring/index.cfm?fuseaction=enter	A five day "train-the-trainer" program
WestEd	http://www.wested.org/tie/techplan/staff_dev/welcome.htm	Suggestions for follow-up.
WestEd	http://www.wested.org/tie/techplan/relatedtools shtml	An assessment rubric

Evaluation is the fifth component of the NCREL Model. According to Guskey (1998), "Good evaluations provide information that is sound, meaningful, and sufficiently reliable to use in making thoughtful and responsible decisions about professional development processes and effects" (http://www.nsdc.org/library/jsd/guskey194.html). On the same Website, he suggests using the following questions to guide evaluative procedures:

- Is this program or activity leading to the results we wanted?

- Is the program better than what was done in the past?

- Is it better than another, competing activity?

- Is it worth the cost?

The Evaluation Design Matrix (http://www.ncrel.org/tech/tpd/res/matrix.htm), which was developed by NCREL, is also a very useful framework for evaluating the impact of staff development. Additional resources for the Evaluation Stage can be found in Table 4.

In summary, effective staff development should involve the stakeholders to assist with developing a clear vision with specific goals and objectives and an assessment of the current situation to determine what is working and what needs to be changed. Once that is done, a cohesive plan for change should be developed that focuses on systemic changes to improving student learning. The

Table 4: Resources for Evaluation

Site	URL	Content
International Society for Technology in Education (ISTE)	http://cnets.iste.org/teachers/t_book.html	Technology standards for teachers
U.S. Department of Education	http://ed.gov/pubs/EdTechGuide/	An Educator's Guide to Evaluating the Use of Technology in Schools
U.S. Department of Education	http://www.ed.gov/pubs/Idea_Planning/section_5.html	Sustaining School-wide Programs through Accountability and Continuous Improvement.

implementation plan should include job-embedded staff developing training with ongoing support. The evaluation should encompass ways to objectively assess how well the plan is working and what modifications, if any, are needed.

Current Professional Development Training for Online Educators

Universities and other education institutions are designing programs that prepare instructors to teach web-based courses. The University of California in Los Angeles, for example, has been at the forefront of online teaching. UCLA offers courses that focus on developing curriculum for online programs and designing assessment tools that evaluate student progress. Teaching and learning models are also shared during each online course that UCLA offers. Advanced courses, such as creating and utilizing multimedia, provide developers of online courses with the knowledge and skills to enhance their teaching modules.

The Illinois Virtual Campus (IVC) offers professional development opportunities to online course developers in different fields, such as business and industry, as well as the academic arena. The IVC online program was developed in collaboration with all Illinois' colleges and universities. The IVC strives to provide training that assists online course developers with goals and objectives for effective pedagogy in web-based classes.

Michigan Virtual University (MVU) has established two strands for their online learning program. The first strand focuses on educators who want to design and teach online courses for high schools and universities. The focus of this strand is to demonstrate how to develop an online learning community that has a strong instructional design component. MVU's second professional development strand reflects the "train-the-trainer" model. The courses in this program focus on teaching administrators of online projects to work with educators that want to become online instructors. Components of this strand include theories, strategies and teaching tools for course development. Once a technology director completes the second strand, he/she can mentor teachers to develop virtual classrooms that ensure effective teaching methodology for online learning.

The Concord Consortium has also been at the forefront of designing and teaching online courses. The Consortium assists online instructors in creating and facilitating web-based instruction. The courses offered by the Consortium demonstrate how teachers can transform current face-to-face curriculum to online learning environments. The program also provides teachers with resources that foster communication and assess student progress.

There have also been programs that offer certification for online teaching. The Master Online Teacher Certificate program was designed by Making the Virtual Classroom a Reality. It is an online training series for educators and administrators who are interested in designing course content for online learning. In order to complete the program and receive a certificate, a participant must take at least nine online courses that relate to Web design principals, developing multimedia, and issues related to online learning such as copyright laws and Intellectual Property. After completing the coursework, an online practicum is required. During the practicum, participants work with a certified instructor and other participants to develop or improve an online course for a particular content area.

The University of Wisconsin - Madison has also established a Distance Education Certification Program. This university prepares future online instructors for their roles as course designers and facilitators. Strategies for teaching online, as well as confronting obstacles and technical challenges, are all part of the coursework required. A participant in the certification program must complete six courses that are tailored to the needs of online learner.

Professional development must be considered a key component in preparing educators to teach online courses. Instructors need to have continuous training in issues directly related to online teaching and learning. As technology continues to change at a rapid pace, online instructors must fully understand how to integrate these new technologies into their online courses.

Online Models for High School Online Course Developers

Online learning has revolutionized the way in which students learn and the manner in which teachers deliver lessons at the high school level as well, and many states have realized the value in offering instructional opportunities through this new form of distance education. Florida has been a pioneer in this area. The Florida Virtual School officially began in August 1997 as a collaboration between two school districts. The first faculty included 15 educators assuming the roles of administrators, teachers and instructional technology facilitators. In five years the Florida Virtual School student population grew to 6,900 participants.

To address the needs of migrant students, the Ohio Valley Educational Cooperative, in cooperation with the Kentucky Department of Education, the University of Louisville, and school districts in Kentucky, developed the Kentucky Migrant Technology Project. Approximately 20,240 migrant students reside in the state of Kentucky. Migrant students often have trouble meeting established academic standards due to the amount of time away from classroom instruction.

The program focuses on migrant students who range in age from 12 to 18 years of age. The program offers online courses in the areas of arts and humanities, math, social studies, and science. Professional mentors who have experience in the area of migrant education provide support and assistance to students involved in the program.

Other online programs such as Mindquest and the Francis Virtual School provide students with the opportunity to make up courses that may have prevented them from receiving their high school diplomas. Mindquest is governed by the State of Minnesota public school system and offers online courses for students who left high school without graduating due to unforeseen circumstances. The online program's curriculum focuses on the adult learner and provides a high school diploma to students who successfully complete coursework for graduation.

Francis Virtual School is a New York State accredited institution which strives to provide online courses to students who are unable to attend face-to-face classes in order to graduate. This virtual school also prides itself on extending the program to students who want to take additional courses to prepare for college.

In July 2000, Michigan recognized the growing population of home school students and established the Michigan Virtual High School to accommodate their needs. Certified teachers in all content areas teach these online courses. Home school students not only have the opportunity to receive high school credit for courses, but they are given the chance to interact with other students who are enrolled in public and private schools throughout the state. The Michigan Virtual University, a private, not-for-profit corporation, operates the Michigan Virtual High School.

Universities are also realizing the value of preparing high school students for college using web-based instruction. The University of Missouri-Columbia established an online high school program, in collaboration with school districts in Missouri, to provide equal opportunities for all students considering college. The program offers Advanced Placement courses which award college credit upon completion.

The University of Texas at Austin has collaborated with school districts in the state to offer a number of online programs to meet the needs of diverse student population. Programs such as the University of Texas High School Diploma Program and the University Charter School provide customized instruction for students who have special needs or are unable to participate in the traditional classroom setting. The University of Texas at Austin also recognizes that many high school students in the state work with family members on farms in different areas of the state. The Migrant Student Program offers online courses to students who are unable to attend classes due to work obligations.

Online learning has provided many opportunities to students who would have not been able to succeed in a traditional classroom. The future of many online programs holds promise for students who require special accommodations for learning.

Recommendations for Developers of Online Professional Development Training

At the beginning of this chapter, we described a situation in which teachers were basically were left alone to implement online courses. Without comprehensive professional development programs, this will continue to happen. The results are uneven instruction for students and frustrating teaching experiences for faculty.

Currently, there are no clear guidelines for professional development for online course developers. Most of the literature focuses on providing staff development to teachers via the Internet rather than preparing educators to teach online. However, educators need to participate in quality professional development so that they can strengthen their courses through the guidance and experiences of others, while reducing the feelings of isolation that are often associated with online course development. Therefore, we recommend those planning professional development for online course developers establish cohorts; set individual goals and objectives; support members during all stages; and promote sustainability.

Establish Cohorts

As mentioned in the models for face-to-face development, the first stage of the professional development process begins by assembling cohorts of educators who are interested in online teaching to assist the development of the process. This is done so that each member can assist with the formation of the staff development plan. We recommend nine to 12 member cohorts. If the members are not pre-selected, there are certain aspects that should be considered for selection.

First, the cohort members should be technically competent. Although competency levels will vary, at the very minimum, cohort members must be able to send email messages, attach files and initiate threaded discussions. In addition, members must be willing to devote time and effort to creating and delivering online courses. Second, communication skills are essential for teaching online because interaction is a key component. Focused communication between online instructors and students leads to a more positive learning environment and minimizes confusion, which can lead to lack of motivation and participation. Thomas (2000) recommends that web-based courses include activities that facilitate interactions between instructors and students and include procedures for monitoring student work closely.

Organization is the third essential skill for online instructors. Harrison and Bergen (2000) found that in reality, teaching in an online format requires instructors to be more organized than in a regular classroom environment. In turn, the students are then able to post their materials and assignments online in an orderly fashion. In the opinions of Pitt and Clark (1997, p. 47), "Online educators must organize situations that address the various facets of learning in order to provide significant experiences for each class participant." Websites should be easy to navigate and well organized. In addition, instructors should use pre-class study questions and advance organizers to encourage critical thinking and participation on the part of the learners (Engineering Outreach, 1995). If the materials are organized to consistently meet the needs of the students, they will become comfortable with the nature of teaching and learning in an online environment.

Set Individual Goals and Objectives

Once the cohort members are selected, the cohort should engage in developing the goals and objectives for the program. Because members will be at different instructional and technical levels, it is important to assess individual needs to determine personal objectives and develop activities that enable all participants to meet their goals. For example, members who have completed or taught an online course may need assistance with time management, while others may need help with course design. Members will be more interested and feel more successful if care is taken to meet their individual professional development needs.

Support Members During all Stages

Instructors need time to plan their courses with mentors or others who are going through the same process. Thomas (2000) recommends that the planning stage begin six months before a specific course is to be offered. He also recommends that instructors be compensated for planning time. All facets of implementation should be resolved during the planning stage. This includes course design, effective instructional strategies, response etiquette, developing comfort with the online course platform (e.g., Blackboard), and determining grading criteria, class participation norms and administrative protocols such as book orders, registration and course evaluations. As part of the planning stage, it is also essential for participants to know how to access technical assistance and to convey this information to students via their class Websites. In addition, instructors should develop procedures for times when they and their students cannot gain access to online courses.

Promote Sustainability

By planning ahead and considering all possibilities, implementation should go smoothly. However, unforeseen circumstances always seem to occur. Therefore, professional development leaders should monitor the implementation stage carefully through online course observations and regular contact with cohort members. In addition, participants should have opportunities for peer observation and review, especially when problems arise. During the implementation stage, instructional support also should continue through frequent meetings with members either through compressed video, online chats or face-to-face meetings to refine instructional strategies and solve problems. Instructional support can also include mentoring, one-on-one tutoring or collaborative activities with peers. McKay and McGrath (2000) support the idea of online mentors and recommend that, "teachers should be exposed to examples of compelling Internet-based lessons prior to developing their own Internet-based curriculum projects" (p. 120). A mentoring program would be a valuable way to introduce new online instructors to the web-based environment, reduce the learning curve and provide more effective learning opportunities for students.

During the evaluation stage of the staff development process, cohort members should meet to discuss successes, revisions and recommendations for improvement. If this stage is omitted, members may lose opportunities for essential feedback from peers and miss valuable insights for improvement. We recommend that the cohort stay together through at least one more implementation stage to apply changes and gain additional comfort with online course delivery.

Chapter Summary

Online delivery involves extensive planning and attention to details that often go overlooked in courses delivered in the typical classroom. Many educators have no training on how to teach an online course, therefore there is a critical need for on-going training on how to convert instructional materials to an online format, use advanced multimedia tools and integrate technology resources into course content. These issues are challenging every first-generation online instructor. However, through relevant on-going professional development, administrative support and follow-up activities, such as mentoring programs, the quality of online instruction should continue to improve with time.

References

The Association for Supervision and Curriculum Development (ASCD). Retrieved December 16, 2002 from the World Wide Web: http://www.ascd.org/index.html.

Berge, Z.L. (1999). Interaction in post-secondary web-based learning. *Educational Technology, 39*(1), 5-11.

Brand, G. A. (1997). What research says: Training teachers to use technology. *Journal of Staff Development, 19*(1). Retrieved October 15, 2002 from the World Wide Web: http://www.nsdc.org/library/jsd/brand191.html.

Concord Consortium. (2002). Retrieved October 15, 2002 from the World Wide Web: http://www.concord.org/courses/designing.

Darling-Hammond, L. (1998). Strengthening the teaching profession: Teacher learning that supports student learning. Retrieved October 15, 2002 from the World Wide Web: http://www.acsd.org/readingroom/edlead/9802/darlinghammond.html.

E-learning for educators: Implementing the standards for staff development. (2001). Retrieved October 15, 2002 from the World Wide Web: http://www.nsdc.org/educatorindex.htm.

Engineering Outreach. (1995). Computers in education. Retrieved October 15, 2002, from the World Wide Web: http://www.uidaho.edu/evo/dist7.html.

Florida Virtual School. (2001). Retrieved October 15, 2002 from the World Wide Web: http://www.flvs.net.

Francis Virtual School. (2002). Retrieved October 15, 2002 from the World Wide Web: http://www.francisvirtualschool.org.

Friedman, E. A. (2000). *Conceptual framework and organizational structure of Alliance+: A national model for Internet-in-education professional development.* Retrieved October 15, 2002 from the World Wide Web: http://k12science.ati.stevens-tech.edu/papers/.

Guskey, T. R. (1998). The age of our accountability: Evaluation must become an integral part of staff development. *Journal of Staff Development 19*(4). Retrieved October 15, 2002 from the World Wide Web: http://www.nsdc.org/library/jsd/guskey194.html.

Harrison, N. & Bergen, C. (2000, January/February). Some design strategies for developing an online course. *Educational Technology, 40*(1), 57-60.

Illinois Virtual Campus. (2002). Retrieved October 15, 2002 from the World Wide Web: http://www.ivc.illinois.edu.

Illinois Virtual High School. (2002). Retrieved October 15, 2002 from the World Wide Web: http://www.ivhs.org.

International Society for Technology in Education. (2002). *National educational technology standards (NETS) and performance indicators.* Retrieved December 16, 2002 from the World Wide Web: http://cnets.iste.org/teachers/t_stands.html.

Kentucky Migrant Technology Project. (2002). Retrieved October 15, 2002 from the World Wide Web: http://www.migrant.org.

Louisiana Virtual High School. (2002). Retrieved October 15, 2002 from the World Wide Web: http://lvhs.doe.apexvs.com.

Making the Virtual Classroom a Reality. (2001). Retrieved October 15, 2002 from the World Wide Web: http://www.mvcr.org.

McKay, M. & McGrath, B. (2000). Creating Internet-based curriculum projects: A model for teacher professional development. *Technological Horizons in Education Journal, 27*(11), 114-124.

Michigan Virtual High School. (2002). Retrieved October 15, 2002 from the World Wide Web: –HYPERLINK "http://www.mivhs.org" —http://www.mivhs.org.

Michigan Virtual University. (2002). Retrieved October 15, 2002 from the World Wide Web: http://www.mivu.org/teaching/.

Mid-Continent Research for Education and Learning. Retrieved December 16, 2002 from the World Wide Web: http://www.mcrel.org/about/sitemap.asp.

Milken Exchange on Educational Technology. (1999). *Professional competency continuum: Professional skills for the digital age classroom.* Retrieved October 15, 2002 from the World Wide Web: www.mff.org/edtech/welcome.html.

Mindquest. (2002). Retrieved October 15, 2002 from the World Wide Web: http://www.mindquest.org.

The National Staff Development Council. Retrieved December 16, 2002 from the World Wide Web: http://www.nsdc.org/educatorindex.htm.

North Central Regional Educational Laboratory. *A vision for using technology.* Retrieved December 16, 2002 from the World Wide Web: http://www.ncrel.org/sdrs/areas/issues/content/cntareas/math/ma2tvisi.htm.

North Central Regional Educational Laboratory. *Learning with technology profile tool.* Retrieved December 16, 2002 from the World Wide Web: http://www.ncrtec.org/capacity/profile/profwww.htm.

North Central Regional Educational Laboratory. (n.d.). *Evaluation design matrix.* Retrieved October 15, 2002 from the World Wide Web: http://www.ncrel.org/tech/tpd/res/matrix.htm.

North Central Regional Educational Laboratory. (n.d.). *Staff development guiding questions development plan for target group.* Retrieved October 15, 2002 from the World Wide Web:http://www.ncrel.org/tech/tpd/res/sdtemplate1.htm.

North Central Regional Educational Laboratory. (n.d.). *Technology professional development: Supporting technology in education with professional development.* Retrieved October 15, 2002 from the World Wide Web: http://www.ncrel.org/tech/tpd/index.html.

North Central Regional Educational Laboratory. (1995). *A Framework for reviewing professional development policies and practices.* Presented as part of a CPRE Policy Brief. Retrieved October 15, 2002 from the World Wide Web: http://www.ed.gov/pubs/CPRE/t61/framwork.html.

Phi Delta Kappan. Retrieved December 15, 2002 from the World Wide Web: http://www.pdkintl.org/kappan/khpartic.htm.

Pitt, T.J. & Clark, A. (1997). *Creating powerful online courses using multiple instructional strategies.* Retrieved October 15, 2002 from the World Wide Web: http://leahi.kcc.hawaii.edu/org/tcc_conf97/pres/pitt.html.

Pogrow, S. (1996). Reforming the wannabe reformers: Why educational reforms almost always end up making things worse. *Phi Delta Kappan, 77*(10), 656-663.

SkyLight Professional Development. Retrieved December 16, 2002 from the World Wide Web: http://www.skylightedu.com/mentoring/index.cfm?fuseaction=enter.

Sparks, D. (2002). *Developing powerful professional development for teachers and principals.* National Staff Development Council. Retrieved October 15, 2002 from the World Wide Web: http://www.nsdc.org/educatorindex.htm.

Sparks, D. & Hirsh, S. (1997). *A new vision for staff development.* Alexandria, VA: Association of Supervision and Curriculum Development.

Sparks, D. & Loucks-Horsley, S. (1989). Five models of staff development. *Journal of Staff Development, 10*(4). Retrieved October 15, 2002 from the World Wide Web: www.nsdc.org/library/jsd/sparks104.html.

Standards for Staff Development (rev.). (2001). Oxford, OH: National Staff Development Council.

Sykes, G. (1996). Reform of and as professional development. *Phi Delta Kappan, 77*(7), 464-467.

Thomas, L. G. & Knezek, D. G. (2002). Standards for technology-supported learning environments. *The State Education Standard, 3*(3), 14-20.

Thomas, W. R. (2000). Electronic delivery of high school courses: Status, trends, and issues. Retrieved October 15, 2002 from the World Wide Web: http://www.sreb.org/programs/edtech/pubs/electronicdeliveryhs/ElectronicDelivery.pdf.

U.S. Department of Commerce, National Technical Information Service. (2000*). The Power of the Internet for learning: Moving from promise to practice.* Washington, DC: The Web-Based Education Commission. (NTIS No. PB2001-105809). Retrieved October 15, 2002 from the World Wide Web: http://www.ntis.gov/search/product.asp?ABBR=PB2001105809& starDB=GRAHIST.

U.S. Department of Education. *An educator's guide to evaluating the use of technology in schools and classroom.* Retrieved December 16, 2002 from the World Wide Web: http://ed.gov/pubs/EdTechGuide/.

U.S. Department of Education. *Sustaining school-wide programs through accountability and continuous improvement.* Retrieved December 16, 2002 from the World Wide Web: http://www.ed.gov/pubs/Idea_Planning/section_5.html.

University of California. (2002). Retrieved October 15, 2002 from the World Wide Web: http://www.ucop.edu/pathways/.

University of California in Los Angeles. (2002). Retrieved October 15, 2002 from the World Wide Web: http://www.uclaextension.org/.

University of Missouri-Columbia. (n.d.). Retrieved October 15, 2002 from the World Wide Web: http://cdis.missouri.edu/MUHighSchool/HShome.htm.

University of Texas at Austin, Distance Education Center. (n.d.). Retrieved October 15, 2002 from the World Wide Web: http://www.utexas.edu/cee/dec/uths/index.shtml.

University of Wisconsin-Madison. (2001). Retrieved October 15, 2002 from the World Wide Web: http://uwex.edu/disted/depd/certpro.html.

Virtual High School. (2002). Retrieved October 15, 2002 from the World Wide Web: http://www.govhs.org/website.nsf.

WestEd. *Model for staff development.* Retrieved December 16, 2002 from the World Wide Web: http://www.wested.org/tie/techplan/staff_dev/welcome.htm.

WestEd. *TechPlan: Technology status assessment - The technology implementation assessment rubric.* Retrieved December 16, 2002 from the World Wide Web: http://www.wested.org/tie/techplan/techasse.shtml.

Wood, F., Killian, J., McQuarrie, F., & Thompson, S. (1993). *How to organize a school-based staff development program.* Alexandria, VA: Association for Supervision and Curriculum Development. Retrieved October 15, 2002 from the World Wide Web: http://www.ascd.org/infocon.

Section IV

Course Development and Implementation

Chapter VIII

Instructional Design Factors and Requirements for Online Courses and Modules

James E. Schnitz
IBM Global Education, USA

Janet W. Azbell
IBM Business Consulting Services, USA

Abstract

The nature of digital content and tools, coupled with the communications capabilities available through online instruction, can, if leveraged properly, provide opportunities for quality instructional delivery. This chapter proposes that — even in an environment of remote, asynchronous, web-based instruction — approaches and the best of effective classroom practices may not be sufficient to address the full range of capabilities the technology provides. Through work done by IBM and the Florida Virtual School (FLVS), principles and models for leveraging the advantages offered by the technology environment and overcoming the difficulties inherent have been worked out in ways that offer significant promise to all providers of virtual schooling.

Introduction

Ms. Alvarez scanned the faces of her charges, and then pointed to the chart on the whiteboard: "The point of price equilibrium is where the supply and demand curves intersect. I know that sounds complex, but it really isn't!" Twenty-two blank faces pointed randomly all over the room. *Let's try this,* she thought. "All it really means is that if the show at the Cineplex seats 250 people and only 100 want to go to the 4:00 p.m. show, they reduce the price for that show time. And if 400 people want to go to the 7:30 p.m. show, they charge more for that show time because people going out for the evening will pay extra to get a seat." *Did anyone follow that one?,* she wondered. A quick glance told her that Khairi and Stephen were staring out the window, the group of jocks in the back of the room was passing notes back and forth, Song Wah was writing down everything as usual, and, wonder of wonders, more than half were actually watching her. *Now let's see who got it:* "Can anyone explain why they charge less for the 4:00 p.m. show?"

LaVon's hand shot in the air. "Yeah, I've noticed that. It's not fair that people who don't work or go to school can pay less to see a movie, and when we want to go out on a date, we have to pay full price! Why don't they charge more during low attendance so they'll make more money from the people who do show up?"

Just the right question. LaVon, you're hired as my straight man! "Because they're thinking about the supply and demand curves! Let's look at what happens on the curves when supply — the number of seats — is constant and demand — the number of people who want to go see a show — either goes up or down. Then we'll see what happens if they open a new screen for a hot show, increasing supply. Then you'll know why you get gouged on Friday night, but a Saturday afternoon date is a real bargain." Forty-four eyes stared straight at her. *Dating and money works every time....*

Twenty minutes later it was obvious that the bulk of the students got the basic idea. The concepts of relative scarcity, diminishing marginal utility, and maximizing opportunity were volubly debated in terms of how many screens and what ticket price should be allocated for the Academy Award winner. But there was still the group in the back who, having had their notes confiscated, were less than actively engaged in the discussion. Their attentiveness earlier had been typically fleeting. *Baseball salaries,* she thought. *Pure supply and demand with no salary cap to confuse the issue, and contraction under consideration to reduce the demand. Two of those kids are on the baseball team. Let's open up that can of worms!*

By the end of the next day, Ms. Alvarez felt comfortable that the basics for understanding the rest of the unit had been well established.

* * * * * * * * * * * * * * *

Ms. Alvarez is a good teacher. Trained in her subject matter and in pedagogy, she knows how to plan and deliver instruction effectively. She is especially good at reading her students' verbal and body language to gain feedback about what is and what isn't understood during instruction so she can adjust her presentation accordingly. With a rich knowledge base and strength in tailoring practical examples on the spot to her students' interests and abilities, she combines the best of planned instruction with artistic and creative interventions to generate high student achievement. It is reasonable to consider her approach a model for what we expect out of highly qualified instruction:

- Content rigor,
- Real world applications of concepts, principles and information,
- Awareness of student readiness to learn,
- Attentiveness to the packaging of information so that it is connected to the interests and abilities of the learners,
- Individualization of content and message to appeal to each and all learners, and
- Rigorous alignment of objectives, methods and ongoing assessments of student learning to ensure productive in-process adjustments to teaching.

Would Ms. Alvarez do as well at facilitating online instruction as she does in a classroom? It's a good question, and we can't be sure of the answer without testing the proposition in actuality. There are no validated predictors yet of which classroom teachers will become quality online instructors. One thing that is certain, though, is that if Ms. Alvarez does not make some significant adjustments in her very successful approach to classroom teaching and learning, she definitely will not succeed at online teaching. Her success, beyond excellence in planning and implementation, depends on observing cues from her students at instructional run-time and drawing upon her knowledge and pedagogic expertise to match the individual characteristics of her students and the packaging of content she wants them to master. The packaging she provides is constantly structured and re-structured as the cues from her students inform her assessment of their processing of information. But the conditions under which online instruction and, particularly, asynchronous online instruction takes place make Ms. Alvarez's practiced approach impossible to apply as is in the virtual environment.

The most obvious differentiating characteristics between classroom and asynchronous online instruction are the absence of run-time student response cues, the spacing and relative sterility of observable responses (periodic e-mail and assignment submissions vs. daily doses of visual, verbal, interpersonal and written feedback), and especially the *a priori* and *a posteriori* nature of instructional decision-making: the reality that all instructional approaches must be built into the online course before students engage, and that instructional interventions can be initiated only after a formal student submission of either an assignment or an e-mail (or fax or, more rarely, a phone call). Essentially, to create an online course environment that equals the best in classroom instruction, the course creators must construct instructional content and processes within the course presentation and assignments that anticipate the differential learning requirements of the class members and embed the creative responses in the course material itself. That which is normally beyond the written instructional plan and ineffable until the moment it is made manifest during classroom interaction must be made richly explicit at the point of online course or module production prior to instructional delivery.

While this set of requirements might seem extremely difficult to address, the nature of digital content and tools coupled with the communications capabilities available through online instruction can, if leveraged properly, provide opportunities for quality instructional delivery that, even in the environment of remote, asynchronous, web-based instruction, approach the best of effective classroom practices. Through work done by IBM (IBM, 2003) and the Florida Virtual School (FLVS) (FLVS, 2003), principles and models for leveraging the advantages offered by the technology environment and overcoming the difficulties inherent have been worked out that offer significant promise to providers of virtual schooling.

The CEO Forum, in its Year 3 Report, specified a number of ways in which digital content and digital learning environments are fundamentally different from conventional, analog, real-time content and instruction (CEO Forum, 2000). Ranging from the ability to randomly access up-to-date, manipulable data to the ability to collaborate and jointly produce sharable outputs, these critical features stem from the fact of digitization of content and the existence of tools for digital communications and collaboration. The characteristics summarized in the two charts (Figure 1 and Figure 2) that follow indicate the most salient of these features for developing the new models for virtual learning. It is in coming to understand the nature of those particular differences that the requirements and structure of the new models can be determined.

The Nature of Digital Content

The relationships within the Digital Content Impact Matrix (Schnitz, 2002) demonstrate the connection between the form and nature of content selected for instruction and the mode of instructional presentation and approach. The more that content is fixed in linear format, as in print materials or analog video, the greater the tendency of the teacher to follow the path of least resistance and greatest familiarity, and teach by presenting information. However, when digitized content is made available and the access modes involve mediated random access or fully manipulable data that can be used by groups of students, discovery learning and construction become dominant instructional modes. Given the limits on presentation in asynchronous virtual learning, the facilitation of student access, manipulation and creation of data offered by digital content and tools enables the creation of online instructional lessons that build the interactive learning processes of student-focused information manipulation and production into the lesson itself.

The very nature of the Internet environment itself helps create the transformations indicated above; but to be used effectively in virtual lessons, teachers must come to understand the nature and implications of the changes for instructional design and learning behavior.

Figure 1: Digital Content Impact Matrix

Digital Content Impact Matrix

Instructional Mode: Content Format:	Presentation Fixed	Mediated Presentation Mediated	Discovery and Construction Manipulable
Content Access Mode: Linear	Books Films/Videos Journals	*"Interrupted" Methods* *(e.g. DRTA)* *Worksheets*	N/A
Categorical	Lists Print Reference Works	*Guided Research*	Data Files
Random	Microfiche *Slides* CD ROM Storage	*Study Guides* *"Interrupted" Methods* *Annotated Files* Algorithmically- structured content	Leggos Math Manipulatives Multi-media Files *Web Pages
Shared	Broadcast	*Web-casts	*e-Mail *Threaded Discussions *Web Page Creation *Streaming Media
Collaborative	N/A	N/A	*Chat Rooms *Synchronous White Board *Common Workflow Tools

NB: Plain text indicates analog content, **bold indicates digital, *and italics indicates content that can be either.*** *Text with an asterisk indicates Internet-based digital content.

The Nature of Online Instruction

The physical classroom and the virtual classroom are radically different. The differences make significant demands on the teacher, the content provider (whether commercially or school-based), and the student. As can be seen in the Digital Content Impact Matrix above, instruction in a digital environment suggests that lessons must, of necessity, move from the predominantly teacher-centered, presentation-oriented conventions of physical classrooms to student manipulations and creation of content online. This implies the need to design online activities that are production oriented rather than receptive.

The role of the online teacher must shift accordingly as the focus of instruction and the control of the learning process shifts from what the teacher presents to what the learner chooses and produces.

The student, too, must adjust to role differences in the virtual school. There are reasons that the retention rate for the Florida Virtual School is far better than that normally experienced by online learning courses. From retention rates as low as 70% in the early years of operations, FLVS has improved its rate to 85% in 2001 and close to 95% in 2002 (Young, 2003) by understanding and directly

Figure 2: Roles and Functions of Teachers and Learners in Web-Based Education

Traditional Learning	Options "Facilitation"	Options "Participation"	Options "Learner Control"
Who? One Teacher and 20 – 30 age peers	Teams of teachers work with groups of students. Older students help younger students	Mentors, resource persons, parents, and community members participate in activities in planning, teaching and learning.	Independent students connect with teachers, mentors, and peers as needed. Teachers access key models and resources as needed.
Where? In a room	Learning facilities include individual workstations plus small and large group areas	Learning environments are extended to other schools and community sites.	Learning opportunities are accessed online from the home, school, or from anywhere.
When? 50 minute session	In -depth study of thematic units occurs in longer time blocks over a shorter term	School programs recognise and provide credit for performance in and out of school rather than for attendance	Students can connect to online resources and courses 24 hours a day, 365 days a year.
How? Face to Face	Interaction with many people Facilitation predominates	Learning activities include online and onsite interactions with other participants	Independent and collaborative learning activities are guided by online teacher and mentor support. Students become producers as well as consumers of knowledge

addressing the skill sets necessary for online learning success. Students are given a screening survey prior to course enrollment to help them decide if they are ready to work in the online environment, and the school provides support during course participation, built into the structure of the courses themselves, to assist with self-direction, comfort with the primarily asynchronous environment, and management of time, task sequencing and task completion.

But even with these differences, the most crucial difference has to do with the way in which the minute-to-minute, day-to-day, and week-to-week interactions between students and teachers in classrooms are replaced by remote, infrequent contacts online. Teachers in classrooms rely on the continuous feedback from student non-verbal and verbal responses during class to inform them as to what is being understood, what explanations must be added, what examples must be brought to bear, how continuity must be constructed and maintained, and how the range of information should be arrayed against the ever-shifting needs of the students in front of them. Teachers in virtual classrooms must rely more heavily on the construction of their materials to carry the transitions, provide for individual differences and preferences in acquiring information, and draw students into the content of the instruction. Virtual practitioners need to attend to the differential characteristics of this new teaching and learning environment as they design the instruction taking place (Seimens, 2002).

Implications For Online Instructional Design Requirements

As a consequence of the differences noted in the nature of virtual schooling and the online instructional environment compared to conventional schooling, there are fundamental differences in the requirements for instructional and curricular content design. To accommodate to the specific characteristics of the virtual schooling environment, online materials must be:

- Visual and dynamic
- Downloadable and printer-friendly
- Randomly accessible and manipulable
- Result in production/interaction
- Qualified and documented (model appropriate permissions and copyright alignments)
- Instructionally-aware of and prepared for remote use
- Fully aware of the audience
- Assessable and accountable
- Easily updatable

Visual and Dynamic

An early, informal study done by one of the authors of this article for WICAT Systems in 1982 (Schnitz, 1982) showed that students, when given online texts from five to 20 unnumbered pages in length containing 19 lines and 40 characters per monochromatic screen, would, in supervised conditions, read a maximum of from seven to nine screens before becoming frustrated and hitting the escape key to do something else. Although we are unaware of any follow-up studies with denser displays of HTML text on color monitors, it is doubtful that the tolerance for online text has increased dramatically. High quality online courseware must use rich visual and auditory displays, including graphics as well as text cues to capture and engage learners. Instructional content cannot afford to be vastly inferior in richness to the wealth of material routinely available in the same environment. At the same time, the content must be dynamic and manipulable to foster interaction, use and reuse of the content by the learners. Static, text-dense displays miss the value-add of Internet-based digitized, communications-involved content.

Downloadable and Printer-Friendly

Concomitantly, and particularly where text density is unavoidable, text should be configured to be easily downloadable and printer-friendly. Online news services have been following this requirement for years by providing access to printer-friendly versions of web-pages that exclude components of the page that are irrelevant to the story. Online courses can provide the same feature to facilitate reading and offline storage of information intended to be static and linear.

Randomly Accessible and Manipulable

Course materials should be randomly accessible and manipulable by the learner. One of the features of Internet-based learning is the ability of the learner to control the order of access and use of the content provided. Given the options available online, needless restrictions in the order of presentation should be avoided at all costs. The charts above indicate that, of all the features of digitized environments, the ability to randomly access and manipulate information has potentially the most dramatic impact on teaching and learning of all the characteristics of digitization. Defeating this advantage through reifying conventional instructional sequencing is the antithesis of what online instruction should do. Navigation aids, quick ingress and egress, and the ability of the learner to determine (within valid instructional parameters) the order in which tasks will be undertaken and material used should all built into the courseware.

Result in Production/Interaction

One of the most obvious differences between physical and virtual classrooms is that class period attendance can not be taken and managed effectively in a virtual environment. Seat time is not a measure on which course credit decisions can be based in virtual schooling. Did the student spend on hour working, or an hour watching a favorite DVD while logged on to the course? Nor are online tests, for user identification and security reasons, sufficient unto themselves. In fact, the only supportable mechanism for granting credit is the aggregate assessments of student productions and work outputs. Hence, it is critical that the design of instruction incorporate all appropriate work outputs and provide the necessary and sufficient enablers to facilitate students in accomplishing the stated goals at a sufficient level of performance. Where a physical classroom may be conducted with somewhat general attention paid to the assessment strategies, a virtual classroom demands explicit planning and execution of assessable tasks and work products in careful alignment with the instructional content if reliable determinations of credit-worthiness are to be made.

Qualified and Documented

There are well over 3 billion searchable Web pages on the Internet as of this writing, with a history of millions of pages added each day (Google.com, 2003). A massive amount of that content is unqualified, lacking citation, evidentiary basis, and even simple reasonableness— and that's discounting fringe content and pornography.

This situation is fundamentally different from the experience of students in schools 20 years ago when the published word was inherently (if not correctly) considered expert, and the written word of students had to be justified through laborious research and citation. The fact is that publication 20 years ago involved significant expense and editorial review for all but the meanest of vanity presses and mimeographs; and then, the form of publication itself was a cue to use differential analyses in judging the contents. Today, anyone with any of a number of inexpensive tools and low-cost to free hosting opportunities can publish anything they want and have it look as legitimate in form and production value as the most traditional and experienced of publishing houses. In such a glut of information from the most suspect to the most legitimate, it is imperative that online content for instructional materials be fully qualified and documented, and that the teaching and learning of skills for both judging the value of unqualified content and for creating qualified content be embedded in the structure of the online instructional offerings. This charge needs to be fulfilled both in terms of the content published, the re-publications and new publications attendant to the students' learning activities, and the instructional mediation provided by the institution offering the course. It also must become an overt standard of instruction in all schools, whether virtual or physical. The ease with which teacher and student production may multiply the amount of content on the Web should not result in equally increasing amounts of unqualified, unsubstantiated pages flooding the search engines.

Instructionally Aware of and Prepared for Remote Use

When analyzing classroom teaching, certain realities and common practices can be readily identified. First, the teacher normally works from some kind of lesson plan that states in some form the objectives to be achieved, the instructional method and approach to be followed, the resources and materials to be used, and the means by which the teacher will be able to tell if the intended learning takes place. What does not appear in the lesson plan is the way the teacher will phrase terminology during a lecture, the extent of probing questions the teacher will ask at key points of a discussion, the rephrasing of a point that has been met by blank stares from the front row and snores from the back, the examples the teacher will generate when a principle turns out to be misunderstood, the linkages the teacher will draw to last week's lesson, and the foreshadowing the teacher will do on the spur of the moment to capture the value of a "teachable moment." In fact, the core of instructional intervention—the act of judging what the learner knows and finding ways to connect new information being taught to the existing knowledge structures perceived will appear nowhere in the lesson plan that encapsulates what the teacher plans to do. All the richness of instruction described above is created at run-time, with the teacher reading and reacting to the verbal and non-verbal inputs of the class as instruction is proceeding. This is the essence of the art and craft of teaching, what the great teacher excels at and what the mediocre teacher struggles with. And none of it is possible in the context of online instruction, particularly in the case of asynchronous delivery.

In online course delivery, if continuity of instruction is to be maintained, if rich, meaningful examples for different types of learners of the same content are to be provided, if the right probing questions are to be asked, if multiple approaches to the same instructional point are to be offered, if the connection from the students' knowledge base to the new material is to be made, then those capabilities must be overtly built into the content of the course at the point of development. That is why, for example, all of the FLVS's courses are built around a motif or a metaphor. The actual structure of the content is developed in terms of the framework of knowing that students can reasonably be expected to have as part of their current knowledge — a travel tour, a set of small businesses, a dinner party, for example. In this fashion, some attributes of meaning for new information can be instantiated from the metaphor, enriching the student's process of knowing through the structuring of the lessons themselves.

Additionally, all FLVS assignments are designed for multiple forms of response, while the content to be mastered is represented in multiple modalities wherever possible. In this fashion, the knowable differences among students can be accommodated at the point of design as a responsibility of the course developer to make explicit in the published content what only becomes apparent normally in verbal form behind the closed door of a classroom. Online content that is unaware of being accessed remotely and asynchronously, and that is unprepared to bear the burden of making itself understood to a wide variety of users, is content that cannot sustain itself.

Fully Aware of the Audience

This requirement is really an extension of the previous one: one size assuredly does *not* fit all when it comes to learning. This is no secret to any teacher, whether in physical classrooms or virtual, whether experienced or in the initial year of teaching. However, the level of attention that must be paid to this need during lesson preparation is much higher for virtual learning than it is for physical classrooms. Where a classroom teacher may adjust teaching at run-time to account for individual differences, as Ms. Alvarez did in our initial example, virtual learning teachers must anticipate those needs and build them into the course and lesson design *a priori*. While the metaphor/motif strategy is used broadly by FLVS to capture as many diverse schemas as possible in one structure, course designers must still particularize different approaches, examples and tasks throughout the material to attend to the needs of the diverse audience taking the courses.

Assessable and Accountable

Measurement needs to be built into the courseware, and needs to attend to the fact that performance (rather than time on task or memorization) is the relevant attribute of evidence of online learning. Formative assessment should be built into the learning activities, and should lead to alternative paths and activities where instances of low performance can be upgraded. Wherever possible, assessable tasks should be authentic, and should result in productive outputs that contribute to the work and/or requirements of the real world at large. Summative assessments should also be performance based, though a mixture of traditional and authentic assessments may be appropriate.

Alignment of assessments to the objectives and methods of learning remain as urgent in virtual learning as in physical classrooms. The alignment should be overt in the course/lesson design, and should be observable to all participants and stakeholders in the education process. Overt links to mandatory and selected standards should be palpable so that the connections from standards to instructional process, content and measured learning results are fully accountable.

Easily Updatable

In the end, online instruction is a software product. Like any software product, it will have to be maintained and upgraded periodically. Several different factors can affect the frequency of maintenance:

- Error fixes: misspellings, factual errors and new information that supercedes previously published data can all require a course or lesson edit.

- Iterations: some task or activity might not have worked as intended during initial use.

- Performance: the lesson might not be paced correctly, or may contain too many tasks, or may contain too many graphics for adequate response time.

- Link failures: built-in URL links may go dead and need replacing, or partner content offerings may have to be changed or upgraded.

- Technology changes: the development tools may change, necessitating a re-implementation of a course.

Unfortunately, the maintenance realities often push developers towards rigidity of formats and instructional approaches to reduce cost of ongoing support. This generates a natural tension between the goals of designers to address the various requirements noted above and the goals of management to contain costs. It is critical to recognize this natural tension, and to strike as productive a balance among the competing requirements as possible.

A Model for Online Instructional Design

How, then, can we take advantage of the best the Web has to offer, respond to the requirements as indicated above, and leverage the ability to link to massive amounts of current content while providing highly motivating, interactive, and visually and auditorally stimulating instruction? IBM developed a model for instructional and curriculum design using Internet resources for e-learning for its *Talking Walls and Talking Walls: The Stories Continue* (IBM, 1999) product, first delivered to the marketplace in 1998. Soon after, the model was employed by the Florida Virtual School as the initial design basis for its online instruction (see Figure 3).

Talking Walls was originally designed (Azbell, 1998) to be effective online instruction for intermediate grade (four through six) students, leveraging web-based attributes as well as locally delivered CD-based content due to band-width limitations at that time. The initial design point focused on a classroom-based implementation, but an analysis of some key features of the model on which the product was based illustrate ways to address the critical virtual course requirements discussed above, and indicate why the model was appropriate as a starting point for the development of asynchronous online curricula.

The Designed Instruction should be Visual and Dynamic

Talking Walls was originally delivered either as a CD that could play on stand-alone machines or that could be installed as a LAN-based network product.

Figure 3: Online Instruction

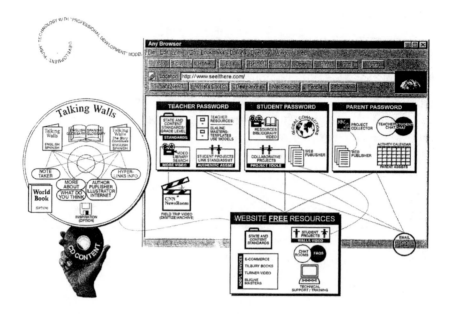

Internet connectivity was featured in either case, as the essence of the instruction was focused on student research and the production of shared work products. Today's technology and bandwidth render the original media approach unnecessary for current online courses; but the approach to teaching and content use by learners remains intact.

The product was based on two popular award-winning trade books that dealt in a colorful, inviting and highly visual way with the sociology, history, psychology, and art of walls around the world. Twenty-eight walls were covered in the two books such as The Great Wall of China, The Berlin Wall, the bookcase wall that hid Anne Frank, and the Dog Wall in the Tokyo subway. Background biographical information on the author, publisher and illustrator as well as video interviews and facilitated teacher workshops were provided on the CD as teaching and learning resources, providing the model for using rich multi-media content as extended and support learning material.

A partnership with Turner Learning (Turner Learning, 2003) [a subsidiary of what is now AOL/Time Warner (AOL Time Warner, 2003)], with full access to the video libraries of CNN (CNN, 2003) permitted the licensing of relevant (and often emotionally powerful) file footage to create rich, multi-media learning environments. The use of content partners and links established in this product became a standard for FLVS courses.

Web-based publishing tools allowed students to submit new walls for consideration as additional content for future additions to the website. This ability to update and add content to the core instructional materials based on learner productivity and work outputs anticipated the requirement that student productivity and performance, rather than time-on-task, become the norm for online learning.

The Designed Instruction should be Downloadable and Printer-Friendly

Talking Walls took advantage of all that the web could offer in the way of being friendly to the end-user. Attachments were added to html pages so that teachers could download to their local machines for printing. Multiple formats for download were offered so that teachers could easily take advantage of the many extension resources provided by the product.

The Designed Instruction should be Randomly Accessible and Manipulable

Because the books were arranged around separate sections, each describing a separate wall, the book itself was randomly accessible and never assumed linear sequence. Menus of choices provided students with full control over the sequence and time allotted to each instructional segment. Within each section, students could select the language of instruction (English or Spanish), and choose to read/read and listen/listen to the story of each wall. Further options included video, web projects, tools, and resources. Selections could be left to the students for exploration and discovery, or could be guided by the teacher to align with particular curricular demands or to meet specific teaching/learning goals. When doing assignments, online content could be accessed and edited to help produce student work.

The Designed Instruction should Result in Production/Interaction and the Designed Instruction should be Instructionally-Aware of and Prepared for Remote Use

(i)   Students and teachers were provided with tools, such as appropriate links to:

- the online version (optional) of the *World Book Encyclopedia (World Book, 2003);*
- the relationship mapping tool (optional), *Inspiration (Inspiration, 2003);*
- an embedded note taking tool;
- web-page publishing tools;
- e-mail; and
- synchronous and asynchronous discussion and chat capabilities as needed for teaching and learning.

The web-based projects required students to research topics related to the walls and respond in a variety of writing genres. This production was collected and could be assessed using the authentic assessment tools linked to the teacher's website. The authentic assessment tools included rubrics, benchmarks or anchor papers, and a scoring tool, which walked teachers through the rubric asking for assessments and comments. These assessments were recorded, stored and could be reported on in a variety of ways.

The Global Projects area allowed teachers at remote locations to join together to complete some projects with the students using the tools indicated above to collaborate remotely to produce a product. This type of interaction closely mimics the current work model in place for so many mobile workers and telecommuters that it truly addresses the requirement to provide access to 21st century skill development reflecting the need of online schools to link to standards such as the Florida Sunshine State Standards (Florida Department of Education, 2003).

The Designed Instruction should be Qualified and Documented (Model Appropriate Permissions and Copyright Alignments)

Talking Walls provided an initial model for using vetted websites (Riverdeep, 2003) aligned with the content of the lessons. Schools were provided with full descriptions and website ratings provided by students and teachers for review by new users. From the outset, the model included using only external sources that had been reviewed and approved.

Attention was paid to the appropriate clearances needed to publish and provide access to this wide variety of materials. Full licensing agreements are in place for access to the copyrighted books and video segments. Letters of agreement are on file for all vetted websites that are included as references and resources linked to student projects and resource databases. Purchase of optional products that can be linked in as tools (i.e., *Inspiration* and *World Book Encyclopedia*) is provided at the correct level to license for student use. Copyright permissions and, sometimes, website linkage letters of agreement are quite often lengthy negotiations and many involved payment up front (Franklin Pierce Law Center, 2003). Maintaining permissions has become a standard operating procedure for FLVS.

The Designed Instruction should be Fully Aware of the Audience

Password protected sites were provided for teachers, students and parents, with content appropriate to each of the targeted audiences. These licensed sites were constantly updated with new resources and provided a way for teachers, students and parents to share information about learning progress.

- *Teachers* had access to state standards alignment of all activities and resources, links to on- and off-line resources, online authentic assessment tools, and an online video library of related footage.

- *Students* had access to online bibliographic references through connections to the school library (optional), global connections to projects shared with students around the country and around the world, and project tools and web publishing tools to post and share project materials with other students and interested parents.

- Parents (local and remote) had access to projects that their student had worked on, as well as projects in progress. Also available were private parent-teacher-student conferences, an interactive parent activity calendar with active learning recommendations for parental involvement in student learning, and web publishing tools for sharing with distant relatives.

The Designed Instruction should be Assessable, be Linked to State Requirements and be Accountable

A key to the instructional model's power was the ability to leverage both local and physical resources (LAN, CD, books) with online resources. Accordingly, a web browser could be launched from the CD to provide access to project-based learning activities aligned to national standards. The projects prompted students to do online research (purposeful research with specific, directed outcomes — not the random surfing that is often labeled research), explore sites and then use the information to create expository writing, keep journals, write biographies, and formulate/defend argumentative/persuasive positions. FLVS uses this concept extensively to engage students with both online and offline learning activities so that the learning objectives dictate the resource, rather than the medium, of primary instruction.

Student work was judged authentically against rubrics and benchmarks. FLVS recognized early on that the performance was the only mechanism that could be used for asynchronous virtual learning, and adopted the concept of authentic assessment of student work wherever productivity was required.

Providing appropriate instruction for asynchronous online instruction is not mysterious. Early codifications of a model were eminently successful, and the use of that model by the Florida Virtual School has shown how the characteristics of virtual learning can be systematically and replicably addressed.

References

AOL Time Warner. (2003). Retrieved February 28, 2003 from the World Wide Web: http://www.aoltimewarner.com/flash.adp.

Azbell, J. W. (1998). *Internal Product Design Document: Talking Walls* and *Talking Walls: The Stories Continue*. Atlanta, GA: IBM Corp.

The CEO Forum. (2000). *The CEO Forum on school technology and education: Year 3 Report*. Retrieved February 28, 2003 from the World Wide Web: http://www.ceoforum.org/reports.cfm?RID=4.

CNN. (2003). Retrieved February 28, 2003 from the World Wide Web: http://www.cnn.com/.

Florida Department of Education. (2003). Retrieved February 28, 2003 from the World Wide Web: http://www.firn.edu/doe/menu/sss.htm.

Florida Virtual School. (2003). Retrieved February 28, 2003 from the World Wide Web: http://www.flvs.net.

Franklin Pierce Law Center. (2003). *Copyright on the Internet.* Retrieved February 28, 2003 from the World Wide Web: http://www.fplc.edu/tfield/copynet.htm.

Google.com. (2003). Retrieved February 28, 2003 from the World Wide Web: http://www.google.com.

IBM. (1999). *IBM talking walls and talking walls: The stories continue* (Software program).

IBM. (2003). Retrieved February 28, 2003 from the World Wide Web: http://www.ibm.com.

Inspiration. (2003). Retrieved February 28, 2003 from the World Wide Web: http://www.inspiration.com/.

Riverdeep. (2003). Retrieved February 28, 2003 from the World Wide Web: http://www.riverdeep.net/talkingwalls/.

Schnitz, J. (1982). *Internal Research Memorandum, IRIS Reading Project.* Provo, UT: WICAT Systems.

Schnitz, J. (2002). *Approaches to Online Instruction.* Ohio SchoolNet Conference.

Seimens, G. (2002). *Lessons Learned Teaching Online.* Retrieved February 28, 2003 from the World Wide Web: http://www.elearnspace.org/Articles/lessonslearnedteaching.htm.

Turner Learning. (2003). Retrieved February 28, 2003 from the World Wide Web: http://www.turnerlearning.com/.

World Book. (2003). Retrieved February 28, 2003 from the World Wide Web: http://www2.worldbook.com/.

Young, J. (2003, February 24). Personal communication.

Chapter IX

The Management of Virtual Classes in School District Digital Intranets

Ken Stevens
Memorial University of Newfoundland, Canada

Abstract

As rural communities and schools decline in size educational policy makers often question their viability. In the Canadian province of Newfoundland and Labrador and in New Zealand, new educational structures based on digital networking, using the Internet, have been developed for the delivery of education to rural schools. Within these electronic educational structures senior students in rural high schools have been provided with extended curriculum choice through a combination of on-site and online instruction. This has led to three challenges: the administration of electronically inter-connected rural schools, the integration of physical and virtual classes, and the need to find pedagogy that is appropriate for e-teaching and e-learning. The new educational structures in rural Newfoundland and New Zealand have extended traditional classrooms in terms of time, space, organisation and capacity.

The Management of Virtual Classes In School District Digital Intranets

As rural communities decline in size, educational policy makers often question the viability of the small schools located within them. Traditionally, senior rural high school students have been encouraged to complete their studies in larger institutions, including boarding schools, most of which are located in urban areas. In many instances, small schools have been closed and their students transported by bus to schools in larger centres.

A problem common to small schools throughout the world is the issue of curriculum choice for senior students. It is difficult to justify the appointment of specialist teachers for very small numbers of students in rural schools. Accordingly, rural high school students often do not have access to the same range of curriculum choices enjoyed by their urban peers who are educated in schools located in larger communities.

The educational policy dilemma of providing resources for small schools in ways that ensure their students have access to educational and, indirectly, vocational opportunities comparable to their urban peers is compounded in countries where it is necessary to maintain viable educational institutions in areas where there are significant economic resources. In Canada, Australia, New Zealand and many of the Nordic countries, schools in small and remote communities are vital to the national economic infrastructure as they are often located near mines, forests, fisheries or agricultural activities. However, it is difficult to attract and retain professional and service personnel in rural areas if local schools are not perceived to be at least as good as those in cities.

The Development of Virtual Classes in New Zealand and Atlantic Canada

When schools are electronically linked so that they can share their teaching resources, often over considerable distances, a much wider curriculum for students can be provided. When schools link classes by audio or video technology and, more recently, by the Internet, "virtual classes" are created. Tiffin and Rajasingham (1995, p. 6) describe the virtual class as a place in which:

"...everybody can talk and be heard and be identified and everybody can see the same words, diagrams and pictures, at the same time."

They further note that the virtual classroom is:

"...an extension of, or alternative to, conventional schools and classrooms."

By linking electronically, schools in rural areas of New Zealand and Canada have provided students with new dimensions to their educational experience by extending and enhancing their remote and isolated classrooms.

In Newfoundland and Labrador, one of the most geographically isolated provinces in Canada, all teachers are able to be linked through the "Stemnet" network. Within this network, the "Stellar Schools" program has been developed to take advantage of recent developments in information and communication technologies in those areas of the province in which there are advanced telephone services. Not all schools in the province are members of the Stellar schools program, but more are able to join as the local telephone company expands its services and provides broadband connections to remote areas.

In the Canterbury area of the South Island of New Zealand, 10 rural schools each faced the threat of closure because of falling enrolments and the relatively high cost of keeping each school open for fewer and fewer students. As each school declined in terms of its student enrolment, fewer areas of the curriculum could be provided to senior students because fewer teachers could be employed. Most schools in the region were in decline and many parents in the rural communities were worried about the ways in which this affected the educational opportunities of their children. In rural areas the school is a special institution because of the central role it has in the life of its community. In the absence of a local school that is able to provide courses of the level and quality students require, many families are reluctant to stay in a rural area. School closure is often therefore associated with population out-migration and subsequent rural economic decline (Stevens, 1995a, 1995b). The solution in the rural Canterbury region of New Zealand was to link small schools (N = 10) with one another electronically with the help of Telecom New Zealand, the national telephone company. By linking with one another to form a 10-site audiographic network to share teaching and learning in the more specialised subjects like Economics, Japanese, Agriculture and French, one teacher was able to simultaneously provide instruction to students in up to ten widely dispersed sites. Teachers in each participating school were willing to collaborate with their colleagues in the other schools in the district to extend educational opportunities for students.

In these examples rural schools have had their geographic and educational isolation reduced by academically and administratively linking with one another to create virtual classes. Today the Internet is the primary vehicle for linking students and teachers across an increasing range of sites.

Teaching and Learning in Virtual Classes in a Canadian School-District Digital Intranet

In the Canadian province of Newfoundland and Labrador, and in other countries that have communities located beyond major centres of population, new educational structures based on digital networking, using the Internet, have been developed for the delivery of education to rural schools (Stevens, 1999). In Newfoundland and Labrador School District No. 8 (The Vista School District), there are 5,165 students enrolled in 18 schools. The schools range in enrolments from 650 down to 40 students. In eight schools in this district there were senior students who wished to study Advanced Placement (AP) courses in four subjects: Biology, Chemistry, Mathematics and Physics. (Advanced Placement courses enable students in their final year of High School throughout North America to begin undergraduate degrees if these courses are passed at grade levels specified by the university of their choice.) The challenge that this presented for the eight small rural schools in the Vista School District was to provide university-level instruction for small numbers of students.

Although AP courses are a well-established feature of senior secondary education in the United States and Canada, it is unusual for students to be able to enrol for instruction at this level in small schools in remote communities. It is rare to find high school students in small and remote communities anywhere in the world who are provided with instruction in university-level studies. The electronic linking of eight sites (or schools) within the Vista School district to collaborate in the teaching of AP biology, chemistry, mathematics and physics created a series of virtual classes in this part of rural Newfoundland and Labrador. This new electronic educational structure became known as the Vista School District Digital Intranet. The four AP teachers came from different schools in the district and were, in fact, the people who developed the AP courses for Internet delivery. Each of the four teachers had a tele-presence in each of the participating schools for that part of the school day during which (virtual) classes were electronically connected, or online.

From the eight schools that together comprised the Vista School District Digital Intranet, 55 students initially enrolled in AP biology, chemistry, mathematics and physics courses. By participating in classes in real (synchronous) time using audio, video and electronic whiteboards over the Internet, combined with a measure of independent (asynchronous) learning, senior students were able to both interact with one another online as well as work off-line in their own community schools. From time to time social occasions were organised so that students could get to know their online AP teachers and the other students in their virtual classes personally.

The development of this new, electronic educational structure in rural Newfoundland was an attempt to use information and communication technologies to provide students with extended educational and vocational opportunities. Many students who were participants in the virtual classes that constructed and deconstructed within the digital Intranet learned about the potential of information and communication technologies while completing their AP courses. Furthermore, many students learned to integrate on-site and online instruction in their daily school lives by participating in virtual and traditional classes.

Three Challenges of Virtual Classes to Traditional School Organization

There are, inherently, three challenges from virtual classes to traditional schools:

- The interconnectedness of schools
- The integration of physical and virtual classes
- The development of pedagogy for e-teaching and e-learning

Virtual classes in rural Canada and New Zealand are located in new educational structures known as school district digital intranets within which schools are electronically interconnected both administratively and academically. This is a challenge to the autonomy of the school.

As schools administratively and academically interconnect, teaching and learning takes place in new ways. A further challenge is to integrate traditional face-to-face and online classes, or to blend physical and virtual instruction.

Teachers have been prepared to teach in their own classes in real or synchronous time. Increasingly, particularly in rural communities in Canada and New Zealand, teachers are teaching across a number of classes within school district digital intranets. Another challenge for the profession is to find appropriate pedagogy for organising teaching and learning in electronic classrooms.

The Interconnectedness of Schools

At a time when the economies of many countries are becoming interdependent, individual schools as well as school systems are able to link with one another. Global economic changes of the last decade have shown that national economic systems cannot survive by sealing themselves off from one another, and neither can national school systems. Many schools today, particularly those in rural areas of countries like New Zealand (Stevens, 2000), Finland (Tella, 1995; Stevens, Kynaslahti, & Salminen, 1996; Kynaslahti & Stevens, 1996), Iceland (Stefansdottir, 1993; Stevens, 2002) and Canada (Healey & Stevens, 2002; Stevens, 2001) are changing by interfacing with one another electronically with profound effects on how they provide education for young people and their families.

There are educational and policy issues associated with schools academically and administratively interconnecting. Schools have traditionally been considered to be autonomous institutions with their own teachers, their own students and their own cultures. Most schools identify a geographical area from which they enrol students. When schools link to other schools to enhance teaching and learning opportunities, as in the case of the Vista School District Digital

Intranet, human resources, in this case, teacher expertise, is able to be shared. Instead of being closed, autonomous teaching and learning spaces, classrooms become open, interactive educational sites. Teachers move electronically from one site to other sites (schools), as do participating students. The space between sites (schools) thereby becomes an educational environment. Classrooms in the Vista School District were expanded to accommodate advanced high school courses so that students in small and remote Canadian communities were able to participate in a new, electronic educational structure.

A second issue associated with the interconnection of schools was the location of power. Normally, power in a school is centred in the office of the Principal and is devolved to teachers. In a digital network, such as the Vista School District Digital Network, power was both shared and transient. Principals experienced teachers entering their schools electronically and leaving at the touch of a button. Power was transient in that it, to a large extent, appeared with electronic teachers and left with them.

Third, the electronic networking of schools provided students with access to a considerably expanded range of teaching expertise and experience and to a wider peer group, albeit, an online one. Many students were challenged to evaluate themselves for the first time in a new and considerably enlarged academic environment. New non-local educational, vocational, cultural and social environments emerged for students beyond their local community schools.

Integrating Physical and Virtual Classes

The question that many schools face today is not whether to develop virtual classes within electronic environments like school district digital intranets, but how new web-based technologies are to be effectively used for improving teaching and learning. The emergence of virtual classes challenges traditional school organisation, the nature and extent of teacher-student interaction and the range of curriculum opportunities that can be provided for learners.

In the example of the Vista School District Digital Intranet, virtual classes co-existed with traditional, on-site classes. As the original intranet has been expanded to include more schools across the province of Newfoundland and Labrador, virtual and physical classes are integrating as students access courses from each.

It is timely to reflect on the meaning of the electronic basis of education. While e-learning uses satellite dishes, the Internet and a range of software as students access courses from computers, their educational space is being expanded. An emerging challenge for the teaching profession is to pedagogically justify the choice of synchronous and asynchronous instruction.

Developing Pedagogy for e-Teaching and e-Learning

Students in the Vista School District Digital Intranet were frequently subject to scrutiny by their peers as they responded through chat-rooms, audio and video with their AP online teachers. The Digital Intranet provided students with access to multiple sites simultaneously, as well as the opportunity to work independently of a teacher for part of the day. The need to prepare for classes before going online became increasingly apparent to both teachers and students if the open, synchronous, science classes were to succeed. The advent of the Digital Intranet had implications for students who had to interact with teachers and their peers in a variety of new ways. The teaching of each of the four AP Science subjects in the Vista Digital Intranet took place within virtual classes that were open between participating sites. Many students experienced difficulty expressing themselves and, in particular, asking questions in virtual classes when they did not know their peers from other small communities. However, as the students became more comfortable with one another, particularly after the first social occasion, inhibitions such as asking questions online were overcome.

A feature of the initial four online AP subjects that were introduced to students through the Vista School District Digital Intranet was that they differed from one another in terms of pedagogy as well as the disciplines they covered. Some teachers favoured large amounts of content being available to students online while others preferred to use the Internet to engage students in interactively solving scientific problems outlined in textbooks. Each of the initial four AP online teachers in the Vista School District Digital Network taught differently from each of the others but in all cases, students were required to take much more responsibility for their own classes. They had to prepare for online classes in much more detail than they were used to doing before traditional face-to-face instruction.

Professional Development Issues for Teaching in Virtual Classes

The development of new ways of providing education in rural Newfoundland and Labrador by bringing schools into collaborative relationships (virtual classes managed within a school district digital intranet) has generated four challenges for teachers:

Issue One: What is an Appropriate Location for E-Teachers — In Schools or Between Schools?

Teachers are appointed *to* schools, but in Newfoundland and Labrador and in New Zealand, a growing number are in fact teaching *between* schools. E-teachers electronically enter and leave a growing number of schools (sites) across rural Newfoundland and Labrador and New Zealand in the course of a school day. Is it now appropriate to recognize the emergence of a new educational professional: the lead teacher with subject expertise and responsibility across a network of schools?

It is common for teachers in rural New Zealand and in Newfoundland and Labrador to express disquiet about the security of their employment as electronic teaching is extended within school district digital intranets. Increasingly, teachers in rural Canada and New Zealand are teaching between schools as well as in them. In Canada several new educational professionals are emerging to manage this situation: e-teachers, m-teachers, instructional designers and webmasters.

E-teachers teaching between schools through the Internet are assisted by m-teachers who mediate between traditional, face-to-face on-site professionals and e-teachers. In most sites where e-learning is taking place, students also receive instruction in physical classrooms. M-teachers are responsible for ensuring that e-students' educational needs are met on-site and mediating, where appropriate, with their e-teachers.

At the school district level there are new positions for instructional design and the management of websites. Instructional design at the school district level is in its infancy but its importance is becoming increasingly apparent to all professionals who are meeting students in virtual classes.

Issue Two: Where should Control be Located in Electronic Teaching and Learning Structures?

Principals in rural New Zealand and rural Newfoundland and Labrador schools have to manage situations where teachers appear electronically in their schools to teach in virtual classes and who subsequently disappear electronically. Where is control appropriately located when schools link electronically to share resources? Who is responsible for e-teachers' conduct while electronically visiting schools (sites) within digital networks? In Newfoundland and Labrador schools are organized within school districts managed by a board. Control of e-learning has increasingly been located in school board offices. In New Zealand schools have been self-managing since the abolition of school boards.

At the present time, many e-teachers in New Zealand and in Newfoundland and Labrador are engaged in providing instruction at the school district level. However, e-learning can be provided anytime, anywhere and need not be restricted to administrative frameworks like school districts. It is possible for e-learning to cross international boundaries and time zones. The location of control of e-teaching is emerging as an issue for educational administrators.

Issue Three: Learning to Teach Collaboratively in Electronic Educational Structures

Rural educators have made considerable advances in bringing online instruction to senior high school classes and currently there are developments to extend this to other areas within schools in Newfoundland and Labrador and in New Zealand. A pedagogical challenge facing educators, curriculum developers and administrators at present is the integration of on-site instruction with online learning to blend physical and virtual education.

A feature of e-learning is that it is essentially collaborative. Computers can link to other computers and the Internet enables information to be accessed by students and teachers from any location. Collaborative learning between sites has been encouraged by some AP teachers in Newfoundland and Labrador but the possibilities of collaborative teaching have not yet been recognized. In a very small network of one-room elementary schools in the North Island of New Zealand, teachers have been observed teaching face-to-face while supervising collaborative instruction in the same classroom and enabling some students to be instructed online by another (one-room) teacher in a local school. Such multi-age, multi-task pedagogy provides an insight into how teachers could support one another by linking classes, as appropriate, and teaching collaboratively between sites.

Issue Four: What is the Future of the Classroom — Physical or Virtual?

How far can educational networking be extended? At present most networks are at the school district level. Is it possible to move beyond the structure of school district intranets to personal intranets so that students are placed in online learning environments that are appropriate to their individual needs rather than in the present administrative framework of a school district? Support for this development through the appointment of m-teachers in Newfoundland and Labrador is already being provided, although students have yet to undertake e-learning other than within school district digital intranets.

Conclusion

The educational use of information and communication technologies has provided learners in rural areas of New Zealand and Canada with new educational opportunities. In each country there are innovative practices in rural schools that both reduce the significance of geographic isolation and provide students with opportunities at least as good as those of their peers who attend large urban schools. The most significant change these developments have brought to small rural schools is considerably extended curriculum choice for senior students. Through the creation of virtual classes, rural students and their families can, in a growing number of communities, obtain similar educational opportunities as those who attend schools in urban areas.

The relationship between virtual and physical classes in rural Canada and New Zealand has technological, pedagogical, administrative and policy implications. Much more financial and personnel support is needed to give teachers and learners in rural communities confidence that the growing range of technologies they use in their electronic educational environments are robust and reliable.

Technology support within and between schools is likely to become a significant budget issue in future as digital intranets expand, multiply and interact with one another.

Most teachers are professionally prepared to teach in classes in schools. The reality for many Atlantic Canadian and New Zealand teachers is that they are required to teach not just in schools, but between schools. Pedagogy to support e-teaching and e-learning and its integration with traditional classroom instruction is a new dimension in teacher education. As traditional classrooms are extended in terms of time, space, organisation and capacity through virtual education, teachers are challenged to develop pedagogy to facilitate the integration of on-site and online instruction.

Little attention has been given to the architecture of classrooms and other learning spaces as physical and virtual learning environments meet. It is time to take a new look at the physical organisation of classrooms in many school districts in Canada and New Zealand to ensure that space is configured appropriately for the seamless delivery of on-site and online education. Students can now learn synchronously and asynchronously in the same physical space. This pedagogical reality is likely to influence school planning in future.

The creation of electronic educational structures and processes in Canada and New Zealand in and between rural communities addresses a fundamental policy and ethical issue in the provision of education — improved access for geographically isolated students to extended educational, and, indirectly, vocational opportunities.

There are educational, sociological, technological and policy implications in the changes that are taking place in and between the virtual classes that link educational sites in rural Canada and New Zealand. There are, accordingly, many research questions to be answered. The largest research question to be answered at this time is whether the structures, processes and emerging pedagogy of e-learning that is shaping rural education in Atlantic Canada and New Zealand can be transferred to all schools, regardless of location.

References

Healey, D. & Stevens, K. (2002). Student access to information technology and perceptions of future opportunities in two small Labrador communities. *Canadian Journal of Learning and Technology (la revue Canadienne de l'apprentissage et de la technologie), 28*(1), 7-18.

Kynaslahti, H. & Salminen, J. (1995). Integration of remote classrooms: Technical and local perspectives. In F. Nouwens (Ed.), *Distance Education— Crossing Frontiers*. Rockhampton: Central Queensland University.

Kynaslahti, H. & Stevens, K. (1996). Mediating local and global knowledge: The emergence of the virtual classroom in Finland and New Zealand. In B. Glastonbury (Ed.), *Dreams and Realities: Information Technology in the Human Services*. Helsinki.

Stefansdottir, L. (1993). The Icelandic Educational Network: Ismennt. In G. Davies & B. Samways (Eds.), *Teleteaching: Proceedings of the IFIP TC3 Third Teleteaching Conference* (pp. 829-835). Amsterdam: Elsevier Science Publishers.

Stevens, K. (2000). Tele-Enseignement et Education en Milieu Rural en Nouvelle Zelande et a Terreneuve, *Geocarrefour: Revue de Geographie de Lyon*. Espaces Ruraux et Technologies de L'Information, 75(1), 87-92.

Stevens, K. (2001). The development of digital intranets for the enhancement of education in rural communities. *Journal Of Interactive Instruction Development, 13*(3), 19-24.

Stevens, K. (2002). Minnkandi Heimur -Rafrænt Net Smárra Skóla- Óvænt Tengsl Íslenska Menntanetsins Við Nýja Sjáland Og Kanada (Making the world smaller: The electronic networking of small schools — some unseen connections of the Icelandic Educational Network in New Zealand and Canada) (K.Erlendsson, Trans.), *Skólavaran, 2*(2), 22-24.

Stevens, K., Kynaslahti, H., & Salminen, J. (1996). Alustavia Tuloksia Koulujen Verkottumisesta Suomessa Ja Uudessa Seelannissa (Some preliminary outcomes rrom networked classes in Finland and New Zealand). *Kasvatus: The Finnish Journal Of Education, 27*(2), 196-205.

Stevens, K. J. (1995a). Geographic isolation and technological change: A new vision of teaching and learning in rural schools in New Zealand. *The Journal of Distance Learning, 1*(1).

Stevens, K. J. (1995b). *Report to the Minister of Education on the development of networks between small rural schools in New Zealand*. Wellington: Rural Education Reference Group.

Stevens, K. J. (1999). A new model for teaching in rural communities: The electronic organisation of classes as intranets. *Prism: Journal of The Newfoundland and Labrador Teachers' Association,* 6(1), 23-26.

Tella, S. (1995). *Virtual School in a Networking Learning Environment.* Helsinki: University of Helsinki, Department of Teacher Education.

Tiffin, J. & Rajasingham, L. (1995). *In Search of the Virtual Class: Education in an Information Society.* London: Routledge.

Chapter X

Virtual Vignettes and Pedagogical Potentials: Insights into a Virtual Schooling Service

Donna Pendergast
University of Queensland, Australia

Cushla Kapitzke
University of Queensland, Australia

Abstract

In 2002 a review of the educational and technical performance of the Virtual Schooling Service being tested in Queensland, Australia, was conducted. The service utilised synchronous and asynchronous online delivery strategies and a range of learning technologies to support students at a distance, who may otherwise have restricted choices in their selection of subjects to study in Years 11 and 12—the final and non-compulsory years of schooling where students are typically aged 16 to 17.

An account of how Activity Theory was used to conceptualise the evaluation is provided. A focus on one element of the evaluation—pedagogical effectiveness—with case studies of actual delivery and receiving classes is incorporated to highlight the pedagogical limitations and potentials of the service. The "productive pedagogies" schema is introduced as a framework for the evaluation of pedagogical effectiveness of the virtual classes. Critical success factors for pedagogical effectiveness are documented, along with a reflection on these elements using Activity Theory. The chapter concludes with an update of the current initiatives being undertaken to enhance the pedagogical effectiveness of the Virtual Schooling Service.

Context—Queensland, Australia

Queensland is the north-eastern state of the Australian continent with a population of around 3.5 million and a land area of 1,727,200 square kilometres. Brisbane, the capital city, is located in the south-eastern corner of the state. Almost half of Queensland's people live in the Brisbane metropolitan area. Roughly half of the state is in the tropical zone, with rain forests on Cape York Peninsula in the extreme north. The remaining land area is arid or semi-arid, where annual rainfall is as low as five inches (13 cm), compared to 160 inches (406 cm) in parts of the northeast coast. The Great Dividing Range separates the fertile coastal strip from vast interior plains. The high population concentration in the southeast corner of the state leaves much of the remaining areas sparsely populated with small remote communities, presenting challenges for the provision of services such as school education (http://www.1upinfo.com/encyclopedia/Q/Qunsld.html).

Education Queensland is the government department with a mandate to provide quality education for all students across the state of Queensland, ranging from the isolated, vastly inhabited zones, to the densely populated urban centres. To support this goal, Education Queensland operates a large decentralised organisation whose facilities and services span the entire state. The organisation operates some 1,320 primary, secondary, distance and special education schools, which are supported by 35 district offices, four facilities service centres, and a central office located in Brisbane. Central Office is organised in a branch structure with each branch having responsibility for specific aspects of educational administration.

The Virtual Schooling Service

In 1999 an innovative pilot project—the Virtual Schooling Service—was commissioned under the auspices of Education Queensland to determine the viability of synchronous and asynchronous online delivery of Year 11 and Year 12 school subjects to small numbers of students where teaching expertise in some subject areas was not available. Until this time, the needs of remote or external students in Queensland were traditionally met by distance education lessons, which were delivered using a combination of print and high frequency radio. The Virtual Schooling Service pilot sought to expand the range of communication channels by which students receive educational services remotely. Since its inception, the service has continued to utilise synchronous and asynchronous online delivery strategies and a range of learning technologies to support students at a distance. At present there are 544 students from 79 schools across the state enrolled in eight subjects (http://education.qld.gov.au/curriculum/service/virtual/).

The Virtual Schooling Service uses an audiographic conferencing system combined with an Internet-based software program for offline access to lesson and learning material. Audiographics conferencing combines loudspeaker phones and computer graphics and enables synchronous communication during lesson time. The web-based resources enable students to flexibly access subject content and the materials of individual lessons, either from home or school, in their own time. The service uses email and telephone contact between individual students and the teacher as well as email discussion lists for ongoing multipoint interaction between students and teacher.

In 2000, a review of the first six-month phase of the Virtual Schooling Service Pilot was conducted (Lundin, Elliott, & Richardson, 2000) and more recently, a team of staff in the School of Education at The University of Queensland were commissioned to review the educational and technical performance of the Virtual Schooling Service during its subsequent years of operation (2000-2001) (Pendergast, Kapitzke, Land, Luke, & Bahr, 2002). This chapter is based on some findings of that review, particularly those considering pedagogical effectiveness.

Theoretical Framework—Activity Theory

The evaluation of the Virtual Schooling Service utilized Activity Theory to inform methodological design and to reflect upon the findings of the study. The components of activity systems are particularly useful for analyzing and understanding learning that takes place in technology-mediated learning environments.

In order to explain the usefulness of Activity Theory, it is helpful to consider its emergence. During the '60s, the key concept for understanding thought and learning was representation. The central tenet of representation theory was that knowledge comprised symbolic mental representations, and learning entailed the manipulation of those symbols. Theories of representation stressed the individual mind and its *acquisition* of schematic structures through mental computation. However, a shift away from representational theories of mind to theories of cultural activity and social practice occurred following the work of the Soviet psychologists, Vygotsky (1981) and Leontiev (1981). In keeping with this shift, Activity Theory focuses on human interaction through engagement in artifact-mediated and object-oriented action. It posits that the relationship between humans and their activities are not direct, but are always mediated. An activity system, therefore, is composed of a subject and an object mediated by tools or instruments (see Figure 1). A subject is a person engaged in an activity. An object (i.e., objective) motivates the activity by giving it purpose and direction. Tools refer to the artifacts that mediate and transform the object into an outcome. They include not only material instruments, but also the social and conceptual resources of thought, language, and culture. Components of the system—subject, object, and tool/instrument—are mutually constitutive, transforming each other in and by the activity.

As theorists developed Activity Theory, they incorporated other levels of mediating factors: the community of actors who share the same object, the norms of that particular group, and the division of labor that emerges within the activity. Divisions of labor can run either horizontally if tasks are spread across community members with equal status, or vertically if tasks are distributed up and down according to hierarchies of status and power. The dynamics of a system and its eventual outcome are constrained by formal (i.e., systemic), informal (i.e., idiosyncratic adaptation during the action), and technical (i.e., mandated) rules, norms, and conventions of the community engaged in the object-oriented action.

Figure 1: Components of an Activity System

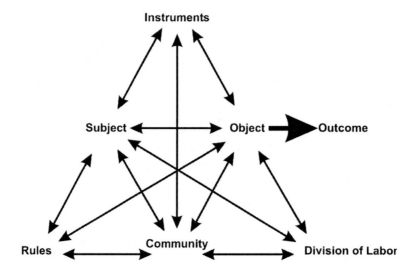

Source: *http://www.quasar.ualberta.ca/edpy597/Modules/module15.html*

Because of their focus on group participation, activity theorists conceive learning as contextualized and participatory activity rather than as the transmission of mental representations such as codified knowledge. As such, Activity Theory is based on constructivist principles and is not concerned with "doing" as disembodied action but as social action occurring to change something in the world. Within this framework, "context" is not an outer or boundaried shell inside which people undertake certain activities. Rather, actors generate context through and with the tools at their disposal and in accord with the object of their action. Context is therefore internal to people because it involves objects and goals. It is also external to them because it involves other people, artifacts, and situated settings for action.

To understand an activity system such as the learning that takes place in online environments, Activity Theory focuses on the interrelation of the components. With respect to the project at hand, Activity Theory enables analyses not only of the human-technology (subject-tool) interaction, but also the subject-object interactions as mediated by the particular technologies at hand. This extends the parameters of analysis from the minds of individuals, and from human-computer interactions as in traditional cognitive psychology research, to the entire activity system.

Because of their inherent complexity, activity systems are characterized by internal tensions and contradictions. Engeström (1999) calls tension that exists within the components of a system—for example, competing objects in a single activity—"primary" tensions. Those that occur between different components of the system—for example, between tools/instruments and objects—he calls "secondary" contradictions. These axes of competition and contradiction are useful for understanding weaknesses or strengths of systems. Tensions and pressures that enter systems become either positive or negative forces for change and development through the disturbance, disorder, and instability they generate.

Activity Theory was used to frame the evaluation of the organizational, technological, and pedagogical outcomes of the Virtual Schooling Service because the elements and dynamics of activity systems provide a useful conceptual lens for understanding learning in technology-mediated contexts. Using Activity Theory as a theoretical lens, we examined the relations of subject and object as mediated by the components that constitute the Virtual Schooling Service as an activity system. These were:

- Subjects (the Education Queensland Virtual Schooling Service community, namely, teaching staff, Study Coaches, students);
- Objects (flexible delivery of curricular material through virtual schooling);
- Outcome (learning outcomes);
- Tools (language, online learning technologies, etc.);
- The classroom micro culture (curricular content, organizational, and pedagogical practices); and
- Division of labor (teachers, learners).

Consistent with Activity Theory, data were collected that (a) documented resources (tools, technological infrastructure) and practices (e.g., tool use, student inquiry, and problem solving); (b) captured the interactions between students and between students and teachers; (c) and described the progress and learning outcomes of students. The specific approach involved several methods of data collection, enabling the triangulation of hypotheses and findings from qualitative and quantitative data. Data were collected at delivery and receiving school sites, with a total of four delivery and seven receiving schools investigated. Receiving site visits were selected, in consultation with relevant staff, to cover a range of variables including: geographic location, subjects delivered, number of students utilising the service, and Index of Relative Socio-Economic Disadvantage.

Data collected at school sites included: observations of delivery or receiving lessons, scoring of pedagogical approach in observed classes, and interviews using structured schedules with delivery teachers, students, administrators and study coaches. Telephone interviews were also conducted with two schools that had withdrawn from the pilot. Two online surveys were developed and administered to teachers and students of the Virtual Schooling Service. The questionnaires consisted of two parts: the teaching (or learning experience) in Virtual Schooling Service classrooms against a productive pedagogy framework with a view to identifying the pedagogic characteristics of the Virtual Schooling Service, and a series of open ended items which allowed teachers or students to locate specific issues they have identified as being a relevant virtue of their experience of the Virtual Schooling Service.

Comprehensive details of the evaluation findings are available elsewhere (see Kapitzke & Pendergast, in press). What is of interest in this chapter is one element of the evaluation—that of pedagogical effectiveness of the Virtual Schooling Service. This draws upon a range of components of the Virtual Schooling Service activity system including the subjects, the objects, the outcome, the tools, the classroom microculture, and the division of labour.

Measuring Pedagogical Success of the Virtual Schooling Service— Productive Pedagogies

The question of how to measure pedagogical effectiveness is an ongoing challenge for educational researchers. In the late 1990s, researchers from the University of Queensland in conjunction with Education Queensland conducted an investigation into school restructuring in this state which incorporated a large-scale study of pedagogical effectiveness of classroom practices, known as the Queensland School Reform Longitudinal Study (QSRLS). The study drew heavily on Newmann's *Authentic Pedagogies* (Newmann & Associates, 1996) because of their importance in terms of the apparent demonstration of a substantive link between classroom practice and student outcomes. However, the researchers identified issues relevant to the Australian context that were missing from Newmann's model and identified approaches to improving the measurement characteristics of Newmann's model. The research team redeveloped Newmann's categories into a broader grid that attempted to encompass the array of factors that, the Australian educational research and curriculum development suggest, make a difference in student achievement. The resultant model was named *Productive Pedagogies* to differentiate it from Newmann's model.

According to the Education Queensland website, *Productive Pedagogies* describes a "common framework under which teachers can choose and develop strategies in relation to what are they teaching and the variable styles, approaches and backgrounds of their students" (http://education.qld.gov.au/corporate/newbasics/html/pedagogies/pedagog.html).

There are four domains of classroom practice that enable "improved and more equitable student outcomes" (Lingard, Ladwig, Mills, Bahr, Chant, Warry, Ailwood, Capeness, Christie, Gore, Hayes, & Luke, 2001, p. 3). These domains are: high degree of intellectual quality, relevance to the learner (connectedness), a supportive classroom environment, and recognition of difference. Twenty elements of classroom observation indicators are grouped under the four dimensions. These are presented in Table 1.

The 20 elements in the four domains of *Productive Pedagogies* were utilised in the Queensland School Reform Longitudinal Study to rate nearly 1,000 classrooms for pedagogical effectiveness on a five-point scale (Lingard et al., 2001). The study found that most of Queensland's face-to-face classrooms are highly supportive learning environments. However, they rated poorly in

Table 1: Domains of Productive Pedagogies

Intellectual Quality	Connectedness	Supportive Classroom Environment	Recognition of Difference
Higher order thinking Deep knowledge Deep understanding Substantive conversation Knowledge as problematic Metalanguage	Knowledge integration Background knowledge Connectedness to the world Problem-based curriculum	Student control Social support Engagement Explicit criteria Self-regulation	Cultural Knowledge Inclusivity Narrative Group identity Citizenship

terms of the other three dimensions of the *Productive Pedagogies* framework (i.e., intellectual quality, connectedness, and recognition of difference). Using this as a benchmark, the Virtual Schooling Service classrooms were compared for pedagogical performance. An explanation of each *Productive Pedagogy* and a sample question used as a prompt for scaling appear in Appendix A.

Inside Virtual Classrooms

For the Virtual Schooling Service evaluation, classroom observations were made using the *Productive Pedagogies* classroom observation scoring system described in the previous section. Each lesson was scored on the 20 elements of the classroom observation schedule and the resultant item scores were collapsed to produce indices of the four domains of the productive pedagogy model—supportive learning environments, intellectual quality, connectedness, and recognition of difference. In addition to being rated on the *Productive Pedagogies* scoring system, short vignettes of the observed classes were constructed so that a sense of being *inside* the teaching and learning process was possible. Three of these classroom snapshots follow.

Year 11 Lesson

The Year 11 Lesson commenced at 2:00 p.m. It was delivered by a male teacher from Alpha Delivery School to a group of 10 students comprising two girls and five boys in the receiving school being observed and three other students at Bravo State High School. The three sites were several hundreds of kilometers from each other. The students worked in pairs at the computers, and were first asked to open a document on the Virtual Schooling Service website. The teacher had prepared a diagram in the document depicting a problem relevant to the topic. He discussed the problem and then told the students to unsynchronize their whiteboards. They were instructed to select one of the 13 whiteboards available to them and to write their names on it to identify their working space.

The students then had to solve the problem by working in pairs using the graphical tablet. The teacher was able to see what each of them was doing, as were the other students in the class. When asked, "Who's stuck?," some of the students answered in the affirmative, so the teacher asked them to assemble on whiteboard 13. He provided assistance by talking the students through some of the difficulties of the problem. One of the students resorted to paper and pen to do the calculations. Others left the graphical tablet and used the keyboard and its numerical symbols to do the equations.

The teacher then summarized the lesson on a clean whiteboard and sought feedback from the students to ensure that they understood. They then turned to a document on the website, which had an activity that he wanted the students to study before the next lesson. The lesson finished with a reminder to those who had not sent in their experiments to do so, and with the usual farewells.

Year 12 Lesson A

Staff at Delta State High School, more than 500 kilometers from the receiving school at Charlie State High School, delivered the lesson. The lesson commenced at 1:30 p.m. There were four female students in the receiving room. There were four computers in the room, but only three were functional, hence one student was sitting beside another sharing the computer. There was one other student in the virtual class, a male student located at Foxtrot High, several hundred kilometers from both the delivery and the receiving classroom being viewed. The class was being delivered in the students' lunch hour due to inconsistencies in timetabling. The students each ate their lunches over the course of the class.

The delivery teacher commenced the lesson with some housekeeping. The purpose of the lesson was to provide an overview of the work for the term. The first task began with the use of the synchronous whiteboard. At this stage, a technical problem forced the Foxtrot student off-line. He was disconnected and spent around three minutes reconnecting to the class under the guidance of the teacher. The class ceased during this time. By now the class had been in progress for 15 minutes, most of which was spent on organization and technical issues.

After remedying the technical problem, the teacher used the initiation-response-evaluation sequence to discuss the overview of the semester. Procedural arrangements regarding student access to the website occurred. During this time, the students at Charlie were distracted—one wrote on the blackboard, two others discussed the coldness of the room, but all managed to respond to the teacher when appropriate. The teacher had no indication the students were off-task.

The teacher then attempted to send a shared document to students. This was delayed by three minutes, during which time students waited for the document to arrive and shared their lunches. Shortly after the document arrived the teacher was disconnected from both the audio and synchronous tools. Students at Charlie State High School chatted with the student at Foxtrot High about their weekend activities. After five minutes, the service provider reconnected the teacher and advised that they would put a trace on the system to try to identify the problem. The teacher then emailed the document to students. Students took turns reading aloud the topics for the semester. Various elements were elaborated upon. The service provider interrupted the class to indicate that they had found the source of the problem and had remedied it.

The next phase of the lesson consisted of students being referred to a PowerPoint presentation. Students read aloud the contents of the PowerPoint presentation, using simple turn taking. The teacher clarified and provided examples. The lesson ended with the usual lesson closing sequences and a reminder for students to complete exercises in their asynchronous classes.

Year 12 Lesson B

One Year 12 lesson of 50 minutes was observed at Tango State High School. The subject was allocated two 50-minute online lessons and three 70-minute offline lessons per week. There were four male students in the class—one at Tango State High School and three at Romeo State High School, several hundred kilometers away. A male teacher at Romeo State High School some 600 kilometers away delivered the lesson.

The lesson opened with some informal chat about a recent public holiday and then moved to the lesson topic. Content was taught on and through a textbook. The students had been asked to read pages 21 through 36 for homework. The lesson was based on this material.

The student used the laptop computer. He opened the Virtual Schooling Service website and brought up the class whiteboard. This contained six information entities and their relationships in diagrammatic form, and was used to teach the topic. Most of the verbal interaction during the lesson between teacher and students comprised discussion of this material, which was based on problems from the textbook. Teacher talk dominated, and consisted of his exposition of the lesson content and numerous initiation-response-evaluation sequences. Although the observed student remained focused on the lesson, his verbal contribution to the lesson comprised of little more than a series of affirmations in the form of "yep." This was usually in response to the teacher's interrogative, "Does that make sense, boys?" While there were four boys in the class, invariably only one of them responded to the query with the monosyllable, "yep."

As well as the textbook, the teacher taught from a complex conceptual schema, or concept map, representing information on certain aspects of the topic. At one stage, he asked one of the boys a question about the map. When the student admitted that he did not know the answer, he was told to "sit down, shut up, and catch up." Notwithstanding the lapse in attention/concentration of the group at Romeo State High School, a session of five minutes of substantive discussion occurred some 45 minutes into the lesson. The student in the room with the researcher did not enter into the conversation. At one stage, while the teacher was talking, this student seemed to leave the lesson by "playing" with other folders and windows. It appeared to be the equivalent of virtual "doodling" or "window gazing."

For homework, the students were asked to "complete Question 2" and email it to the teacher so he could check it before the next lesson. Some agitated discussion from the Romeo State High School students followed as they claimed that they had no offline lessons before then and so had no access to a computer to send the email message. The teacher proceeded to make three alternative suggestions on how they could complete the work and send the file to him. The students remained unconvinced, and the issue remained largely unresolved. The lesson closed with the teacher telling them to email him if they had any problems.

These three lessons were selected to give the reader an insight into the praxis of the Virtual Schooling Service classrooms.

Pedagogical Effectiveness of the Schooling Service

Productive Pedagogy scores for each of the four domains were lower than the benchmarked Queensland School Reform Longitudinal Study (QSRLS) face-to-face classes in receiving (student sites) Virtual Schooling Service class-

Table 2: Mean Scores* for Each Productive Pedagogy Domain

Classroom Type	Intellectual Quality	Connectedness	Supportive Environment	Recognition of Difference
Delivery	2.00	2.05	2.94	1.61
Receiving	1.86	1.52	3.05	1.20
QSRLS Standard	2.27	1.90	3.06	1.40

Source: Pendergast et al. (2002)

* On a 5 point scale where 5 is the most effective pedagogical practice

rooms (see Table 2). Interestingly, the delivery sites, where the teachers relaying the lesson are located, rated higher than the receiving sites (student classrooms) on all domains (with the exception of supportive environment). This could mean that while teachers employ techniques across the four domains that are pedagogically of a higher rating in the delivery strategies in their classes, what the students' receive/experience is mediated such that their experience of the strategies received a lower rating. Furthermore, given that most of Queensland's face-to-face classrooms rated poorly in terms of intellectual quality, connectedness, and recognition of difference, the comparatively lower rating raises concerns about the pedagogical effectiveness of the Virtual Schooling Service.

In addition to the observation and analysis of classrooms using the *Productive Pedagogies* domains, delivery teachers, students, study coaches, and Virtual Schooling Service coordinators, as well as administrators at both delivery and receiving schools, were interviewed and asked to identify the factors that facilitate the success of the virtual schooling pilot. Three categories of critical success factors were determined: organizational, technological, and pedagogical. The critical success factors for effective pedagogy are of interest in this chapter and are summarized in Table 3.

All subjects in the Virtual Schooling Service activity system, including the school coaches themselves, identified the effectiveness of the study coach as a critical success factor for pedagogical effectiveness. As the system currently operates, receiving schools have study coaches who typically perform an administrative function at the receiving school site. However, this contrasts with the expectations of the delivery teachers who place higher expectations on the person(s) in this role, envisaging the study coach as their embodied link to

Table 3: Critical Success Factors—Pedagogy

Delivery Teachers	Students	Virtual Schooling Service Coordinators and/or Study Coaches	Administrators
• Effectiveness of study coach • Reliability of delivery medium • Technoliteracy of delivery teacher • Student learning style • Controlled class sizes • Opportunity to meet students • Professional development of teachers	• Effectiveness of study doach • Reliability of delivery medium • Competence of delivery teacher • Student learning style • Controlled class sizes • Offline learning tasks • Support of peer group • Opportunity to meet with virtual teacher	• Effectiveness of study coach • Technoliteracy of delivery teacher • Student learning style • Controlled class sizes • Offline learning tasks	• Effectiveness of study coach • Technoliteracy of delivery teacher • Professional development of teachers

students, providing guidance, and motivational and procedural support. Several delivery teachers, along with students, suggested this was the most important factor to facilitate effective learning. The relationships between study coach and other subjects were a primary tension within the Virtual Schooling Service activity system.

Delivery teachers and students identified the unreliability of the delivery medium as a key factor affecting pedagogy in the virtual classroom. This subject-tool interaction of the activity system frequently led to secondary tensions and was evident in Year 12 Lesson A included in this chapter. Here, most of the lesson was affected by technological problems. This was consistently observed by the researchers to be a factor affecting the pedagogical effectiveness of intended strategies. The inability to predict dropouts and downtime in lessons required delivery teachers to have contingency pedagogical approaches in place at all times, though in some cases complete breakdowns occurred, including contingency plans. These interruptions to lessons were typically frequent and lengthy in duration, and limited the range and complexity of strategies that teachers were likely to utilise. This proved to be the most significant factor in impeding pedagogical success in the Virtual Schooling Service.

Administrators, delivery teachers, and study coaches all noted the technological literacy of the delivery teacher to be a significant factor affecting pedagogical success. This tended to focus on the teacher's ability to utilise the technology available for the virtual classes. The Year 11 lesson included in this chapter demonstrates a teacher who could be considered to be competent at using the available technology. Students were interested not only in the technological literacy of the teacher, but also their general competence as an effective teacher. Students recognised the difference between teachers who were technically skilled and those who were less skilled at using this technology. But, in the students' view, the unskilled teachers were "better teachers" because they were more challenged and these teachers went beyond transmission of knowledge as the primary teaching strategy. Virtual Schooling Service students were more likely to prefer a "better teacher" than a technically skilled teacher. There were contradictions in terms of site provision and educational outcomes. For example, it was possible for sites to have poor equipment and site facilities, yet students were pleased with their learning outcomes. This provides evidence for the pedagogical reality that learning with and around technology is not technologically driven but is the product of effective pedagogical relationships between students and teacher. This is an important finding from this research and represents a primary stressor using the Activity Theory framework. Linked with this aspect was the finding that the professional development of teachers was also recognised particularly by school administrators and delivery teachers as being crucial to pedagogical success. There was criticism by both groups of the limited professional development opportunities offered to virtual teachers, particularly in the arena of modifying pedagogical approaches to suit virtual schooling.

Student learning style was also considered to be a significant factor affecting pedagogy in the virtual classroom. Characteristics such as self-reliance, maturity, and time management skills, combined with technoliteracy, were seen as critical factors. Capacity to complete offline and asynchronous independent learning tasks was considered to be equally as important as the technical skills to participate in online classes. As the analysis of lessons using the *Productive Pedagogies* framework showed, students were more likely to experience teaching that focused on them being receivers of content, transmitted in simple ways, with little opportunity for the development of deep thinking. This led to student passivity and compliance, with occasional disengagement and boredom. This scenario is evident in Year 12 Lesson B, where the student disengaged from the class. The teacher is often unaware of this lack of engagement due to the students being "invisible" to the teacher. Despite this, the evaluation found that most students enjoy and are relatively pleased with their learning outcomes from Virtual Schooling Service lessons. They find the high level of autonomy and self-regulation a challenge, but believe that it will be better for them in the long-term with respect to lifelong learning.

Another factor identified by students, delivery teachers, and coaches as being a critical factor for pedagogical effectiveness was the importance of controlling class size—generally for technical performance reasons. In some of the larger classes observed, the likelihood of technical shutdowns was increased. The implications of this technical requirement had the effect of restricting teaching and learning strategies to those suitable for small groups. Again, the relationship between subject-tool (students and teachers/technological equipment) in this activity system has produced a primary tension.

Students recognised the value of their peers as an important element for individual learning. Small class groups were likely to facilitate the development of a degree of intimacy among students, both in the isolation of one school site and with classmates in other locations. This bond was critical to some students remaining in the virtual class, demonstrating a strength in the activity system. This primary component contributed to enhanced student learning. Also within the subject component of the activity system, the opportunity for some delivery teachers and receiving students to meet each other during a visit by the teacher to the school site, or by students attending school camps or similar activities, was consistently reported by both groups to have enhanced their pedagogic effectiveness.

The offline learning tasks were noted by the students and the study coaches to be critical as a pedagogical success factor. A wide variation was observed in the expectations delivery teachers demanded of offline learning, and students and study coaches generally found this to be the least guided and poorly conceptualised aspect of the learning processes. Some students utilised the offline class time to catch up on other subjects, while in other cohorts of students this time was fully integrated into the overall learning of the subject. This was an element within the Virtual Schooling Service model that provided wide scope for improvement.

Activity Theory— Reflecting on the Virtual Schooling Service Pedagogy

From an Activity Theory perspective, Education Queensland's Virtual Schooling Service Pilot was established for the purpose of providing the flexible delivery of school curricular subjects (object) via online technologies (tools) with the intention of providing "quality education appropriate to the needs of students and society" (outcome). Based on the corpus of data, it is apparent that vibrant real and virtual communities exist in and around the Virtual Schooling Service. Nevertheless, consistent with Activity Theory, a number of competing priorities and contradictory practices are at play within that learning and teaching community. These tensions ultimately affect the quality of the Service's stated outcomes. What follows is a discussion of one overriding primary tension and one secondary tension within the activity system of the Virtual Schooling Service.

The overriding primary tension characterizing the Virtual Schooling Service system in its attempts for pedagogical effectiveness is the available technology (tool). The tension comprises the disparity between the education system's expectation of schools to provide appropriate technological infrastructure for effective virtual learning, and the current realities of online connectivity and bandwidth capability afforded them. Both technical and technological issues were paramount in inhibiting learning. Nevertheless, because receiving schools need the Virtual Schooling Service to maintain the viability of their curricular offerings, they persist with the Service as it currently stands. In spite of technical inadequacies and their consequent pedagogical implications, the majority of students enjoy their virtual lessons.

The *Productive Pedagogies* observation checklist, surveys, and class vignettes show that the microculture of Virtual Schooling Service classrooms is, in large measure, defined by the print-based culture and hierarchical social relations of traditional face-to-face classrooms. Pedagogical practices are typical of teacher-centred, textbook-based approaches of industrial-era schools. In most observed lessons, students sat quietly or responded to teacher questions in monosyllabic utterances.

The delivery teacher truly "delivered"—subject content was transmitted from deliverer to receiver in a unilinear fashion. As material tools, the web-based technologies enable instruction to occur, but what has been overlooked to date is attention to the cultural factors mediating and remediating that delivery. Online technologies in and of themselves are not going to produce desired outcomes unless the cultural components (i.e., community, rules, and norms) align with and are conducive to that effect. This was not the case with the activity system of the Virtual Schooling Service. Rather, a secondary tension existed between the educational potential of the technology and the institutional site— its communal and cultural norms.

As an educational innovation emerging at the beginning of the 21st century, the Virtual Schooling Service is a transitional learning space, a hybrid of two models: industrial and "information age" education. Virtual schooling combines new and old communications technologies, and new and old learning and teaching practices, as part of the subtle shift that is occurring from print to digital culture. It imitates some features of the older medium, but also claims to improve them. Remediation comprises cultural competition between or among technologies and activity systems. Whilst virtual schooling attempts to refashion the learning space by eliminating the need for the physical presence of teachers, it nevertheless retains some of the social and pedagogical practices of the industrial activity systems from which it is emerging.

Enhancing Pedagogical Effectiveness in the Virtual Schooling Service

Three recommendations relating to pedagogy were made in the review:

- that delivery teachers be provided with time release for development of curricular materials;
- that Virtual Schooling Service teachers undergo tailored professional development in the productive pedagogies framework to address pedagogical repertoires that are currently limiting the potential of virtual schooling; and
- that delivery teachers and coaches work more closely together in providing a more integrated service for students.

Of particular interest are the initiatives now underway to address the second of these recommendations. Since the release of the report, the Virtual Schooling

Service has facilitated an induction on *Productive Pedagogies* for new employees. This will be followed with professional development for all virtual teachers. The aim of the professional development is not to adopt *Productive Pedagogies* as a formulaic solution to enhancing pedagogy in virtual schooling, but to develop a contextualized, virtual schooling version of *Productive Pedagogies*—a potentially timely and valuable contribution to virtual education.

Acknowledgments

The authors wish to acknowledge their colleagues, Professor Allan Luke, Dr. Mark Bahr, and Mr. Ray Land, along with the staff, students, and schools involved in the Virtual Schooling Service for their participation in and contributions to the original research project.

References

Engeström, Y. (1999). Activity Theory and individual and social transformation. In Y. Engeström, R. Miettinen, & R. Punamaki (Eds.), *Perspectives on Activity Theory* (pp. 19-38). Cambridge, MA: Cambridge University Press.

Kapitzke, C. & Pendergast, D. (In press). Virtual schooling: Productive pedagogies or pedagogical possibilities? *Teachers College Record.*

Leontiev, A. N. (1981). The problem of activity in psychology. In J. Wertsch (Ed.), *The Concept of Activity in Soviet Psychology.* Armonk, NY: Sharpe.

Lingard, B., Ladwig, J., Mills, M., Bahr, M., Chant, D., Warry, M., Ailwood, J., Capeness, R., Christie, P., Gore, J., Hayes, D., & Luke, A. (2001). *The Queensland School Reform Longitudinal Study Supplementary Material.* Brisbane, Australia: Education Queensland.

Lundin, R., Elliott, B., & Richardson, A. (2000). *The Queensland Virtual Schooling Service: An Evaluation of the Pilot Project. January-June 2000.* Brisbane, Australia: Department of Education.

Newmann, F.M. & Associates (1996). *Authentic Achievement: Restructuring Schools for Intellectual Quality*. San Francisco, CA: Jossey-Bass.

Nunan, T. (1992). *Student Support as a Factor Affecting the Quality of Australian Distance Education: The Findings of the Project to Investigate Quality and Standards in Distance Education*. Institute of Distance Education: Deakin University.

Pendergast, D., Kapitzke, C., Land, R., Luke, A., & Bahr, M. (2002). *Virtual Schooling Service Pilot – Two Year Review*. Brisbane, Australia: The University of Queensland.

Vygotsky, L. (1981). The instrumental method in psychology. In J. Wertsch (Ed.), *The Concept of Activity in Soviet Psychology*. Armonk, NY: Sharpe.

Appendix A

Source: Education Queensland, see http://education.qld.gov.au/corporate/newbasics/html/pedagogies/pedagog.html

Recognition of Difference

Cultural Knowledges are valued when more than one cultural group is present and *given status* within the curriculum. Cultural groups can be distinguished by gender, ethnicity, race, religion, economic status, or youth.

Are diverse cultural knowledges brought into play in the lesson?

Inclusivity is identified by the degree to which non-dominant groups are represented in classroom practices by participation.

Are there deliberate attempts made to increase the participation of all students of different backgrounds?

Narrative in lessons is identified by an emphasis in teaching and in student responses on such things as the use of personal stories, biographies, historical accounts, literary, and cultural texts.

Is the teaching principally narrative or expository?

Group Identity is manifested when differences and group identities are both positively developed and recognised while at the same time a sense of community is created. This requires going beyond a simple politics of tolerance.

Does the teaching build a sense of "community" and identity?

Citizenship is developed when the teacher elaborates the rights and responsibilities of groups and individuals in a democratic society and facilitates its practice both inside and outside the classroom.

Are there attempts to engage or foster active citizenship?

Connectedness

Connectedness to the World measures the extent to which the lesson has value and meaning beyond the instructional context, exhibiting connection to the larger social context within which students live.

Does the lesson and the assigned work have any resemblance to or connection to "real-life" contexts?

Problem-Based Curriculum is identified by lesson in which students are presented with a specific real, practical or hypothetical problem (or set of problems) to solve.

Does the lesson focus on the identification and solving of intellectual and/ or real world problems?

Knowledge Integration is identified when knowledge is connected across subject, boundaries do not exist.

Does the lesson range across diverse fields, disciplines and paradigms?

Background Knowledge is valued when lessons provide explicit links with students' prior experience. This may include community knowledge, local knowledge, personal experience, media and popular culture sources.

Is there an attempt to connect with the students' background knowledge gained from a range of sources?

Intellectual Quality

Higher-Order Thinking requires students to manipulate information and ideas in ways that transform their meaning and implications. This transformation occurs when students combine facts and ideas in order to synthesize, general-ize, explain, hypothesize or arrive at some conclusion or interpretation. Manipulating information and ideas through these processes allows students to solve problems and discover new (for them) meanings and understandings.

Is higher order thinking and critical analysis occurring?

Deep Knowledge concerns the central ideas of a topic or discipline. Knowledge is deep or thick because such knowledge is judged to be crucial to a topic or discipline.

Does the lesson engage with operational fields in any depth, detail or levels of specificity?

Deep Understanding is shown when students develop relatively complex understanding and demonstrate them by discovering relationships, solving problems, constructing explanations, and drawing conclusions.

Does the students' work and response evidence depth of understanding of concepts or ideas?

Substantive Conversation is evident when there is considerable teacher-student and student-student interaction about the ideas of a substantive topic; the interaction is reciprocal, and promotes coherent shared understanding.

Does classroom talk break out of the IRE pattern and lead to sustained dialogue between students and between teachers and students?

Knowledge as Problematic involves presenting an understanding of knowledge as being constructed, and hence subject to political, social and cultural influences and implications.

Are students critiquing and second-guessing texts, ideas and knowledge?

MetaLanguage instruction is evident when there are high levels of talk about: talk and writing; how written and spoken texts work; specific technical vocabulary and words; how sentences work or don't work; meaning structures and text structures; and issues around how discourses and ideologies work in speech and writing.

Are aspects of language, grammar, technical vocabulary being foregrounded?

Supportive Environment

Student Control examines the degree of student influence on the nature of activities and the way they are implemented.

Do students have any "say" in the pace, direction or outcomes of the lesson?

Social Support is present in classes when the teacher supports students by conveying high expectations for all students: these expectations include that it is necessary to take risks and try hard to master challenging academic work; that all members of the class can learn important knowledge and skills; and that climate of mutual respect among all members of the class contributes to achievement by all.

Is the classroom a socially supportive, positive environment?

Engagement is identified by on-task behaviours that signal a serious investment in class work; these include attentiveness, doing the assigned work, and showing enthusiasm for this work by taking initiative to raise questions, contribute to group tasks and help peers.

Are students engaged and on-task?

Self-Regulation by students is high when teachers are not making or not having to make statements that aim to discipline students' behaviour or to regulate students' movements and dispositions.

Is the direction of student behaviour implicit and self-regulatory or explicit?

Explicit Criteria are frequent, detailed and specific statements about what it is students are to do in order to achieve. This may involve overall statements regarding tasks or assignments, or about performance at different stages in a lesson.

Are criteria for student performance made explicit?

Chapter XI

The Collaborative Critical Incident Tool: Supporting Reflection and Evaluation in a Web Community

John M. Carroll
Virginia Tech, USA

Dennis C. Neale
Virginia Tech, USA

Philip L. Isenhour
Virginia Tech, USA

Abstract

We describe an evaluation tool used by teachers and researchers to study the impact of computer-mediated collaborative and communication technologies used in K-12 education. Standard usability engineering methods and tools focus on individual users at a single workstation. Networked collaborative systems, however, present the challenge of multiple users interacting at a variety of times and places. We developed a Web forum tool to capture and display user critical incident reports and threaded discussions of these reports by users, evaluators and system developers. Our Collaborative Critical Incident Tool (CCIT) is effective at evoking detailed usability evaluation information, as well as reflective analysis of usability issues from diverse points of view among stakeholders in the system.

Introduction

In this chapter we describe an evaluation tool used by teachers and researchers to study the impact of computer-mediated collaborative and communication technologies used in K-12 education. Standard usability engineering methods and tools focus on individual users at a single workstation. Networked collaborative systems, however, present the challenge of multiple users interacting at a variety of times and places. We developed a Web forum tool to capture and display critical incident reports and threaded discussions identified and reported by users, evaluators and system developers. Our Collaborative Critical Incident Tool (CCIT) is effective at evoking detailed usability evaluation information, as well as reflective analysis of usability issues from diverse points of view among stakeholders in the system.

Evaluating the quality and effectiveness of user interaction in networked collaborative systems is difficult. There is more than one user, and typically the users are not physically proximal. The "session" to be evaluated cannot be comprehensively observed or monitored at any single display, keyboard or processor. It is typical that none of the human participants has an overall view of the interaction (a common source of problems for such interactions). The users are not easily accessible either to evaluators or to one another.

There is no simple solution to the evaluation problem for networked collaborative systems. To a considerable extent, evaluation work in this domain focuses on investigations of techniques in isolation (for example, substitution of multi-user widgets for single user widgets; Begole, Rosson, & Shaffer, 1999) or on rather coarse, aggregate assessments of systems (for example, quantitative measurement of volume of accesses as an indicator of user acceptance; Rosson, Carroll & Messner, 1996). It would be useful to supplement these sources of evaluation data with detailed, qualitative reports of personal usage experiences. But it is difficult to do this because the use of these systems is distributed in time and space.

In this chapter we describe an evaluation method that recruits the already-pervasive medium of Web forums to support collection and discussion of *critical incidents*: episodes that stand out in memory as being especially positive or negative. We describe a Web forum tool created to support this discussion, the CCIT. The notion of "critical incident" is adapted from Flanagan (1954) who debriefed test pilots to inventory flight episodes. Flanagan's method has become a mainstay of human factors evaluation; it has been used extensively to study the causes of human error in aviation, military systems and medicine (Meister, 1985; Shattuck & Woods, 1994). Many variations of the technique have been developed for formative usability evaluations of human-computer interactions (Carroll, Koenemann-Belliveau, Rosson, & Singley, 1993; del Galdo, Williges, Williges, & Wixon, 1987; Neale & Kies, 2000). For example, in "remote" usability testing, users can submit online critical incident forms to evaluators during a session (e.g., Thompson & Williges, 2000).

Our method is a social-participatory variation of the critical incident technique, and contrasts with other approaches in several ways. For example, we follow other Internet forums, like newsgroups, in attributing contributions to authors; that is, contributions are not anonymous. Anonymity is important in contexts where there are possible punitive consequences of reporting an incident, or retribution from regulatory or enforcement entities, as can be the case in aviation or medical incident reporting. However, in circumstances where users play active roles on the development team, anonymity is often neither necessary nor desirable. In our case study, critical incident reports often became critical incident discussions among users, and among users, developers and evaluators.

Users can post a critical incident report to the forum at any time. Subsequently, other users, as well as evaluators and system developers, can post threaded replies. Users who post critical incident reports may then post comments on the replies posted by developers and evaluators. In other critical incident approaches, it is not typical to interact with users beyond collecting reports. In particular, users do not have the opportunity to interact with one another to develop interpretations of their own data. However, permitting follow-up questions and other conversational elaboration and refinement of original reports can make the data richer. The CCIT exploits the affordances of networked communication, namely, that critical incident information can flow in both directions, and that users, developers, and evaluators can work together to improve designs. While users increasingly are involved in requirements development (Carroll, Rosson, Chin, & Koenemann, 1998) and early design (Kyng, 1995; Muller et al., 1995), it is not typical currently to involve them directly in the analysis and interpretation stages of evaluation.

An example of the kind of critical incident report we are concerned with might be a teacher's description of how a group of students struggled with leadership and division of labor issues as they organized themselves to carry out a physics experiment with lenses and mirrors on reflection and refraction. Using the CCIT, another teacher could post an interpretation about how a particular impasse arose, and suggestions about how to help the students resolve their issues and continue making progress. In our research, the groups of students typically include members at two or more school sites who work together using Internet tools. Thus, the critical incidents and their resolutions often involve computer and communications technology interventions.

In the balance of this chapter we describe the development of the CCIT. The tool was motivated by the challenge of evaluating the use of a regional infrastructure to support school science collaborations. We describe the development of the tool, illustrate its use with a summary of some sample data, and discuss design tradeoffs we are aware of now and our immediate further plans.

Background: The LiNC Project

Our study was carried out in the context of the LiNC project (for "Learning in Networked Communities"). This project is a partnership between Virginia Tech and the public schools of Montgomery County, Virginia, USA. The objective of the project is to provide a high-quality communications infrastructure to support collaborative learning. Montgomery County is located in the rural Appalachian region of southwestern Virginia; in some schools, physics is only offered every other year, and to classes of only three to five students. Our initial vision was to give these students better access to peers through networked collaboration (Carroll et al., 1998).

Over six years (1995-2000), we developed and investigated the virtual school, a Java-based networked learning environment, emphasizing support for the coordination of synchronous and asynchronous collaboration, including planning, note taking, experimentation, data analysis, and report writing. The central tools are a collaborative notebook and a workbench. The notebook allows students to organize projects into shared and personal pages; it can be accessed collaboratively or individually by remote or proximal students. The software employs component architecture that allows notebook "pages" of varying types (e.g., formatted text, images, shared whiteboard). The workbench allows groups including remote members to jointly control simulation experiments and analyze data. The virtual school also incorporates email, real-time chat, and video conferencing communication channels (see Eales, Neale, & Carroll, 1999; Isenhour, Carroll, Neale, Rosson, & Dunlap, 2000; Koenemann, Carroll, Shaffer, Rosson, & Abrams, 1999).

The project included six middle and high school science teachers, and about a dozen university students and faculty. The teachers worked at two middle schools and two high schools. One high school and one middle school were located in the town of Blacksburg, the major town in Montgomery County. The other two schools were located in a rural area about 15 miles from Blacksburg. The teachers taught the standard Virginia physics and physical science curriculum to students in grades 6, 8 and 12. Two hundred to three hundred students per year participated in the project.

The university participants can be divided into principal investigators, developers and evaluators. The principal investigators were academic faculty at Virginia Tech. They helped to identify goals and strategies, but were not regularly involved in day-to-day project activities. Developers were research associates and graduate research assistants in computer science who were responsible for designing, implementing, installing, and maintaining software. Evaluators were research associates and graduate research assistants in computer science, education, human factors and psychology who were responsible for assisting teachers and students in using the technology, for observing and recording classroom activities, and for analyzing usage data.

Through the course of this project we have found that the virtual school technology transforms classroom activity in many ways. For example, the dependencies in class schedules among various schools entailed by networked collaboration are alien to both school administrative procedures and teacher professional practice. This is particularly interesting since no one anticipated it. Before the virtual school enabled rich, real-time collaboration, teachers and administrators were enthusiastic without qualification, now that the possibility exists, complications are more apparent. A more technical-level example of how the virtual school has transformed classroom activity is the emergent importance of community mentoring. The teachers we work with have a significant history of recruiting community mentors for school science projects. However, it has turned out that the virtual school provides an attractive communications infrastructure for mentoring; it allows mentors to interact with groups of school students without having to always travel to school sites (Gibson, Neale, Van Metre, & Carroll, 1999.)

The pervasive and systemic effects of the virtual school on school administration, teachers' practices and classroom activity comprise a formidable object for evaluation. Thus, to evaluate a mentoring interaction, one needs to understand the low-level, moment-by-moment actions, perceptions, plans, interpretations, and experiences of students and mentors in a series of collaborative sessions that can extend over several months. One needs to understand how each of these sessions supports the students' learning of science concepts and skills, how they support the teachers' curriculum objectives and government standards of learning, and how they support the mentors' personal and professional goals and intrinsic interest in participating in school activities.

The Development and Use of the Collaborative Critical Incident Tool

Requirements Interviews. Our initial concept for a critical incident reporting tool derived from two prior web-based forum projects. We developed the Blacksburg Electronic Village (BEV) HistoryBase as a design history system for the development of a community networking project (Carroll, Rosson, Cohill, & Schorger, 1995). The HistoryBase presents a collection of design documents, public relations materials and community reports describing the development of the BEV from a variety of viewpoints. Users, in this case residents of Blacksburg, Virginia, were able to post comments to any of these documents. We developed the Web StoryBase as a forum for stories about personal Internet experiences, a shared archive for the vast and fragmented "community" of the World Wide Web (Rosson et al., 1996).

As the first step in developing a critical incident reporting tool and forum for users, we conducted requirements interviews with four LiNC teachers. There were two meetings, each involved two teachers and two developers. We briefly discussed the notion of providing the teachers with a tool to post their classroom observations, and to participate in discussing the observations of their colleagues. They were all initially positive about this concept, indeed, all offered examples of how such a tool might have been useful to them in recent days and weeks. We, the developers, showed them some simple screen layouts (HTML form mockups printed on paper), and asked them to consider how they might use such a tool.

In our meetings with the teachers, we emphasized (1) that a critical incident reporting forum would be a more direct way to get feedback on the virtual school software to the developers; (2) that it would provide a means for developers to propose new functions or to describe problems and work-arounds for existing functions; (3) that it would provide a means of sharing experiences with other teachers; (4) that it would create a searchable history of classroom experience that might be used in the future to plan classroom activities; and (5) that it would provide a remote window into the various classrooms for the project's evaluation people. We showed them several paper mock-ups of possible screen designs. One of these was just a layout template of input fields for author's name, author's email, a set of pre-defined classification keys, and fill-in fields for classification keys, incident date, incident location, and incident description. Another was a more streamlined version, without fields for classification keywords. We also mocked-up the presentation of a posted critical incident report; this mock-up was pretty densely hyperlinked.

The teachers raised several issues. They were concerned that the critical incident reports might be quite lengthy, and that it would be difficult to indicate the specific portion of a report to which a comment was directed. They wanted a fast-path function to contribute a report similar to one already submitted, the ability to say "ditto" was the way they put it. They asked that the tool provide teacher and class period identifier information as automatically as possible, to minimize the overhead of contributing. They emphasized the importance of being able to print out critical incident reports and discussions. Perhaps because we had (optimistically) emphasized the volume of data that might eventually be produced, and because they had all had significant recent experience with World Wide Web search engines, the teachers were concerned about how to manage long lists of hits. They responded to our paper mock-ups of screen designs by elaborating categories of what we had called keys: They suggested a "Type of Impact" classification with the initial categories technology, education and social interaction; they suggested an "Importance" category with the values low, medium and high; they suggested an "Activities" category which would have as values the names of the various in-class projects that teachers were using.

We have adopted an incremental approach to developing the Collaborative Critical Incident Tool. We focused on developing fairly lightweight support for the core tasks of contribution and discussion of critical incidents. We wanted to examine the feasibility and potential utility of these basic capabilities for involving users in the evaluation of networked collaborative systems.

Design of the Tool. The CCIT is a threaded discussion forum used primarily by teachers, evaluators and developers in the project. Although only those who directly observed critical incidents reported them, everyone participated in the discussion of incidents. The root of each thread is a critical incident report, consisting of a description of a critical incident and an author comment. Users can post comments to a critical incident report, and comments on comments. Authors of reports and comments specify short-hand descriptions that serve as subject titles for each item. These short descriptions are used as items in an indented list that provides a complete mapping of the critical incident database; in the map, the short-hands are link anchors providing single-click access to reports and comments.

Access to the CCIT is protected by password. The first screen displays a statement of purpose and definition of *critical incident*, a list of the critical incidents currently posted — listed by their author-supplied names, and a link to add a new critical incident, as in Figure 1.

When a user selects a posted critical incident for the first time, the critical incident description and author comment are displayed, and the user is prompted to rate the critical incident on a 7-point scale, anchored by "not critical" and "critical" with respect to usability, learning, collaboration, communication, and/or teacher practices. The criticality rating is indicated by selecting a radio button, as in Figure 2. Once the rating is saved, the user jumps to the discussion forum for that critical incident.

The discussion forum displays the critical incident name, description, and author comment at the top of the page, followed by a table of the obtained criticality ratings from all users who have viewed that report. Below this is a link to "Add comment," followed by an indented list mapping of the discussion so far. Figure 3 presents an example.

*Figure 1: Main Page for Collaborative Critical Incident Tool *

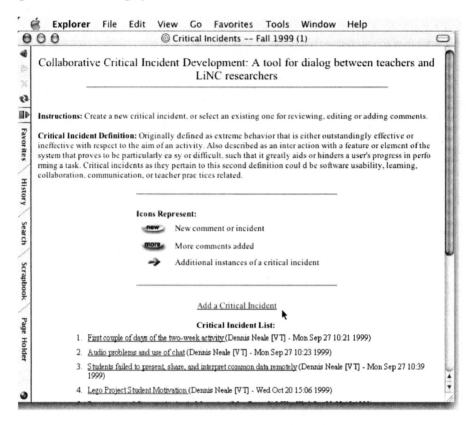

* A statement of purpose and definition of critical incident are displayed permanently with a key to special symbols (new comment or incident, more comments added to an incident report already posted, additional instances of a critical incident). Below this orientation information is the list of critical incidents currently posted — listed by their author-supplied names (only the top of the list is visible in the figure). At the bottom of the list is a link to add a new critical incident.

In Figure 3, a sixth-grade teacher has posted a critical incident report with the name "LEGOS-levers," saying that some eighth graders in a different school had prepared a lesson on levers for her students. As a comment on her own report, she added that she thought the scope of the lesson might have been too ambitious; her students could not finish it during the class period. She suggested that she and the eighth grade teacher might develop a pre-test to ascertain what the students know before such a lesson. This would also be useful in assessing what they learn from the lesson.

Figure 2: Criticality Rating Indicated by Selecting a Radio Button *

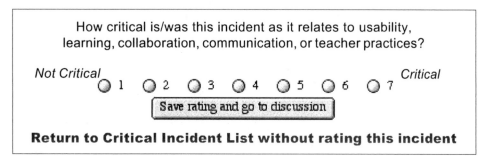

* *When a user selects a posted critical incident for the first time, the critical incident description and author comment are displayed, and the user is asked to rate the critical incident on a 7-point scale, anchored by "not critical" and "critical" with respect to usability, learning, collaboration, communication, and/or teacher practices.*

The posted discussion of the LEGOS-levers critical incident report has focused on the feasibility and utility of pre-testing. An evaluator posted a comment asking how pre-testing is related to current debates about assessment in educational outcomes, and whether teachers ever do systematic pre-testing. An eighth grade teacher, not one involved in the levers lesson, responded to this comment, saying that pre-testing is not used widely because it is one more task in an already-overloaded curriculum, and that the student differentiation it describes is difficult to make use of because it would require an even greater variety of tracks and options in the curriculum.

Comments are organized into threads presented as indented lists. Items are grouped under the comment to which they refer in order of submission. Thus, in Figure 3, the eighth grade teacher's comment was the first response posted to the evaluator's comment on new forms of assessment. At the level of critical incident reports (e.g., Figure 3), only the titles of comments are displayed. To view a comment users select the comment title from the list. The full comment is then displayed, embedded in the list context, that is, with all of the preceding and following comment titles in the view. Thus, users are able to understand the context of a particular comment by maintaining a frame of reference to the entire discussion. This is useful when discussion threads are lengthy and when they involve embedded threading.

Users can reply to a critical incident or to a comment using a form which prompts for a name and a text pane which accepts ASCII or HTML. We used the "Re:" convention, common in email clients, for suggesting a default comment

Figure 3: Main Page for the LEGOS-Levers Critical Incident

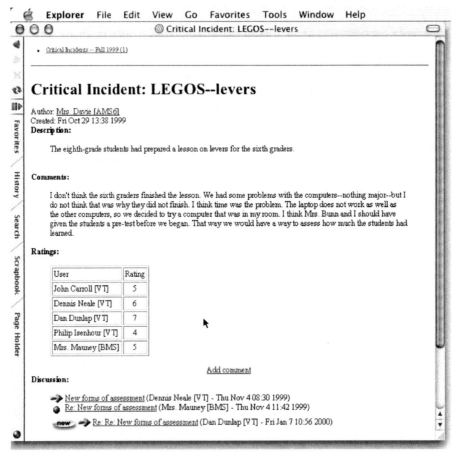

*   *At the top of the page is a link to the parent page (the list of Fall 1999 critical incidents — Figure 1). The critical incident description and comment provided by the author, a middle school science teacher, appear next, followed by the ratings of those project members who have viewed the critical incident report. At the bottom of the figure is the discussion to date, consisting of a comment by an evaluator and a response from a second middle school teacher.*

name, and assume ASCII text as a default. When responding to a prior comment, the comment being referred to is always displayed in the form. We found that users had to continually jump back to what they were commenting on if the item was not displayed while composing the comment. We want to encourage users to bring additional evaluation data into these discussions, so we also provide a check box to indicate that the comment describes another occurrence of the critical incident. Comments which include further critical incident data are subsequently marked in the indented list display of the discussion by being prefixed with a special icon. Adding a critical incident report also triggers a form, in this case consisting of a prompt for a name and two text panes, for a critical incident description and author comment. The description area is intended to be an objective account of the circumstances surrounding the incident. The author comment section is used for providing a subjective assessment of the incident, including causes leading to the incident, implications for users and the system, possible re-design solutions, etc.

The rating display only appears on a user's first viewing of a critical incident. Subsequently, selecting a critical incident name in the list of critical incidents on the initial screen causes a direct jump to that critical incident's discussion forum. The list of critical incidents is annotated with a "new" icon when a critical incident has not yet been viewed by the user, by a "more" icon when the critical incident has been viewed before but items have since been added to that critical incident's discussion, and by an "additional instance" icon when a comment has been author-classified as including additional critical incident data. These icons help users understand whether they need to rate the new incident or simply view additional content. In both cases the icons immediately alert users to new content.

The initial screen also contains notification and configuration functions. The notification function provides a form to create an email notification that a critical incident report has been posted. The form lists all posted critical incident reports. Check boxes are used to indicate that a critical incident name should be included in the notification. The email that is generated includes the URL for the CCIT to facilitate its access by recipients. The default recipient is the LiNC project mailing list, and the typical use of this function is to notify project members that a new critical incident has been posted in order to solicit their comments. The configuration function allows users to customize a variety of display parameters and privileges. Groups of contributors, administrators and viewers can be defined, and restrictions on re-editing contributed incidents and comments can be defined. In addition, header text, footer text and icons can be specified. Access to the CCIT configuration is typically restricted to those users in an administrator group.

Example Critical Incident. Figure 4 presents a typical example of a critical incident report. In this case, a middle school teacher posts a comment about a group of her students working on a bridge project with a group of high school students at a different school location. She describes it as a "continuing saga" because she has posted other critical incidents about the group previously, and this one reflects a shift in her viewpoint and understanding of the group's collaborative interaction.

The context for this critical incident report included several other reports and provoked further discussions addressed to perceived problems in the networked collaboration among students in a middle school and a high school. Students and teachers in both schools felt that their remote counterparts were not contributing enough. Interestingly, the underlying issue was more a matter of collaborative awareness than of cooperation: Session logs and in-class observations showed that quite a lot of relevant work and interaction was taking place. The teachers had concluded that the collaboration had broken down because their students were not video conferencing, but in fact students were

Figure 4: Example Critical Incident Drawn from the Spring 1999 Database

Critical Incident: Bridge collaboration -- the continuing saga

Author: Mrs. Mauney [Blacksburg Middle School]
Created: Thu May 13 10:18 1999

Description:

Yesterday, the group of three boys in my classroom who are working with two of Mark's kids actually tested their bridge in class. Shanan recorded it digitally for the benefit of the partners at Blacksburg High School (BHS). With a little prompting from me one of the group members got on the VS early this morning to post their results. I was expecting a cursory sentence or two but he took his job far more seriously and actually drew a picture of their bridge to go along with the explanation. He then wrote out the procedure they had used so the partners at BHS could compare their methods. He was disappointed that the digital pictures weren't there because he wanted the BHS guys to see what happened.

Comments:

Several things surprised me about this scenario (dare I use the word)? The guys here and one in particular were really surprised their bridge held up 36 pounds of weight -- he expected much less -- there was real excitement in their results. I think this is why they were fairly anxious to share this with the other guys at BHS. I feel certain they are hoping the high school bridge does much worse -- interestingly enough each group predicted the other group would do better. At any rate this group has been very interesting because their level of interaction has fluctuated significantly and the early problems that involved personalities seem to have been forgiven if not forgotten. These groups actually have had more give and take than I realized and in the end they may actually be a group that really relied on each other for shared data necessary to write up their experiment.

using chat to discuss hypotheses and bridge construction materials. The evaluators used the CCIT to share this information.

This example demonstrates the utility of critical incident discussions in developing shared understanding of usage experiences in networked collaborative systems. The incident described would have been difficult for the other teacher or for the evaluators to fully understand without this type of extended and enriched discussion. Although other methods, such as interviewing, can elicit rich information, the other teacher or the evaluators would have had to ask just the right questions. This is particularly difficult for teachers as users since teachers work in relative isolation from professional peers; not even colleagues within a school know one another's classroom context in detail (Tyrack & Cuban, 1995). It is even more difficult in our situation since the teachers are working with a novel networking infrastructure and application software. An asynchronous critical incident discussion allows the description and analysis to be incrementally developed, first through the initial written report, and then through the ensuing interaction with colleagues.

A total of nine people (including teachers, evaluators and developers) rated and participated in the discussion evoked by this critical incident report. On the criticality scale of 1 to 7, participants' mean rating was 4.8. Following the initial posting, evaluators made five comments, teachers contributed four, developers two. The structure of the comments is diagrammed in Figure 5. The original report elicited three direct responses, one from another teacher (the teacher whose students were collaborating with those of the teacher who posted the report), one from an evaluator, and one from a developer. The teacher's response elicited a response from the teacher who had originally posted the critical incident report, which in turn elicited a response from an evaluator. The developer's response to the original critical incident report elicited two direct responses, one from the evaluator who responded to the original report, and one from the teacher who responded to the original report. And so on. The critical incident discussion involved three main issues: One was problems of managing remote collaborations among students (Issue 1), a second was competition among students (Issue 2), and a third was complications of gender (Issue 3). As indicated in Figure 5, Issues 2 and 3, competition and gender, tended to be discussed together.

The middle school teacher who posted the incident was pleased, and a bit surprised, that her students are apparently collaborating successfully with the high school students. The cooperating high school teacher is still skeptical; in

Figure 5: Discussion Structure of Comments Posted to a Critical Incident Report

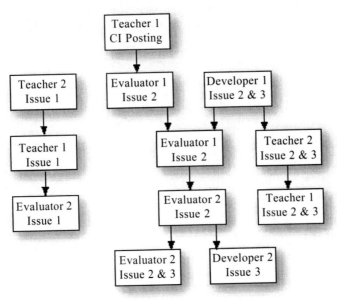

his response to the critical incident report, he suggests that his students just have more experience with collaborative interaction, and more refined ways of talking about it, but may not actually be doing all that much or benefiting from it. The middle school teacher responds that in networked collaborations much goes on that teachers cannot directly observe: "My guys are pretty quiet and don't require the level of attention that others demand so its easy to overlook the fact that they probably knew what they were doing all along." The two teachers did not finally resolve their different perspectives in this interaction, but at least they expressed their different views. This is the first step towards the development of a shared understanding, and it places the issues under discussion before all other members of the project team.

Competition (Issue 2) became a moderately controversial discussion thread. One of the evaluators suggested that a cross-school competition might increase student involvement in the bridge design project. Both teachers strongly objected to this idea. The high school teacher (Teacher 2) declared, "Regardless of how nicely anybody asks, I'll never have competition as a part of my classroom...on any level; no matter how subtle." Through the discussion, however, the idea of competition got transformed into *comparing results*, and the concept became generally accepted as an important technique for facilitating distributed learning. This, in turn, led to a general conclusion about the design of activities for the virtual school: Networked collaborations should integrate physical sub-activities at each of the collaborating sites, and each group should have a result or conclusion that is their own, and which they can share and compare with their remote partners.

Gender (Issue 3) is often raised in discussions of networked interactions (e.g., Sproull & Kiesler, 1991). The student group discussed in the original critical incident was all boys. One evaluator suggested that a propensity for competitiveness by males might have contributed to the group's apparent motivation to share and compare their results with their high school counterparts. The group's teacher continued to reject this account, and interpreted the group's behavior in terms of personalities and personal motivation. The example incident described above illustrates one of 15 critical incidents reported and discussed over a 57-day period. A separate paper presents a detailed analysis of the use of the CCIT and its role in our evaluation of the virtual school (Neale et al., 2000).

Experience and Observations

Like any forum, the CCIT requires deliberate administration. There was no pre-existing practice among the LiNC project members of accessing the forum and contributing critical incident reports and discussion. We made a concerted effort in the spring semester of 1999 to identify and post critical incidents for which we expected some difference of opinion.

Ironically, in a close-knit group there are often social obstacles to reporting and discussing some potentially significant critical incidents. For us one such type of critical incident is that in which teachers' classroom practices appear to be in conflict with the overall LiNC project goals of supporting collaborations among students. For example, several critical incident reports described problems with schedules and assignments. Schedules and assignments are difficult to manage even within a single classroom. When students in different schools collaborate, multiple teachers must manage schedules and assignments, and must coordinate their management. This is a good example of the sort of problem the teachers wanted to work on, but which they also cannot afford to get wrong.

For our type of technology intervention to succeed in the school context, it is extremely important for us to identify and address collisions with teacher goals and practices. The teachers we work with are sometimes caught between their LiNC-oriented goals and their immediate responsibilities to their students and school administration. The teachers want to explore new teaching practices and classroom activities enabled by the virtual school, but they are also expert practitioners operating within the context of current schools. They have immediate-term job responsibilities and well-established and proven-effective skills to meet those responsibilities. When there is a conflict between project goals and standard practice, they must often choose standard practice. But they are reluctant to discuss these conflicts in person.

We found that teachers were more likely to address these issues using the CCIT, and posting this kind of critical incident attracted lively discussion from the teachers as well as other project members. In some specific ways it seemed superior to trying to confront these important but awkward issues face-to-face: Asynchronous forums allow contributors to refine their comments until they have expressed their views precisely as intended, and thereby reduce the chance of mis-speaking and unintentionally polarizing the discussion or embarrassing a colleague. In general, we have found that the best critical incidents are those that address moderately controversial issues: The most and the least controversial critical incident reports are those most likely to be neglected by colleagues. For example, evaluators raised the issue of differences in teachers' strategies for intervening during distributed student group work. In face-to-face meetings, teachers were always careful not to criticize their colleagues' teaching approaches, even though there were concerns that differences among teachers sometimes caused problems for students. The CCIT allowed teachers to express these concerns in a less confrontational manner, giving balanced rationale for differences in approaches.

The findings provided in this chapter focus on 15 critical incidents reported over a 57-day period. This material represents typical usage of the tool for a classroom project. In the data presented the "Evaluator" group included all members of the research team. Critical incidents were categorized into software usability, learning, collaboration, communication, and teacher practices. Table 1 provides a summary of critical incidents reported. The table shows the order of submission, who submitted the incident, the number of comments, the structure of the dialog, and the length of the discussion. Breadth indicates the discussion broadening from prior comments and ideas, and depth is a measure of the discussion deepening on the same topic.

Table 1: Summary of Critical Incident Contributions

CI Submitter	Evaluator Comments	Teacher Comments	Breadth x Depth	Discussion (Days)
1 Evaluator	2	2	3 x 2	12
2 Evaluator	5	2	3 x 3	12
3 Teacher	4	1	4 x 2	12
4 Evaluator	3	0	2 x 2	6
5 Evaluator	5	3	4 x 3	17
6 Teacher	5	3	5 x 3	36
7 Teacher	3	2	4 x 2	15
8 Evaluator	5	8	4 x 8	49
9 Teacher	3	1	2 x 2	2
10 Evaluator	8	5	6 x 4	18
11 Evaluator	7	10	6 x 6	35
12 Teacher	7	4	5 x 4	7
13 Teacher	3	2	3 x 3	6
14 Evaluator	1	2	2 x 2	3
15 Evaluator	2	3	4 x 3	2
Totals	63	48		

Our original expectation was that teachers would be the main providers of critical incident reports, drawing from their first-hand classroom experience, and that developers and evaluators would be involved more as discussants. As it turned out, teachers often became involved as discussants for critical incidents contributed by evaluators and developers. For this project, nine of the 15 critical incidents reported were submitted by evaluators and developers; six were submitted by teachers. Four of the initial five critical incidents were submitted by evaluators. To this extent, the researchers seeded the activity, and subsequently teacher participation increased. It did turn out that contributions by teachers typically brought to light facts and perspectives we would not otherwise have had access to.

Teachers were able to contribute substantially without any training. We provided a description and comment area in the CCIT to help provide structure for the reporting of incidents. Initially we were concerned about whether teachers could make the distinction between an objective description and subjective interpretation. We wanted to gather both the facts constituting events, but also relevant background and perspective for understanding the larger context in which individual events occurred. The format was successfully used by both evaluators and teachers. In fact, teachers often followed the format more closely than evaluators. Teachers were very explicit about what constituted an event and how the event was contextualized by concomitant details and interpretation. Evaluators were sometimes more theoretical, incorporating interpretations that reflected integration across issues and data.

Evaluators often posted reports of things they have observed but not fully understood in order to elicit clarifications and explanations from the teachers. This was an extremely useful channel for the evaluators to have. It was like bringing all the classroom personnel together each week for a data interpretation workshop — something we could not actually do. In one case teachers provided critical information regarding deadlines slipping on project deliverables. This helped evaluators construct a model of collaborative workspace awareness that included components for project planning tools. Ratings also provided evaluators with valuable information about how much agreement there was concerning the significance of a critical incident to the various stakeholders. Table 2 shows the mean ratings and standard deviations for incidents broken down by evaluators versus teachers. This table provides a measure of initial quantitative agreement between participants.

Teachers post information that is unique to their classrooms and often inaccessible to evaluators and other teachers. Sharing this information helps them explain to other teachers and researchers why they took a particular action that had consequences for project outcomes. For example, a teacher reported a conversation with her students that took place at a time other than during project work, where her students explained why they were not willing to fully work with remote students. The teacher used this incident to explain her actions for not forcing the students to collaborate. In a single classroom or for teachers collaborating in the same building, these issues naturally get worked out. The evaluators and the remote teacher could have easily misconstrued the circumstances leading to breakdowns in this project group.

Commenting on reports submitted by others also turned out to be a role shared across researchers and teachers. Out of the 111 comments contributed to 15 critical incident reports for this project, teachers contributed 43% and researchers 57%. We found it encouraging that commenting tended to cross the boundaries of subgroup constituencies. Figure 6 shows the direction of responses between evaluators and teachers. Evaluators responded more to teachers than to other evaluators, and teachers responded more to evaluators than to other teachers. Although discussions within the same group often turned

Table 2: Critical Incident Ratings

CI Submitter	Mean Rating 7-point	SD	Mean Evaluator Rating	Mean Teacher Rating
1 Evaluator	4.8	0.46	4.7	5.0
2 Evaluator	6.4	0.53	6.6	6.0
3 Teacher	6.3	0.50	6.3	6.0
4 Evaluator	3.9	1.37	4.6	2.7
5 Evaluator	5.3	0.95	5.6	4.5
6 Teacher	6.0	0.94	6.4	5.7
7 Teacher	5.9	0.93	5.7	6.5
8 Evaluator	5.8	0.67	5.7	6.0
9 Teacher	6.0	0.94	5.4	6.3
10 Evaluator	5.1	1.73	5.7	3.5
11 Evaluator	5.4	0.74	5.2	5.7
12 Teacher	4.8	0.44	4.8	4.7
13 Teacher	6.4	0.53	6.4	6.7
14 Evaluator	4.2	1.20	4.3	4.0
15 Evaluator	4.4	1.51	3.5	5.5
Mean Total Rating:			5.4	5.4

out to be valuable, cross-group interaction was one of our primary objectives for use of the tool. This information turned out to be invaluable for understanding the full context of critical incidents and their consequences.

Critical incidents are salient usage events; this is their definition. Thus, it is more or less a given that people will notice critical incidents, and quite likely that they will discuss critical incidents. Members of the LiNC project — teachers, evaluators and developers — have always talked about critical incidents. For example, one or two particularly significant episodes have often been raised for discussion at project meetings. However, all-hands, face-to-face project meetings are rare (about one per month over the past two years). And, in any case, these face-to-face discussions tended to be brief, incompletely documented, and often dominated by the person who first reported the incident. When we began using the CCIT, the discussion length for a critical incident for this project varied from two to 49 days, with the average discussion length for a critical incident being 15 days. Discussing these events over longer periods of time allowed additional evidence supporting or refuting interpretation of an event to surface, and it allowed reflection by all group members.

Figure 6: Direction of Responses to Others in the CCIT

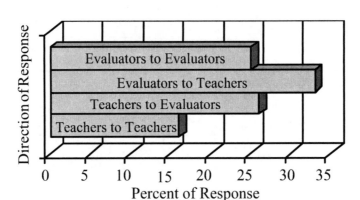

The example critical incident in Figure 4 illustrates this. The high school and middle school students working in this group project appeared to take the project far more seriously as time went along. Fairly subtle and incidental differences in experimentation across locations due to communication errors helped the students learned that procedural changes can cause large outcome differences. The concept-in-action of comparing results from distributed physical experiments emerged through the course of this process. This is a relatively deep concept at this level of science learning.

The role of critical incident reports as a kind of evaluation data has been enhanced tremendously by the CCIT. Reporting no longer is delayed until people meet face-to-face. Discussion is no longer restricted to what can be articulated during a meeting. Participation is no longer limited to who knows the most, who thinks or talks the fastest, or who happens to attend a given face-to-face meeting.

Further Work

We envision several avenues for further development of the CCIT. For example, there are several refinements in the user interface we want to investigate. Once a participant has returned to the CCIT, the "new" and "more" icons simplify the task of locating previously unread content. For lengthy discussions, however, this approach could be augmented by links that let the user jump directly to new comments without having to scroll though the list of titles for previously read comments.

Participants currently give a rating to each incident when they first read the incident. We have used this measure in the evaluation as a global indicator of the severity or significance of the event. And the standard deviations of rating are used as an initial measure of divergence across participants. By looking at inter- (across teachers and evaluators) and intra-group ratings and comparing these with standard deviations, the divergence can be attributed to within or across groups. Although we had planned to use these measures later in the analysis for a broader understanding of the data, they became an important motivating factor in the use of the tool: participants were interested in and motivated by seeing how others rated the incident. The table with ratings gave a quick snapshot of how others perceived an incident. Subsequent discussion sometimes modulated opinions on the criticality of an event, suggesting that the ability to provide a post-discussion rating could be useful. Giving continual feedback in the form of a simple rating with some indication of discrepancies across groups may help orient users globally to how the group feels about an incident at any given time. In addition to each participant's rating, we plan to represent means and standard deviations in the form of simple "overall severity" and "group agreement" scales.

An important area for more strategic development is integration with our virtual school software. Since users typically do not continuously run and reload their web-based forums (as they in effect do with their email clients), they must explicitly return to forums to read new contributions. The CCIT's email notification functionality is an attempt to mitigate this, though it needs to be further automated and perhaps have options to (at the contributor's or reader's request) send notifications for new comments on incidents rather than only for new incidents. Since the teachers, evaluators and developers often work in the virtual school environment, and since many critical incidents are observed in and pertain to this environment, it might be useful to add the ability to open the CCIT easily while reviewing student work, either through a button or menu item in the virtual school notebook or a link on the web-accessible version of notebook content.

Better integration of CCIT with the virtual school might also have implications for the type of critical incident data we can gather through this technique. Currently, most of our critical incidents seem to address larger process issues, for example, regarding the conduct of classroom activities. Through the course of these discussions, design issues for the virtual school software often emerge.

It could be that anchoring the CCIT more directly in the virtual school would have the effect of more directly evoking a greater number of software issues more directly. Another consequence of more direct integration of the CCIT and the virtual school is that we could explore the possibility of making some CCIT discussions accessible to the students participating in the virtual school project.

Another avenue for further work involves representing relationships among critical incidents. Empirical usability studies have shown that the traditional concept of discrete critical incidents with singular, proximal causes can be elaborated. The causes of observable critical incidents are not always discrete, nor are they always proximal to the observed effect. Sets of causally related episodes of user interaction, each of which is itself less than a critical incident, can comprise a "distributed" critical incident (Carroll, Koenemann-Belliveau, Rosson, & Singley, 1993). Such patterns indeed can have powerful and wide-ranging effects on the usability and usefulness of systems. One approach to representing such relationships would be designate a special type of comment in the CCIT to indicate possible relationships to other critical incident reports and to provide links to those reports and their discussion threads.

The current CCIT implementation includes the ability to mark comments that describe additional examples of a critical incident. Users can also manually add links to other critical incident pages, but this requires writing html tags and remembering or copying and pasting URLs. Automating this process, minimally by allowing selection of other comments/incidents by title, would simplify cross-referencing. Keyword searching (a generally useful addition by itself) would also aid location of older relevant incidents and comments.

A final direction is transferring and implementing our model of critical incident reporting and discussion in other K-12 settings, and perhaps beyond school settings. We are currently developing two new K-12 projects that will allow us to explore this. In one project, we are investigating ways to support teacher professional practice and professional development with Internet collaboration tools. One of the classroom practices we are supporting involves gathering student feedback via email after each class discussion. We think a forum could also support teacher professional development through peer discussion of shared incidents. The second project is much like the original LiNC project, but focuses on investigating tools and techniques for enhancing awareness of one's collaborators and shared work. The "new" and "more" images in Figure 1 are examples of support for this kind of awareness (Carroll, Neale, Isenhour, Rosson, & McCrickard, 2003).

We are also trying to develop and apply the model beyond K-12 settings, and in larger scale projects. To this point, the CCIT manages relatively small databases of a couple dozen critical incident discussions. Our core project team currently involves six teachers and five university researchers who are developers and evaluators in various combinations. During the past two school years, our practice has been to create a new CCIT database for each new school year. This raises the question of how the approach can scale to serve larger projects teams who may wish to maintain critical incident databases over longer periods of time. We would not expect critical incident databases to ever raise digital library-scale issues, but we can easily imagine a database of several hundred discussions.

In the HistoryBase project (Carroll et al., 1995), we organized a database of approximately 400 design documents by the date to which they referred. Users interacted with a graphical timeline, selecting a quarter to see a temporally ordered list of documents pertaining to that quarter. For example, selecting the second quarter of 1995 displays list of 69 documents. A larger database of critical incidents could be presented in this manner; the lists associated with quarters would be names of critical incident reports prefixed with an expansion caret to give access to embedded comments. As part of a National Science Foundation project to evaluate the use and social impacts of the Blacksburg Electronic Village, we will implement a critical incident forum for the entire Internet-using population of Montgomery County, Virginia — approximately 65,000 people (Carroll & Rosson, 2001).

Conclusion

A large set of issues pertain to generalizing this case study. We studied a group of teachers, developers and evaluators designing and understanding new collaboration technology and classroom activities. However, many aspects of this case are potentially general. Various types of knowledge workers and their organizations are currently adopting, and sometimes struggling with, new collaboration technology and with the consequences for new work practices that are entailed by this technology. The collaborative critical incident technique could be employed in such circumstances. Such possible extensions raise some of the orienting issues. Consider for example anonymity. In our rather intimate design collaboration, anonymity did not make sense. But in larger-scale workplace contexts, it might be extremely important.

Critical incidents alone do not provide solutions to problems. Practical answers come from appropriate analysis and interpretation. Miester (1985) described three major problems with critical incident analysis: (1) selecting a frame of reference for describing incidents, (2) inductively developing incident categories, and (3) determining the level of specificity for reporting incidents. Flanagan (1954) argued that most errors are not made in the collection and analysis of critical incidents, but in their interpretation. The CCIT allowed sustained and interactive revision, amendment, storage, and documentation of critical incidents over a long period of time. Participants often refined and modified critical incidents as more interaction took place and more information about events became recognized. The tool also acted as a repository of important events that were referred back to time and again in the course of long-term activities. Over time, additional examples of earlier incidents were elaborated and connected in the threaded discussions. Thus, the tool facilitated reflection, iteration, multiple interpretation, and reinterpretation of critical incidents involving the full participation of users.

We are encouraged by the utility of the CCIT in the LiNC project and will continue to develop and investigate this sort of evaluation tool. We feel it definitely has provided an effective channel for evoking, sharing and discussing evaluation data in our project. Moreover, and of critical importance to our project, it achieves this while also providing a more active and more equal role for users in the interpretation of early evaluation data within the system development process.

Acknowledgments

We are grateful to Craig Ganoe for assisting with the requirements study, and to Mary Beth Rosson for planning discussions about the design. We thank Kathy Bunn, Peggy Davie, Dan Dunlap, Mark Freeman, Alison Goforth, Suzan Mauney, and Fred Rencsok for feedback on the design of the CCIT. We benefited very much from referee comments and suggestions in the review process. This work was supported in part by the Hitachi Foundation, the National Science Foundation, and the Office of Naval Research.

References

Begole, J. M. A. (1999). *Flexible collaboration transparency: Supporting worker independence in replicated application-sharing systems.* Unpublished Ph.D., Virginia Polytechnic Institute and State University, Blacksburg.

Carroll, J. M. & Rosson, M. B. (2001). *Better home shopping or new democracy? Evaluating community network outcomes.* Paper presented at the Proceedings of CHI 2001: Conference on Human Factors of Computer Systems, New York.

Carroll, J. M., Koenemann-Belliveau, J., Rosson, M. B., & Singley, M. K. (1993). *Critical incidents and critical threads in empirical usability evaluation.* Paper presented at the People and Computers VIII. Proceedings of the HCI'93 Conference, Cambridge, UK.

Carroll, J. M., Neale, D. C., Isenhour, P. L., Rosson, M. B., & McCrickard, D. S. (2003). Notification and awareness: Synchronizing task-oriented collaborative activity. *International Journal of Human-Computer Systems, 58,* pp. 605-632.

Carroll, J. M., Rosson, M. B., Chin, G., & Koenemann, J. (1998). Requirements development in scenario-based design. *IEEE Transactions on Software Engineering, 24*(12), 1156-1170.

Carroll, J. M., Rosson, M. B., Cohill, A. M., & Schorger, J. (1995). *Building a history of the Blacksburg Electronic Village.* Paper presented at the Proceedings of the ACM Symposium on Designing Interactive Systems, New York.

delGaldo, E. M., Williges, R. C., Williges, B. H., & Wixon, D. R. (1987). A critical incident evaluation tool for software documentation. In L. S. Mark, J. S. Warm, & R. L. Huston (Eds.), *Ergonomics and Human Factors* (pp. 253-258). New York: Springer-Verlag.

Eales, R. T. J., Neale, D. C., & Carroll, J. M. (1999). *Desktop videoconferencing as a basis for computer supported collaborative learning in K-12 classrooms.* Paper presented at the ED-MEDIA, World Conference on Educational Multimedia, Hypermedia & Telecommunications, Charlottesville, VA.

Flanagan, J. C. (1954). The critical incident technique. *Psychological bulletin, 51*(4), 327-358.

Gibson, S., Neale, D. C., Carroll, J. M., & VanMetre, C. A. (1999). *Mentoring in a school environment.* Paper presented at the Proceedings of CSCL'99 Computer Supported Cooperative Learning, Mahwah, NJ.

Isenhour, P. L., Carroll, J. M., Neale, D. C., Rosson, M. B., & Dunlap, D. R. (2000). The virtual school: An integrated collaborative environment for the classroom. *Educational Technology and Society, Special Issue on "On-Line Collaborative Learning Environments", 3*(3). Retrieved from the World Wide Web: http://ifets.ieee.org/periodical/.

Koenemann, J., Carroll, J. M., Shaffer, C. A., Rosson, M. B., & Abrams, M. (1998). Designing collaborative applications for classroom use: The LiNC Project. In A. Druin (Ed.), *The Design of Children's Technology* (pp. 99-122). San Francisco, CA: Morgan-Kaufmann.

Kyng, M. (1995). Creating contexts for design. In J. M. Carroll (Ed.), *Scenario-Based Design for Human-Computer Interaction: Envisioning Work and Technology in Systems Development* (pp. 85-107). New York: John Wiley & Sons.

Miester, D. (1985). *Behavioral Analysis and Measurement Methods.* New York: John Wiley & Sons.

Muller, M., Tudor, L., Wildman, D., White, E., Root, R., Dayton, T., et al. (1995). Bifocal tools for scenarios and representations in participatory activities with users. In J. M. Carroll (Ed.), *Scenario-Based Design: Envisioning Work and Technology in System Development* (pp. 598-601). Santa Monica, CA: Human Factors and Ergonomics Society.

Neale, D. C., & Kies, J. K. (2000). *Symposium on recent advances in the critical incident technique.* Paper presented at the Proceedings of the 44th Annual Meeting of the Human Factors and Ergonomics Society, Santa Monica, CA.

Neale, D. C., Dunlap, D. R., Isenhour, P., & Carroll, J. M. (2000). *Collaborative critical incident development.* Paper presented at the Proceedings of the 44th Annual Meeting of the Human Factors and Ergonomics Society, Santa Monica, CA.

Rosson, M. B., Carroll, J. M., & Messner, D. (1996). A Web StoryBase. In M. A. Sasse, R. J. Cunningham, & R. L. Winder (Eds.), *People and Computers XI: Proceedings of HCI '96* (pp. 369-382). London: Springer-Verlag.

Shattuck, L. G. & Woods, D. D. (1994). *The critical incident technique: 40 years later.* Paper presented at the Proceedings of the Human Factors and Ergonomics Society 38th Annual Meeting, Santa Monica, CA.

Sproull, L. & Kiesler, S. (1991). *Connections: New Ways of Working in the Networked Organization.* London: MIT Press.

Tompson, J. A. & Williges, R. C. (2000). *Web-based collection of critical incidents during usability evaluation.* Paper presented at the Proceedings of the 40th Annual Meeting of the Human Factors and Ergonomics Society, Santa Monica, CA.

Tyrack, D. & Cuban, L. (1995). *Tinkering toward Utopia: A Century of Public School Reform.* Boston, MA: Harvard University Press.

Chapter XII

Science Net: A Virtual School for the Extension (Science) Education of the Public in Singapore

Leo Tan Wee Hin
Nanyang Technological University, Singapore

R. Subramaniam
Nanyang Technological University, Singapore

Abstract

A university-science center partnership called Science Net has been functioning as a virtual school for the extension (science) education of the global public in general and the Singapore public in particular. This chapter describes the design, implementation mechanics and learning

potential of this online school for non-formal science education, and
suggests that it is an innovative experiment to expand the communicative
space of learning in society.

Introduction

The advent of the Internet is impinging in multi-dimensional ways on various aspects of societal endeavors. A personal computer and a network connection are sufficient to open up new vistas in the Internet as well as mine the World Wide Web for a range of resources and information.

One area that the Internet has impacted very significantly is in education. Starting to dissolve the perimetric boundaries of traditional education structures in both the institutional and curricular domains, it is redefining the way education is being disbursed as well as opening up new genres of learning. Online learning is now beginning to be recognized as an important aspect of the educational dispensation (Chen, Ou, Liu, & Liu, 2001; Lupo & Erlich, 2000; Maes, 2001; Sanders & Morrison-Shetlar, 2001). Almost all schools and universities, at least in the developed world, have a web presence and their portals feature an abundance of learning resources.

The "dotcoming" of schools has led to an important development with far-reaching implications: the opening of a virtual annex which mirrors their traditional roles and objectives in some ways. Such virtual schools have mushroomed in large numbers in the USA and in Canada, especially at the K-12 level, and have spawned a plethora of online learning communities. Leveraging the Internet to foster distance learning among a group of students who are geographically dispersed, their impact has been sufficient to generate a number of studies (for example, Clark, 2001, and references therein). Whilst they have yet to mature fully, as the technologies and standards of delivery are still evolving, they are continuing to proliferate with a view towards catering to diverse learning needs.

While traditional schools are fundamentally institutionalized to support the needs of the industrial economy, virtual schools, in contrast, are a reaction of the opportunities engendered by the emerging knowledge-based economy, also known as the information economy. The knowledge economy puts a premium on intellectual resources, in contra-distinction to human resources per se.

A key prerequisite is information and communication technology skills, which helps people to avail themselves of the opportunities that the networked economy offers for their learning needs. Thus, virtual schools are strategically positioned to rise to the challenges of the knowledge economy as well as help bridge the digital divide. The proliferation of virtual schools and other online learning portals is a recognition of their potential to cater to diverse learning needs. Virtual schools can cater to both formal and non-formal educational needs. The latter aspect often addresses enrichment needs, but also complements the formal educational needs in some ways. A distinct advantage of virtual schools over conventional schools is that they are able to cast the net wide over the Web and garner a critical mass of learners so as to capitalize on their available manpower and training resources. Even catering to special interest groups or those with unique learning needs becomes an economically viable option because of the geographic reach afforded, unlike traditional schools.

In Singapore, a variant of the virtual school, called Science Net, has been in operation since 1998. It is hosted on the website of the Singapore Science Centre (http://www.science.edu.sg), an institution for the promotion of non-formal science education, and is not to be found in the portals of other science centers or science museums. What is unique about Science Net is that it is a web-based platform to promote the public understanding of science. The global public, including students, can seek answers or explanations to any of their scientific queries, doubts or misconceptions via this forum. In promoting the public understanding of science through science centers (Tan & Subramaniam, 1998, 2003a) scientific societies (Tan & Subramaniam, 1999), and the Internet (Tan & Subramaniam, 2000), there is a tendency to overlook the curiosity dimension of the public — Science Net attempts to fill this niche.

A brief background to the question-and-answer format of Science Net is now presented so that the ensuing discussion can be better appreciated in context. The Singapore Science Center has been popularizing science and technology to students and the public in multi-dimensional ways since its establishment in 1977. A best selling science magazine, *Singapore Scientist*, that it has been publishing since its opening has a popular section called *The Scientist Answers*. In this section, students get their doubts in science cleared by the scientific staff of the science center. However, the quarterly nature of this print publication means that only a limited number of questions can be answered in any issue. On an average of five questions and answers per issue, this works out to about 20 questions and answers a year, or about 200 questions and answers in 10 years. And the huge pile of questions awaiting answers means that a valuable opportunity is foregone to address learning needs. When the Internet became a buzz-word in the mid-1990s, and Internet penetration rates in Singapore started to increase, a decision was made to open a virtual annex of the science center. This virtual science center features information about the science center, virtual exhibits and a range of science learning resources (Tan & Subramaniam, 2003b) Among the science learning resources featured here is the online equivalent of *The Scientist Answers*, called Science Net. A significant reason for instituting this section is the need to encourage the public to keep abreast of developments in science and technology by providing them a platform for use in clarifying any doubts that they may have in science. Freed from the frequency schedule and page limitations of the print medium, the Science Net has enabled *The Scientist Answers* section to be scaled up dramatically on the web. In fact, the number of questions and answers published in the first twenty years of *The Scientist Answers* section was exceeded within a few months of operation of Science Net!

The posting of science-based questions by the public, and the providing of answers or explanations constitute an important aspect of furthering the public understanding of science. Questions are often posted by the public because they have doubts or misconceptions about a topic or concept for which they seek enlightenment as part of their attempts to understand the world around them. No institutional mechanism is generally available to service such learning needs of the public in an effective and timely manner — the Science Net comes closest to this model.

The Science Net is a good example of a "learner interaction with experts" forum. Published studies of the effectiveness of learner interaction with experts are, however, lacking in the primary journal literature, presumably because the field is new and is still evolving. Whilst Science Net is unique in that it is the only such forum to be hosted on the web of a science center or science museum, and is backed by a large ensemble of scientists, there are other variants of this service on the web. A brief commentary is presented of some of these versions:

1. *Ask the Experts (http://www.sciam.com/askexpert_directory.cfm).*

   Administered by the *Scientific American* magazine, this service features nine categories in science. An average of one answer to a question is posted every week.

2. *Science Made Simple (http://www.cedarnet.org/ahs/science.html).*

   This is a subscription service (US$9.95 for 10 online issues), which entitles students to access answers to various science questions posted by online subscribers.

3. *Ask an Expert (http://www.slb.com/seed/en/ask/q_and_a/index.htm).*

   Only a limited range of topics in science is covered by this service, and the database of questions and answers is rather small.

4. *Ask Dr Universe (http://druniverse.wsu.edu/sendquest.asp).*

   Hosted by the Washington State University, one can ask any question — not just in science — and answers will be obtained from its faculty. However, the database of questions and answers is not large.

5. *Ask A NASA Scientist (http://imagine.gsfc.nasa.gov/docs/ask_astro/ ask_an_astronomer.html).*

   Hosted by NASA, a good range of questions and answers on various aspects of space and astronomy is featured here. Typically, it takes about one to two weeks for one answer to be posted.

6. *Ask the Experts (http://www.physlink.com/Education/AskExperts/).*

   This is a site which caters to questions and answers in physics and astronomy. The database, however, is not large.

7. *Ask Dr Math (http://mathforum.org/dr.math/).*

   A good collection of questions and answers in mathematics is featured here.

8. *ScienceNet (www.sciencenet.org.uk).*

   Hosted in the United Kingdom, this site features questions and answers on a range of science topics. However, it entertains questions from only within the United Kingdom.

9. *Ask Discover Magazine (http://www.discover.com/ask/).*

   Hosted by the Discover Magazine, it entertains questions on the world of science. The categories covered, as well as the database of questions and answers, is rather limited.

10. *Newton BBS (http://newton.dep.anl.gov/).*

    Hosted by the Argonne National Laboratories in Illinois, USA, this site covers 14 categories in science, mainly for K-12 educators and students. It has fielded more than 10,000 questions since 1991.

11. *The Last Word (http://www.newscientist.com/lastword/).*

 Hosted by New Scientist magazine, this site features the print version of the questions and answers which appear weekly in the magazine. A good collection of questions and answers featured since 1995 has been assembled here.

These sites, though serving a very useful purpose, do not provide as comprehensive or as frequent coverage as Science Net, which reaches out to both generalist and specialist audiences, and is backed by more than 100 scientists. Some of the sites also have restrictions — for example, ScienceNet entertains only questions from within the United Kingdom, while Ask the Experts fields only questions in physics and astronomy.

With five years having passed since the launch of Science Net, a wealth of experiences and insights have been accumulated on the operation of this virtual school. The time is thus opportune to comment on its impact and effectiveness.

The purpose of this chapter is four-fold:

(a) to describe the design of the Science Net,

(b) to discuss its implementation mechanics,

(c) to explore the learning potential in this forum, and

(d) to present a commentary on its place in the virtual schools community.

Design of Science Net

From the outset, Science Net was conceived of as a virtual school to promote non-formal science education on the website of the Singapore Science Center. It was recognized that with the challenges posed by the Internet, science centers will have to reengineer aspects of their operational philosophy so as to take cognizance of the new realities of the information age. In this context, the website of the Singapore Science Center was set up to host general information about the science center, virtual exhibits and other educational resources. The Science Net is a key component of the latter offerings.

The portal of the Singapore Science Center is hosted on a high capacity server, which is able to service thousands of simultaneous access by the online public.

We estimate that the Science Net itself occupies close to 40% of the operating server space.

The database of questions and answers is organized according to broad schema and sub-classifications. There are seven categories and nearly 70 sub-categories (Table 1) in Science Net.

Table 1: Classification of Questions and Answers in Science Net

Category	Sub-categories	Sub-categories
Computer Science / Information Technology / Mathematics	Computer systems Computer vision & machine intelligence Database Internet	Mathematics / Algorithms Network & Communications Programming languages / Computer software Robotics/Automation Security & Encryption
Earth Science	Agriculture / Farming Auroras/Northern lights Geology & Geophysics	Meteorology Natural resources Oceanography / Hydrology
Engineering / Technology / Engineering Materials	Acoustics Aviation Biotechnology / Bioengineering Civil / Structural Engineering Electrical Engineering Electronic Engineering	Food Technology Industrial / Production Engineering Materials Science / Polymers Mechanical Engineering Optical Engineering / Photography
Life Sciences	Animal behavior / Zoology Biochemistry / Biophysics Botany Ecology / Environment General Biology Genetics / Reproduction Genomics / Bioinformatics Human Anatomy Marine Biology	Microbiology Molecular & Cell Biology Neuroscience / Vision Pharmacology / Medicine / Disease Physiology Safety / Health Systematics / Taxonomy Human Behaviour / Psychology
Physical Sciences	Analytical / Clinical Chemistry Fluid Dynamics General Chemistry General Physics High Energy / Particle / Plasma Physics Lasers / Optics / Photonics	Magnetism / Electricity Mechanics / Waves / Vibrations Organic / Theoretical Chemistry Relativity Theoretical / Quantum Physics
Astronomy & Space Science	Astrophysics / Cosmology Comets /Asteroids / Meteors General Astronomy Observatories / Telescopes Planetaria / Constellations	Milky Way / Galaxies Radio Astronomy Search for Extra-Terrestrial Intelligence Space Exploration Satellites Solar System
Others	Science policies Tips on passing science examinations Etc.	

The schema and sub-categories are a reflection of the need to classify the labyrinth of questions and answers into a coherent format that would permit a rational basis for guided exploration. The classification is necessarily guided by the variety of questions that have been posted so far. New categories are added as and when these are needed. From an operational standpoint, the organizing of content in multifarious ways has the advantage that visitors need not download entire files in order to access the Science Net section — this would be rather time-consuming on a slow network. Also, the classification has the advantage of promoting directedness in the learning experience, as a user is more likely to access categories of interest to him.

Accessing the database can be by one of three ways — clicking the *Full List of Questions*, sieving by category and sub-section, or by perusing via year of posting. It is recognized that a multiplicity of access options does serve the varying needs of online visitors.

The aesthetics of the section has been assured by the use of a simple layout, presence of a design motif without flamboyant elements, minimal use of colors and graphics, and use of simple fonts to present information. No multimedia is featured in the section. These strategies help to minimize ocular discomfort, and make the requisite subset of the section less bandwidth-intensive for access — important considerations in ensuring that the site continues to stay breezy and popular.

Navigation aids are provided on all pages in order to help visitors move from one category to another in a seamless manner.

A noteworthy aspect is that the section is updated almost every day — an important consideration in ensuring its dynamism and vibrancy.

Implementation Mechanics

Since its introduction in 1998, more than 19,000 questions have been posted by the public, not only from Singapore, but also from other countries. Nearly 6,000 of these questions have been answered by the organizers: the others are repeat questions, school homework assignments (which is strongly discouraged), and, to a very small extent, unanswered questions.

It needs to be recognized that a single institution cannot take on the colossal task of answering all the questions posted because of the diversity of expertise and the number of personnel that would be needed for such an exercise. To address this challenge, the two premier universities in Singapore, the National University of Singapore and the Nanyang Technological University, were also inducted as co-organizers of this section. Science centers and universities make natural partners because they share a common focus in education. Such a partnership is also necessary to endow the section with even greater credibility and in building up the database, important considerations in drawing visitors. The two universities provide faculty, more than 100 academics, who, together with (science) graduate staff of the Singapore Science Center, help to answer questions closest to their field of specialization. A number of questions have two answers — this is more a consequence of some interesting or tricky questions being directed simultaneously to two experts. Besides decreasing the response time of getting at least one answer for the question, the strategy also offers the public the benefit of obtaining perspectives from different experts. Often, it may not be that easy to answer a question — such questions are then posted on the website itself, soliciting for answers. Hyperlinks are provided for in some answers; this is not to be construed as a quick-fix solution for answers that are brief, but more as an extension of the textual narrative and also as a recognition that there needs to be a limit on the length for each answer. More importantly, the use of hyperlinks encourages visitors to continue their learning experience, an important consideration in their extension education.

To facilitate easy posting of questions by the global public, user-friendly features are incorporated into the section. They are required to register by keying in brief details of their personal particulars before entering the question. This helps to capture a profile of the visitor as well as help personalize the question, in that the person who posted the question is acknowledged next to the question in the database if his question is selected for answering by the organizers. A click-button sends the question to the Science Net coordinator, who then decides on the appropriate course of action. This is a tricky process involving quite some decision making: has the question been answered before, is it a school homework assignment, is it a question for which the answer can be readily found by consulting standard books, or is it a question which will help to add quality and build up the database? If the latter is the case, then the question is routed to the relevant expert in the resource panel. It has to be noted that all these are time-consuming procedures and labor-intensive tasks.

To ensure that the public does not post questions which have already been answered, a search protocol is available. This allows key words describing a concept or topic to be entered in order to facilitate checking. Based on analyses of server logs, about 35% of the questions posted by the public have been found to be previously answered. For such cases, an e-mail response is sent, directing them to the relevant section of the Science Net — a rather time-consuming exercise. Posting of school homework assignments is common, and is strongly discouraged.

Answers to questions are usually restricted to about a screen length in order to minimize cognitive overload. Lengthy explanations that would require the online visitor to connect at different cognitive levels have generally been avoided. In answering the questions, a balance between scientific exactitude and popular appeal is generally sought to be achieved, so that as many people as possible can be reasonably expected to benefit from the answers given. The nature of some of the questions posted often makes it a challenge to structure a response which oscillates between the needs of the neophyte and the expert!

Some examples of questions and answers extracted from the database of Science Net are presented in Figures 1 and 2.

Figure 1: Example of Science Net Entry in General Physics

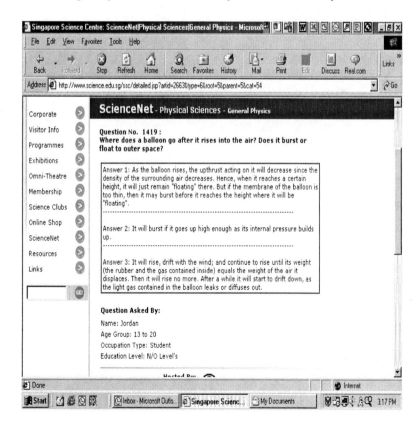

Figure 2: Example of Science Net Entry in Astronomy

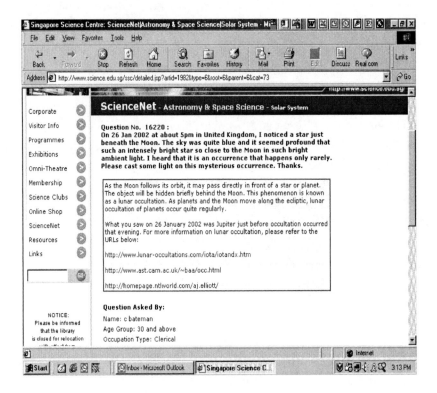

Access to Science Net is free and is available to anyone with a network connection. The rich repository of information available in this section draws visitors from across the globe. No intellectual copyright restrictions are placed — the entire database is downloadable for free if required! It is the global public's participation that has helped to generate a vast database of intellectual resources in a public domain.

The process by which university faculty become involved has been a key factor in ensuring the success of the Science Net section. In Singapore, the two premier universities, the National University of Singapore and the Nanyang Technological University, encourage staff to get actively involved in communitarian work related to their professional expertise and which benefits society at large. This constitutes an important aspect of the annual appraisal of faculty, besides their teaching, research and administrative duties. Typically, the weight assigned for external interaction is about 10%, with the exact quantum depending on the professorate nomenclature of the staff concerned.

This arrangement has been an important factor in ensuring that a reservoir of scientific talent is available to draw upon in building up the Science Net section.

From the university point-of-view, the Science Net has been a useful opportunity to show to the public that scientists are not living in ivory towers or divorced from ground realities but are, in fact, also providing useful linkages to society through their public service. It is an example of how communities of interest — scientists, with their specialist expertise, and the online public, hungering to satiate their curiosity — can engage in mutually enriching partnerships to achieve important educational goals. Without this partnership, the massive corpus of knowledge residing on Science Net would not have been achieved.

Assessment of Learning Potential

As the Science Net is a forum for the public to obtain answers to their scientific queries, it is difficult to comment on the effectiveness of the learning which takes place. Several facts, however, attest to the efficacy of the learning potential:

(a) As answers are generally pitched at the popular level, it is reasonable to assume that they are quite amenable to comprehension by the online public.

(b) The large number of questions posted and answered does indicate that the site is drawing online visitors and fulfilling a useful role. Data in Table 2 show that the site has grown in size and complexity over the years.

Table 2: Distribution of Questions Posted on Science Net by Year

Year	Number of questions posted
1998	2,064
1999	3,686
2000	5,664
2001	4,382
2002	3,208
TOTAL	**19,004**

Assuming that each answer occupies about half an A-4 size paper, the Science Net section itself comes to about 3,000 pages.

(c)   Analyses of server logs have generated a wealth of data on the popularity of the section. For the two-year period from January 1, 2001 to December 31, 2002, 24.8% of the total hits registered at the virtual science center have been for the Science Net section. This translates to a daily average of 17,533 hits and 3,771 page views for Science Net (Table 3). That is, the Science Net section is helping to significantly draw more online visitors to the virtual science center. About 20% of the surfers are from Singapore, with others predominantly from the Western world as well as some from other parts of Asia.

Table 3: Website Statistics of Singapore Science Center for the Period from January 1, 2001 to December 31, 2002

Section	Total hits	Average hits per day	Total number of page views	Average number of page views per day
Virtual Science Center	52,377,282	71,749	10,208,973	13,984
Science Net	12,799,165	17,533	2,753,308	3,771

We now comment on the cognitive dimension of the learning engaged in by users. Since the activity focuses on learner interaction with experts through questions and answers, it is different from traditional learning contexts. For an activity to conform to the constructivist philosophy, four pedagogical aspects would have to be demonstrated (Taylor, 1992; Phillips, 1998; Gance, 2002).

• The user must be cognitively engaged in wanting to explore the environment for new information

• The user must be immersed in a learning context that admits of problem-solving situations

• There must be interaction with the learning environment through a hands-on, dialogic mode

- The user must be ensconced in a social setting which permits interaction with other learners and mentors

When users access the Science Net, it is clear that they seek to bridge gaps in their understanding of a particular topic or satiate their curiosity about some matter. This posits the stance that the user wants to explore the environment for new information through appropriate cognitive engagement. The learner is thus motivated to be self-directed and independent in his learning attempts. The first postulate of the constructivist philosophy is thus essentially satisfied. As for the second postulate, it is unlikely that this is fulfilled, as the essentially dialogic nature of the question and answer approach leaves little room for authentic problem-solving situations. The third postulate is significantly satisfied, since one can argue that the interaction with the Science Net section is basically a hands-on session, with the computer mediating the learning experience; the presence of hyperlinks in a number of answers also provides a platform to continue the learning experience. Moreover, the question and answer format mirrors somewhat a conceptual dialogic session, that is, an interaction between the learner and the material. The fourth postulate is partially satisfied in that there is learner interaction with experts by those who post questions, though there is no interaction with other users.

Thus, one can see both the constructivist and didactic philosophy at work in the Science Net section. Whilst the nature of the question and answer format is consistent with the behaviorist and information transfer model pertaining to the didactic view, the shift from teaching to learning required of the user does endow the section with significant strains of constructivism, since he is now empowered to take control of his learning needs in order to construct or extend his own understanding of a topic. Scope is thus afforded for the learner to integrate new knowledge gained with his pre-existing knowledge in order to expand the cognitive dimension of his knowledge about the topic.

Science Net also meets the general knowledge needs of science students in Singapore schools since it is not reasonable to expect teachers to be able to fully satiate the general knowledge questions in science frequently asked by students as part of their attempts to understand the world around them. Commonly, the maxim given is: *Post it on the Science Net*. This opening of a communication channel has been helpful in further strengthening linkages of the Singapore Science Center with schools.

Commentary Vis-à-Vis Virtual Schools

Since its introduction in 1998, Science Net has developed into a virtual school for the extension education of the online public, especially in Singapore.

Science Net has a number of parallels with traditional virtual schools:

- They are both Internet-based.

- They both cater for education: whilst traditional virtual schools cater to students, Science Net caters to both students and the general public.

- They both leverage instructors to at least help mediate the learning experience; whilst traditional virtual schools rely on teachers, Science Net leverages on university teachers and other graduate staff.

Its differences with conventional virtual schools are as follows:

- It uses only electronic text to disburse instruction, unlike most virtual schools, which use audio and/or video for conferencing as well.

- It does not provide assessment of learning.

- The interaction between the question poster and the question answerer is on a one-off basis, unlike in traditional virtual schools where it is more sustained.

The differences are more a result of Science Net evolving as a variant of the virtual school concept with respect to the promotion of non-formal science education. Rigors in assessment and interaction are generally played down in such environments, as the intent is more to popularize science and technology.

We envisage that future developments in Science Net would be along the following lines:

- Its global positioning means that there will continue to be a large pool of people to post questions, and thus help to build up the database further.

- Multimedia files are likely to be incorporated in order to complement text explanations for certain questions.

- Live interaction with experts on topical issues in science and technology is a possibility, especially with the maturation, affordability and pervasiveness of technologies related to videoconferencing and broadband access.

- Articles on popular issues are likely to be posted in order to complement text resources; that is, the knowledge base in respect of answers to questions would be expanded further through a medley of other resources.

The long-range outlook for virtual schools of informal education is bright, especially for those related to science. After all, science and technology have become integrated into society and the economy to a large extent. With the emergence of the knowledge economy, new challenges will surface and virtual schools, because of their web-centric positioning, would be able to address the arising challenges more effectively than traditional schools. Virtual schools of informal education will thus mushroom in order to cater to various needs and special interests, for example, foreign languages, enrichment lessons, etc., and thus contribute towards personal fulfillment, pluralistic learning needs, and life-long learning. Emerging technologies which are likely to make an impact include those related to broadband access, for example, asymmetric digital subscriber line, hybrid fiber co-axial cable, and asynchronous transfer mode, as well as those related to delivery platforms, such as Blackboard. The former suite of technologies will help to speed up access to the Internet as they become more ubiquitous and affordable, while the latter assortment of technologies will enhance instructional needs, all helping to enhance the quality of the learning experience.

The experience of Science Net suggests that it is possible to extend its applicability to other informal learning environments. Possible areas could include national history, culture, philosophy and a range of enrichment needs. The challenge is to assemble a team of experts and host the section on the website of a suitable institution. Universities wishing to build bonds with the local community can also replicate this experience to address appropriate learning needs.

Conclusion

Science Net has established itself as a virtual school for the extension (science) education of the public in Singapore. Opening a gateway to a wealth of resources, and transcending the fixations of space, time, and other barriers, it has been an innovative experiment in reaching out to the online public as part of their continuing education in science and technology. By enlarging the communicative space of learning, it reinforces the perception that the learning environment transcends traditional education structures. Perusing the various questions and answers on the site is also an educationally enriching experience, and this fulfills a niche in resource-based learning. By presenting learning opportunities which cater towards personal fulfillment, enrichment, and life-long learning in non-formal science education, Science Net has matured as a key virtual infrastructure in the educational setting of Singapore — thus contributing in its own unique way to the development of a learning society among students and the public in today's networked world!

Acknowledgment

We thank Mr. Edwin Teng, Technical Manager at the Singapore Science Center, for his assistance in generating statistical profiles from server logs for this study.

References

Chen, G.D., Ou, K.L., Liu, C.C., & Liu, B.J. (2001). Intervention and strategy analysis for web group learning. *Journal of Computer Assisted Learning, 17*, 58-71.

Clark, T. (2001). *Virtual Schools: Trends and Issues*. Phoenix, AZ: WestEd/ Distance Learning Resource Network.

Gance, S. (2002). Are constructivism and computer-based learning environments incompatible? *Journal of the Association for History & Computing, 5*, 1-5.

Lupo, D. & Erlich, Z. (2000). Computer literacy and applications via distance learning. *Computers & Education, 36*, 333-345.

Maes, J.T. (2001). Quality in an e-University. *Assessment and Evaluation in Higher Education, 26*, 465-473.

Phillips, D.C. (1995). The good, the bad and the ugly: The many faces of constructivism. *Educational Researcher, 24*, 5-12.

Sanders, D.W. & Morrison-Shetlar. (2001). Student attitudes towards a web-enhanced instruction in an introductory biology course. *Journal of Research on Computing in Education, 33,* 251-262.

Tan, W.H.L. & Subramaniam, R. (1998). Developing nations need to popularize science. *New Scientist, 2139,* 52.

Tan, W.H.L. & Subramaniam, R. (1999). Scientific societies build better nations. *Nature, 399,* 633

Tan, W.H.L. & Subramaniam, R. (2000). Wiring up the island state. *Science, 288,* 621- 623.

Tan, W.H.L. & Subramaniam, R. (2003a). Science and technology centers as agents for promoting science culture in developing nations. *International Journal of Technology Management, 25*(5), 413- 426.

Tan, W.H.L. & Subramaniam, R. (2003b). Virtual science centers: Web-based environments for promotion of non formal science education. In A.K. Aggarwal (Ed.), *Web-Based Education: Learning from Experience* (pp. 308-329). Hershey, PA: Idea Group Publishing.

Appendix

School	Location	URL
Abbington Hill Online School	Bricktown, New Jersey	http://www.business.inc.com/abbingtonhillschool
Advanced Academics	Norman, Oklahoma	http://www.advancedacademics.com/home
Alabama Online High School	Tuscaloosa, Alabama	http://www.aohs.state.al.us/index.html
Alpha-Omega Academy On-Line	Chandler, Arizona	http://www.welcometoclass.com
APEX Learning Systems	Bellevue, Washington	http://www.apexlearning.com
ArabesQ Online Academy	St. Louis, Missouri	http://www.arabesq.com/
Arkansas Virtual High School	Dardanelle, Arkansas	http://arkansashigh.k12.ar.us
Athena Academy	Colombia, Missouri	http://www.athena.edu/academy
BabbageNet School (the)	Port Jefferson, New York	http://www.babbagenetschool.com/
Basehor-Linwood Virtual Charter School	Linwood, Kansas	http://vcs.usd458.k12.ks.us/
Birdville Virtual School	Birdville, Texas	http://www.birdville.k12.tx.us/cf/Virtual/VirtSchl.htm
Brigham Young University Independent Study	Salt Lake City, Utah	http://ce.byu.edu/is/site/index.dhtm
CAL Online	Clovis, California	http://www.cusd.com/calonline/Default.htm
CCS Web Academy	Fayetteville, North Carolina	http://www.ccswebacademy.net/
ChildU - "The Learning Odyssey"	Fort Lauderdale, Florida	http://www.childu.com
Choice 2000 Charter Online High School	Perris Union School District, California	http://www.choice2000.org
Christa McAuliffe Academy	Yakima, Washington	http://www.cmacademy.org/
Clintondale Virtual High School	Clinton Township, Mississippi	http://www.clintondalevhs.org/
Colorado On-line School Consortium	Littleton, Colorado	http://www.col.k12.co.us/
Compuhigh Online High School	Fairmont, West Virginia	http://www.compuhigh.com/
Cool School	Eugene, Oregon	http://coolschool.k12.or.us/
Delta Cyber School	Delta Junction, Alaska	http://www.dcs.k12.ak.us/
Dennison On-Line Internet School	Los Angeles, California	http://www.dennisononline.com/
E.COT (Electronic Classroom of Tomorrow)	Columbus, Ohio	http://www.ecotohio.org/index.htm
E2020	Grand Rapids, Michigan	http://www.e2020inc.com

School	Location	URL
Eagle Christian High School	Missoula, Montana	http://www.montana.com/eagle/Home.html
ECO 2000 Consortium	Washburn, Maine	http://www.eco2000.org/consortium/index.htm
Educational Program for Gifted Youth	Stanford University, California	http://www-epgy.stanford.edu
Eldorado Academy	Nederland, Colorado	http://www.eldoradoacademy.org/
Electronic Charter School	Elkhart, Kansas	http://onlineecs.org/
Electronic High School	Utah	http://www.ehs.uen.org/
E-School	Honolulu, Hawaii	http://www.eschool.k12.hi.us
Evergreen Internet Academy	Vancouver, Washington	http://eia.egreen.wednet.edu/
Florida Virtual School	Orlando, Florida	http://www.flvs.net
Francis School	New York	http://www.francisschool.com/
Fraser Valley Distance Education School	British Colombia, Canada	http://www.fvrcs.gov.bc.ca/
Garden Schools	Branson, Missouri	http://www.gardenschools.com/
Gridlink Online Education System	London, England	http://atschool.eduweb.co.uk/ctrh/home.htm
Gwinnett County Online Campus	Lawrenceville, Georgia	http://gwinnettk12online.net/
Illinois Virtual High School	Springfield, Illinois	http://www.ivhs.k12.il.us/welcome/index.html
Indiana University High School Diploma Program	Bloomington, Indiana	http://www.indiana.edu/~iuhs/
International High School	Oceanside, California	http://www.internationalhigh.org
Internet Academy	Federal Way, Washington	http://www.iacademy.org/
Internet High School	Woodbridge, Virginia	http://www.rmhs.org/Internet.htm
Internet Home School.Com	Prescott, Arizona	http://www.internethomeschool.com/
James Madison High School	Norcross, Georgia	http://www.jmhs.com/?code=9941
JeffcoNet Academy	Lakewood, Colorado	http://jeffcoweb.jeffco.k12.co.us/access/academy/index.html
Juneau Cyber School	Juneau, Arkansas	http://jcs.jsd.k12.ak.us
K12	McLean, Virginia	http://www.k12.com
Kentucky Virtual High School	Frankfort, Kentucky	http://www.kvhs.org

School	Location	URL
Keystone Virtual High School	Keystone National High School, Pennsylvania	http://www.keystonehighschool.com
Laurel Springs School	Ojai, California	http://www.laurelsprings.com/default.asp
Learning Park Virtual School	Sedona, Arizona	http://www.learning-park.com/Index.htm
Louisiana Virtual Classroom	Baton Rouge, Louisiana	http://www.lcet.doe.state.la.us/distance/
Maryland Virtual High School of SCI. and Math	Silver Spring, Maryland	http://mvhs1.mbhs.edu/
Michigan Virtual High School	Lansing, Michigan	http://www.mivhs.org
Mindquest	Bloomington, Minnesota	http://www.mindquest.org/
Missouri Virtual School	Springfield, Missouri	http://mvs.smsu.edu/
Monte Vista On-line Academy	Monte Vista, Colorado	http://monte.k12.co.us
Nevada Virtual High School	Ely, Nevada	http://www.nvhs.org/
New Mexico Virtual School	Santa Fe, New Mexico	http://www.intelligented.com/nmvs/
New York State External Diploma Program	New York, New York	http://www.nyadulted.org/distance.htm
North Dakota Division of Independent Study	Fargo, North Dakota	http://www.dis.dpi.state.nd.us/
NorthStar Academy	Sherwood Park, Alberta, Canada	http://www.northstar-academy.org/pages/ushome.htm
Northwest WebSchool	Hillsboro, Oregon	http://www.nwwebschool.org/
Oak Meadow Online School	Putney, Vermont	http://www.oakmeadow.com/OnlineSchool2.htm
Oakland Virtual School	Oakland, Michigan	http://www.oakland.k12.mi.us/ovconnect/index.html
Odyssey Charter School	Las Vegas, Nevada	http://www.odysseyk12.org/
Oklahoma State University Extension	Stillwater, Oklahoma	http://extension.okstate.edu/k12.htm
Plano ISD eSchool	Plano, Texas	http://www.planoisdeschool.net
Potter's School (The)	Ledyard, Connecticut	http://www.pottersschool.com/
Regina Coeli Online Academy	Louisiana	http://www.reginacoeli.org/
Rock Hill Virtual High School	Rock Hill, South Carolina	http://www.rock-hill.k12.sc.us/departments/vhs/
Rocky View Virtual School Program	Calgary, Alberta, Canada	http://www.rvvs.com

School	Location	URL
Salem Keizer Online,	Keizer, Oregon	http://skonline.salkeiz.k12.or.us
Scholars' Online Academy	Louisiana	http://www.islas.org/
SeeUonline	Matanuska-Susitna, Alaska	http://www.seeUonline.org
Southern Oregon Online School	Oregon	http://www.soesd.k12.or.us/it/soos/
Stanford University Education Program for Gifted Youth	Stanford, California	http://www-epgy.stanford.edu/
Sycamore Tree Online	Costa Mesa, California	http://www.sycamoretree.com/
TEACH The Einstein Academy Charter School	Morrisville, Pennsylvania	http://www.einsteinacademymycharterschool.org/
Texas Virtual School	Houston, Texas	http://www.texasvirtualschool.org
Trent Schools (The)	Bloomington, Indiana	http://www.theschools.com
University of Californian Extension On-line (the)	Berkeley, California	http://explore.berkeley.edu/subdiscipline.asp?value=6.&action=Internet
University of California College Prep Initiative	Santa Cruz, California	http://uccp.ucsc.edu/
University of Missouri High	Colombia, Missouri	http://cdis.missouri.edu/MUHighSchool/HShome.htm
University of Nebraska Distance School, (Class.com)	Lincoln, Nebraska	http://www.class.com/
University of Oklahoma Independent Learning High School	Norman, Oklahoma	http://ouilhs.ou.edu/
University of Texas Austin Continuing Education	Austin, Texas	http://www.utexas.edu/cee/dec/uths/index.shtml
VILAS	Vilas, Colorado	http://www.vilas.k12.co.us/vilas/vilas.htm
Virginia Internet High School	Virginia	http://www.internet-high.com/va/home.htm
Virtual Greenbush	Topeka, Kansas	http://www.virtualgreenbush.org/
Virtual High School @PWCS	Manasssas, Virginia	http://www.pwcs.edu/pwcsvirtualhs/
Virtual High School	Concord, Massachusetts	http://www.govhs.org/website.nsf
Virtual School @ Liverpool	Liverpool, New York	http://www.liverpool.k12.ny.us/virtual.html

School	Location	URL
Virtual School for the Gifted	Melbourne, Victoria, Australia	http://www.vsg.edu.au/
VirtualHighSchool.Com	Ontario, Canada	http://www.virtualhighschool.com/
Western Penn Cyber Charter School	Midland, Pennsylvania	http://www.wpccs.com/
Westside Virtual HS	Omaha, Nebraska	http://wvhs.westside66.org/
Willoway Cyber School	Wernersville, Pennsylvania	http://www.willoway.com/
WISE Internet High School	Woodbridge, Virginia	http://www.rmhs.org/Internet.htm
Zipstar Academy	Richmond, Virginia	http://offcomputer.roshd.ir/zipstar/content.htm

About the Authors

Catherine Cavanaugh, PhD, is assistant professor in Curriculum and Instruction at the University of North Florida, USA. She has been an educator since 1982. She taught science to children in the Caribbean and Florida, and directed an educator professional development center. As assistant director of the Florida Center for Instructional Technology, she developed online resources for teachers and studied distance education effectiveness. Her distance education experience includes producing distance learning programs for children, teaching distance workshops and courses to teachers, and publishing on the topic.

*   *   *   *

Janet W. Azbell is a managing principal for the Global Education Industry in IBM Business Consulting Services, USA. Dr. Azbell has 10 years of elementary teaching experience and four years at the university level. Dr. Azbell serves on the Education Council for Western Governor's University. Prior to joining IBM Business Consulting Services, Dr. Azbell was the Global Solutions Manager (Manager of Courseware Development) for IBM K-12 Education. Six years of prior industry experience culminated as Vice-President for Professional Development and Product Implementation. Dr. Azbell has published articles on technology implementation, professional development, and the impact of change on teachers and teaching.

Rachel Sellers Bordelon received her PhD in 2000 from Louisiana State University in Curriculum and Instruction. Currently, she is teaching online courses for Walden University, USA. She is also an adjunct professor for Lesley University in the Technology in Education Program. She has taught courses for Louisiana State University. Previously, Rachel worked at the Louisiana Center for Educational Technology, a division of the Louisiana Department of Education. During this time, she conducted research on the Louisiana Virtual School and served as the project coordinator for the Louisiana Educational Advancement and Development with Technology (LEADTech) Program.

John M. Carroll is professor of Computer Science, Education, and Psychology, and directs the Center for Human-Computer Interaction at Virginia Tech, USA. His research interests include methods and theory in human-computer interaction, particularly as applied to networking tools for collaborative learning and problem solving. He has written or edited 12 books, including *Making Use* (MIT Press, 2000), *HCI in the New Millennium* (Addison-Wesley, 2002), and *Usability Engineering* (Morgan-Kaufman, 2002, with M.B. Rosson). He was elected to the CHI Academy, and is a member of the National Research Council's Committee on Human Factors, and received the CHI Lifetime Achievement Award from ACM.

Terence W. Cavanaugh, PhD, is visiting assistant professor in curriculum and instruction at the University of North Florida, USA. With degrees in science education and instructional technology, his areas of expertise include curriculum design, instructional technology, assistive technology, and teacher education. In addition to his college teaching, he has more than 15 years of middle and high school teaching. He taught science and technology in the U.S. and the Caribbean, is the author of a book on integrating media into science education, and has developed educational technology materials for organizations integrating technology and curriculum, distance education, and methods for teaching special needs learners.

Margaret Haughey, professor, Educational Policy Studies, University of Alberta (Canada), is editor of *JDE*, the *Journal of Distance Education*, and a long time proponent of alternatives to site-based schooling. She has been an instructor, designer, producer, administrator and researcher in a variety of media-based initiatives in the K-12 and post secondary sector. Her most recent book is *Using Learning Technologies. International Perspectives on Practice*, edited with Liz Burge (2001) and she is currently exploring the components of K-12 e-learning environments that are most conducive to student success.

Janice M. Hinson received her EdD in 1993 from the University of Virginia in Curriculum and Instruction. She is an associate professor in the Department of Educational Leadership, Research and Counseling and serves as the coordinator of the Educational Technology Graduate Concentration. As part of her duties, she teaches a course entitled *Professional Development for K-12 Technology Integration*. This course is offered both online and face-to-face.

Philip L. Isenhour is a research associate with the Center for Human-Computer Interaction at Virginia Tech, USA. His research is currently focused on design of adaptable software infrastructure for distributed and collaborative applications, particularly in support of classroom activities and teacher knowledge management.

Sharon Johnston is the director of Curriculum and Instruction at Florida Virtual School, USA. Dr. Johnston's responsibilities include the supervision of courseware development and validation. Dr. Johnston, a National Board Certified Teacher, wrote her doctoral dissertation on "Online Discourse as a Constructivist Approach to Learning." For nine years, Dr. Johnston, as a College Board consultant, has facilitated the Advanced Placement English Literature and Composition for the AP Institute at University of Central Florida. Twice she has won the Walt Disney Teacherrific Award. Dr. Johnston earned her EdD in Curriculum and Instruction from the University of Sarasota.

Cushla Kapitzke is a lecturer in the School of Education at the University of Queensland, Australia. Major publications include *Literacy and Religion* (John Benjamins) and an edited volume, *Difference and Dispersion: Educational Research in a Postmodern Context* (Post Pressed). She has published in *Educational Theory, Teachers College Record, Educational Technology and Society*, and *Journal of Adolescent & Adult Literacy*. Her research interests include the political economy of new technologies and literacies, and information capitalism. Cushla can be contacted at c.kapitzke@mailbox.uq.edu.au.

Gaye Lang currently serves as the Deputy Secretary's regional representative for the US Department of Education, Region VI. Prior to taking this assignment, Dr. Lang served as project manager for Houston Independent School District Virtual School, USA. Her career in education includes roles as a classroom teacher in elementary and middle school, secondary assistant principal, elementary principal, Regional Service Center Field Service Specialist and university adjunct professor. Her educational background includes a Bachelor of Arts Degree in Elementary Education, Master of Arts Degree in Teaching and Administration from Pepperdine University, and Doctorate of Education in Cultural Studies, University of Houston.

Dennis C. Neale was a research associate with the computer science department at Virginia Tech (USA) during the time of this work. Currently, he is a PhD candidate in the Industrial and Systems Engineering Department at Virginia Tech. His research interests include designing and evaluating computer-mediated collaboration and communication technologies and video systems for mobile computing.

Donna Pendergast is program director and lecturer in teacher education at the University of Queensland, Australia. Dr. Pendergast has worked in secondary schools, technical colleges and university contexts in the area of teacher education. She utilizes postmodern theoretical approaches, with a strong emphasis on body theory and discourse analysis. Dr. Pendergast has a strong research background, having been involved in national and international collaborative research ventures, including research into the effectiveness of virtual schooling and middle schooling practices. She has published in *Teachers College Record, Teaching Education* and other professional journals. Donna can be contacted at d.pendergast@mailbox.uq.edu.au.

Glenn Russell spent nearly 20 years teaching in country and suburban schools in Victoria, Australia, before joining Griffith University, Queensland, where he received his doctorate in 1998. He has developed an international reputation in virtual schooling, cyberspace, and educational uses of hypertext. He is part of the faculty of Education at the Peninsula Campus of Monash University, in Victoria, Australia. His current research involves ethical uses of information and communications technology in school education, educational futures in globalized environments, and responsibilities in online schools.

James E. Schnitz has been a professional educator for more than 30 years, including teaching at high schools and at the University of Texas at San Antonio. Dr. Schnitz has been developing products and strategies for using technology in public education since 1981, and has spoken and published widely on the subject for both national and international audiences. Since joining IBM (USA) in 1994, Dr. Schnitz has worked on strategies for IBM's Reinventing Education projects and on disseminating the findings from those projects into the education market. Dr. Schnitz has a PhD.

Ken Stevens is a New Zealander who is professor of Education at Memorial University of Newfoundland, Canada, where he holds the Chair of TeleLearning and Rural Education, a research position established with assistance from Industry Canada. His previous appointments were at Victoria University of Wellington in New Zealand and James Cook University in Australia. His major research interest is the development of pedagogy for telelearning to take advantage of recent developments in multi-media technologies for classrooms. He lives in Canada and New Zealand.

R. Subramaniam has a PhD in Physical Chemistry. He is an assistant professor at the National Institute of Education in Nanyang Technological University and Honorary Secretary of the Singapore National Academy of Science. Prior to this, he was acting head of Physical Sciences at the Singapore Science Center. His research interests are in the fields of physical chemistry, science education, theoretical cosmophysics, museum science, telecommunications, and transportation He has published several research papers in international refereed journals.

Leo Tan Wee Hin has a PhD degree in Marine Biology. He holds the concurrent appointments of director of the National Institute of Education, professor of Biological Sciences in Nanyang Technological University, and president of the Singapore National Academy of Science. Prior to this, he was director of the Singapore Science Center. His research interests are in the fields of marine biology, science education, museum science, telecommunications, and transportation. He has published numerous research papers in international refereed journals.

Index

International Journal of Distance Education Technologies (JDET)

The International Source for Technological Advances in Distance Education

ISSN:	1539-3100
eISSN:	1539-3119
Subscription:	Annual fee per volume (4 issues):
	Individual US $85
	Institutional US $185
Editors:	Shi Kuo Chang
	University of Pittsburgh, USA
	Timothy K. Shih
	Tamkang University, Taiwan

Mission

The *International Journal of Distance Education Technologies* (**JDET**) publishes original research articles of distance education four issues per year. **JDET** is a primary forum for researchers and practitioners to disseminate practical solutions to the automation of open and distance learning. The journal is targeted to academic researchers and engineers who work with distance learning programs and software systems, as well as general participants of distance education.

Coverage

Discussions of computational methods, algorithms, implemented prototype systems, and applications of open and distance learning are the focuses of this publication. Practical experiences and surveys of using distance learning systems are also welcome. Distance education technologies published in **JDET** will be divided into three categories, **Communication Technologies, Intelligent Technologies, and Educational Technologies**: new network infrastructures, real-time protocols, broadband and wireless communication tools, quality-of services issues, multimedia streaming technology, distributed systems, mobile systems, multimedia synchronization controls, intelligent tutoring, individualized distance learning, neural network or statistical approaches to behavior analysis, automatic FAQ reply methods, copyright protection and authentification mechanisms, practical and new learning models, automatic assessment methods, effective and efficient authoring systems, and other issues of distance education.

For subscription information, contact:	For paper submission information:
Idea Group Publishing	**Dr. Timothy Shih**
701 E Chocolate Ave., Suite 200	**Tamkang University, Taiwan**
Hershey PA 17033-1240, USA	tshih@cs.tku.edu.tw
cust@idea-group.com	
URL: www.idea-group.com	